God's Promise of Redemption

a story of fulfilled prophecy

D. Robert Pike Ph. D

Acknowledgments

The Word of God

The power of his spoken word, a power beyond compare
Is harnessed now for you and me, for all of us to share.
The Word of God has **SO MUCH POWER**, much more than we can know.
It reaches down inside a man, and pierces to the soul.

A lightning bolt with all its might, is but a speck of sand
When you compare the Word of God, you hold within your hand.
So never fear what man can do, if you have trusted Christ,
The Word of God has made it clear, that he has paid the price.

With these words, I wish to acknowledge our awesome savior, Jesus Christ, God the Father, and the Holy Spirit, without whose inspiration, this work would not have been possible. I could not consider any work on theology without acknowledging my deepest gratitude to the only true God.

That poem was inspired by those encouraging words of Hebrews 4:12:

"For the word of God is living and active and sharper than any two-edged sword, and piercing as far as the division of soul and spirit, of both joints and marrow, and able to judge the thoughts and intentions of the heart."

Yes, there is awesome power in the Word of God. Thank you Lord, for this wonderful gift! It is my prayer that I present this work in the spirit of truth.

A book on theological concepts is often a team effort, and that is true of this volume. I would like to give my sincere heartfelt gratitude to all those below who helped me in the production of this work.

First of all, my loving wife Ida, who continually pushes me to pursue the work that God has given me to do, while at the same time trying to keep me from the sin of overcommitting myself.

Thank you my dear close friends, Fred and Barb Singleton. Our discussions and discoveries together have helped to pave the way for this volume.

Thank you, George and Carol Dannenberg. Every error you found while reading helped make this production better.

I would like to thank Ron Workman for his insights on publishing, and his wife Marjorie for her continual emphasis on prayer, and their continual friendship and support in many ways beyond the production of this book.

Many thanks to Charles Meek, for helping me in more ways than I can mention, including the convincing logic of his book "Christian Hope through Fulfilled Prophecy," his tireless work on various websites, and his fearless dedication to truth! As with all who seek the truth of the Parousia, we have our minor differences. This book celebrates the things with which we agree.

Thank YOU, the reader, for your decision to read this work. Seeking the truth of God's Word is my obsession. I encourage you to continue to seek truth in accordance with 1 Thessalonians 5:21: "But examine everything *carefully;* hold fast to that which is good;"

And finally, I wish to thank my primary editor and proofreader, Julie McAllen, who has put in many countless hours of work helping to make sure that I was consistent in my use of terms and capitalization, as well as doing a thorough job of proofreading. I took to heart every one of your suggestions in this publication.

To God be the glory for his magnificent grace to us who have put our trust in him, and for not giving us what we really deserve.

God's Promise of Redemption

God's Promise of Redemption

CONTENTS

Foreword

When Rob sent me his manuscript for chapter 3, he asked if a "normal" person could understand what he dissected in Daniel and I replied that a "normal" person wouldn't bother to read his book. What I meant by that statement was that a person would have to already have some interest in eschatology in order to get past the introduction. And if they do, then they've probably already had some experience with Daniel. But it was in that question that I understood Rob's heart and reason for this book.

Rob's not out to argue. He's not out to impress anyone with biblical terms at the exclusion of the average reader. His focus is to exalt Jesus Christ in such a way that anyone can understand and experience the joy he has. As he wrote to me in an email, *"my favorite chapter is chapter 11 which brings it all together, with an absolute highlight on the supremacy of Christ and what he has done for us in redemption. When I proofread it myself, I wanted to stand up and shout from the rooftops how blessed we are because of the fulfillment of the promises of God and how much it impacts our lives every day and in every way!"* It's that attitude that makes it an honor to recommend this book.

In a culture currently dominated by a futurist interpretation, Rob has taken a brave step to proclaim the fulfillment of the promises of God. As one who shares his fulfilled view, my concern is the same as his; will an open-minded reader also see it if explained well?

Therefore, I endeavored to read each chapter as if fulfillment were a new concept to me and allowed the author to teach it. Along the way, I was educated and encouraged. I also discovered Rob's gifts as a leader and shepherd. In taking the lead to proclaim the fulfillment of God's promises and the glories of his kingdom, Rob's sensitivity in how he shares it also reveals the right shepherd's heart.

The role of a Christian is to exalt Jesus Christ and lay down if necessary for others to see him. We're not laying down when we pound our views (right or wrong) into the other person without that sensitivity. When discussing the Bible, Rob and I both know how conversations can quickly escalate to unproductive arguments, but I've observed on Internet forums and in this book, Rob's humble desire to exalt Christ and not promote a view simply for argument's sake.

I first met Rob in an on line discussion. We share a common background as former Jehovah's Witnesses and had read one another's posts on a Facebook group for people who've left the Watchtower Society. After viewing the testimony I had shared at the 2011 Witnesses Now for Jesus conference in Pennsylvania, Rob took the time to send me a personal message. Through the years, I've come to know many former Jehovah's Witnesses, but it's a rare treat to find one who also shares my fulfilled view.

Coming to Christ through a study of Scripture without much exposure to the current trend of teaching in today's Church, I assumed fulfillment was just "normal" Christianity. Upon entering the Church, I was quite frankly surprised to discover how many Christians were unfamiliar with the present kingdom. Perhaps that is because not enough has been said or written about it from the perspective of fulfilled prophecy. The sermons and books that deal with the topic of prophecy often persuade Christ's followers to look to future fulfillment by focusing on present distresses. But at the closing of this book, Rob asks, "Isn't it wonderful to know that our Lord Jesus did what he said he would do?" It's good to focus our attention on his fulfilled promises!

I love God's Church. May we never stray from the foundation of praising God for what he has done through Christ. As it says of our Lord Jesus in 2 Corinthians 1:20: "For as many as are the promises of God, in Him they are yes; therefore also through Him is our Amen to the glory of God through us." And so it is my prayer that upon reading this study of Bible prophecy, you will join Rob in wanting to stand up and shout from the rooftops how blessed we are because of the fulfillment of the promises of God!

Keep yourself in God's love,
Julie McAllen

Former Jehovah's Witness redeemed by Jesus Christ

Prologue

God's Promise of Redemption
A story of fulfilled prophecy

There was a prophetess named Anna who was the daughter of Phanuel. My guess is that you have never heard of her. There is not much written about her. From Luke's Gospel, we know she was a prophetess, and not much else. We do know that the Lord inspired Luke to write about her around the time of the birth of our Lord. There is no reason to believe that this 84-year-old widow from the tribe of Asher, had any special talents. She obviously was not rich or among the well-educated of Israel. Why did God decide to include her in Luke's account of his beloved Son Jesus as he began his earthly existence?

Anna's inclusion in Luke's Gospel says a lot about God's view of his servants who routinely serve out of love, but seldom get recognition. There were more than likely a lot of eighty-four year old widows in Jerusalem, and probably very few of them were even noticed by those living in the city. This might have been the case with her too, but she had great worth in the eyes of God.

As we look at the account in Luke we can paint a picture in our minds. Jesus was eight days old and was due to be circumcised. Following the law of Moses, he was taken to the temple in Jerusalem to be presented before the Lord. Luke records that one of the most righteous and devout men, Simeon was on hand to perform the ritual. Mary and Joseph marveled to learn about the powerful role Jesus was to play in the future (Luke 2:21-35).

But then the account focused on Anna:

> Luke 2:36 And there was a prophetess, Anna the daughter of Phanuel, of the tribe of Asher. She was advanced in years and had lived with *her* husband seven years after her marriage,
> Luke 2:37 and then as a widow to the age of eighty-four. She never left the temple, serving night and day with fastings and prayers.
> Luke 2:38 At that very moment she came up and *began* giving thanks to God, and continued to speak of Him to all those who **were looking for the redemption of Jerusalem.** (emphasis mine)

The word redemption comes from the root word redeem, which means to free from captivity by payment of a ransom. Already when Jesus was eight days old, **Luke mentions a prophetess speaking about God's promise of redemption!** It was front and center in the mind of this special woman of God. From this we also see that God had a special calling on Anna's life. Despite becoming a widow after only seven years of marriage, because she made herself available, and had faith in God's promise of redemption, God used her to proclaim it. The result of her faith was that she saw the fulfillment of God's promise. She **knew** that Jesus was the Messiah, **the blessed redeemer** for whom she had been waiting. And she was able to welcome her King into the world with thanksgiving, telling everyone about him **and the redemption he would provide**.

We can learn a good lesson about faith from this. And that lesson is that we can have **unwavering faith** in the promise of God. But let's look at this promise a little closer.

In the book of Genesis, man was told that he could eat from every tree of the garden except for one:

Gen 2:15 Then the LORD God took the man and put him into the garden of Eden to cultivate it and keep it.
Gen 2:16 The LORD God commanded the man, saying, "From any tree of the garden you may eat freely;
Gen 2:17 but from the tree of the knowledge of good and evil you shall not eat, for **in the day that you eat from it you will surely die.**"

Thus, God told Adam that if he ate of the fruit of that tree, he would die **the same day**. Soon after this we read that Eve was deceived by the serpent and ate of the fruit. She then gave it to Adam to eat, and he ate it:

Gen 3:1 Now the serpent was more crafty than any beast of the field which the LORD God had made. And he said to the woman, "Indeed, has God said, 'You shall not eat from any tree of the garden'?"
Gen 3:2 The woman said to the serpent, "From the fruit of the trees of the garden we may eat;
Gen 3:3 but from the fruit of the tree which is in the middle of the garden, God has said, 'You shall not eat from it or touch it, or you will die.'"
Gen 3:4 The serpent said to the woman, "You surely will not die!
Gen 3:5 "For God knows that in the day you eat from it your eyes will be opened, and you will be like God, knowing good and evil."
Gen 3:6 When the woman saw that the tree was good for food, and that it was a delight to the eyes, and that the tree was desirable to make *one* wise, **she took from its fruit and ate; and she gave also to her husband with her, and he ate.**

So now this immediately raises the question of God keeping his first promise. Did Adam die that same day? Most people would say NO! Adam did not die in that same 24 hour period. He did die in that same thousand year period. To support this they may use:

2 Peter 3:8 But do not let this one *fact* escape your notice, beloved, that with the Lord one day is like a thousand years, and a thousand years like one day.

But the truth is that *__he did die in that exact same 24 hour period__* that God mentioned! You say, "How can this be, Genesis 5:5 tells us that Adam lived for 930 years on the earth."

But God was not speaking of **physical death** here. He was speaking of **spiritual death.** They died in the sense of *__being separated from God, and they knew it__*. This is why they reacted as they did when God approached them. They hid from God. They knew they were now separated from God. There is never any record of speaking to them again after Chapter 3 of Genesis. We will elaborate on this later. But this disobedience on Adam's part was not something which was unforeseen by God. God is omniscient. That means he knows everything that is going to happen. And God already had a plan for redeeming man from this disobedience. This is often referred to as the Covenant of Redemption. No, God did not have a contingency plan of what he would do in case man disobeyed. He had a Covenant in place that was made in heaven. It was the Father's plan and involved the Son coming to earth to complete the plan. R.C. Sproul explains it this way:

> So, we believe that there was a covenant made among the persons of the Godhead (Father, Son, and Holy Spirit) prior to creation. We often say that in the economy of redemption, the Father sends the Son into the world to redeem His people; the Son accomplishes that redemption by His work of obedience; and the Holy Spirit then applies the work of Christ to the people of God. The Spirit illumines the Word of God for us, regenerates our spirit to new life, draws us to the Son, and reconciles us to the Father. Thus, in biblical categories, redemption is a Trinitarian work from beginning to end. The great truth that rests on the concept of the covenant of redemption is that redemption was not an afterthought in the plan of God. **It was not God's Plan B**, which he was forced to come up with to correct the mess humanity made out of creation. No, **before he created the world, God had an eternal purpose of redemption**, a plan for redeeming His people in this world, and all three persons of the Trinity were in complete

agreement about it. Thus, the idea of covenant is rooted and grounded in the character of God Himself.[1] (emphasis mine)

This knowledge of God concerning disobedience extended to the people of Israel. God warned them and they disobeyed. Even while they were moving toward Canaan in the wilderness; and even after they had seen all of the magnificent miracles of God, they made a golden calf and **started worshiping it.** God could have destroyed them then, but because he had a plan in place, he showed them grace. God had Moses lead them to the Promised Land, but because of their lack of faith, he made them wander in the wilderness until that faithless generation died off. Moses died and was buried and did not get to enter the Promised Land.

Another man was anointed to take over for Moses, a man originally named Hoshea, but was called Joshua by Moses. (Num. 13:16) By anointing him, Moses obeyed God. Joshua, whose name is the same in Hebrew as Jesus, was **not** named such **by accident.** The name which signifies saved, a savior, or salvation, or the salvation of Jehovah; referring, no doubt, to his being God's instrument in saving the people from the hands of their enemies, and leading them from victory to victory over the different nations inside the land. Eventually they came to be in possession of the land. But soon they started disobeying again. The historical section of the Bible shows constant disobedience. The result of their disobedience was predicted by the prophets. And just as God predicted through the prophets, foreign armies continually invaded their lands. When this happened, even though they knew they had disobeyed God, and were receiving the wrath of God's promise, they felt hopeless.

This feeling of hopelessness is also what those early disciples felt after they saw their Savior nailed to a cross and buried in a borrowed tomb... hopelessness and broken hearts. Isn't this how you feel when the storms of life settle upon you? This is what you feel when you lose a job, or when your marriage starts to drift away. This is what you feel when sin seems to take over your life. This is what you feel when a family member is suffering with pain from some debilitating disease. ***But through it all, there is a solution!*** Yes! Due to the covenant of redemption made in heaven, that answer is Christ.

Yes, in the midst of all of this feeling and experience of hopelessness, despair, and broken hearts, Jesus is that long-awaited answer… he is the answer to the promise that God will be present with us through all of the challenges of our lives. Jesus is that great prophet who called *us to trust in his promises* and the faithfulness of our great God. Jesus is that great high priest who took his sacrifice to the Most Holy in Heaven, *once and for all time.* He is the one who carries all of our sorrows and weakness. Jesus is also that great King who leads us to "green pastures" as we commit to follow him with all of our hearts (Psalm 23:2). He has rescued us from sin and death. He has brought us to a place of faith in him, and one that grows as we continue the process of sanctification. He is present **in us** through his Holy Spirit. This book asks the question: Is this promise of redemption fulfilled? Can we **trust the Lord** Jesus to deliver on every promise that he ever spoke?

Did God redeem mankind from this original curse? For as he said to the serpent in Genesis 3:

> Gen 3:15 And I will put enmity between you and the woman,
> And between your seed and her seed; He shall bruise you on the
> head, and you shall bruise him on the heel."

This was not an idle threat. The rest of the Bible deals with this issue. Will we see in future chapters the finality of the entire story? Does it show that God lives up to his word? The Old Testament shows us that God made a lot of good promises, as well as terrifying promises. The prophets recorded the future and laid it out before the nation in fine precision. If they refused to obey, their future would be bleak, maybe even devastating to them. Ninety percent of the time they ignored the prophets or killed them for what they predicted. The prophets Isaiah and Micah predicted the appearance of the Messiah hundreds of years in advance, but these prophecies also fell on deaf ears.

God kept his terrifying promises. He destroyed the city of Jerusalem through the hands of King Nebuchadnezzar of Babylon after warning the nation of Israel numerous times. He allowed this king of Babylon to destroy the magnificent temple of Solomon. And even though the city and the temple were eventually rebuilt, the second temple was a far cry from the first. After seeing that this people whom Moses himself called "a stubborn people" (See Deut. 9:6,13), were indeed never going to repent from their evil works, and after what was spoken through the prophet Malachi, God stopped speaking through the prophets for a period of 400 years.

But even though all of this time passed, we see that God **still did not** forget his promises. The words of the prophet Malachi came to life when John the Baptist appeared on the scene. He fulfilled the prophecy in Malachi:

> Mal 4:4 "Remember the law of Moses My servant, *even the* statutes and ordinances which I commanded him in Horeb for all Israel.
> Mal 4:5 "Behold, **I am going to send you Elijah the prophet before the coming of the great and terrible day of the LORD.** (emphasis mine)

The Lord Jesus himself said that John the Baptist was this predicted Elijah:

> Mat 11:11 "Truly I say to you, among those born of women there has not arisen *anyone* greater than John the Baptist! Yet the one who is least in the kingdom of heaven is greater than he.

Mat 11:12 "From the days of John the Baptist until now the kingdom of heaven suffers violence, and violent men take it by force.
Mat 11:13 "For all the prophets and the Law prophesied until John.
Mat 11:14 "And **if you are willing to accept** *it,* **John himself is Elijah who was to come.**
Mat 11:15 "He who has ears to hear, let him hear. (emphasis mine)

Jesus' most famous prophecy is outlined for us in the Synoptic Gospels. He told the disciples that there would be a time of great trouble in which there would be wars in the surrounding nations, a time in which the temple and the holy city would be destroyed. He told them that *they would be persecuted,* hounded by false prophets and false Christs. And he pointed his finger at the ones behind the persecution in Matthew 26:64, and told them that **THEY would see him return** "in the clouds with great power and glory." This followed up what was originally told to his disciples as recorded in Matthew chapter 24, Mark chapter 13, and Luke chapter 21. But the timing of this, as recorded in these three Gospel accounts, is what has sparked much controversy:

Mat 24:34 "Truly I say to you, **this generation will not pass away until all these things take place.**
Mat 24:35 "Heaven and earth will pass away, but My words will not pass away. (emphasis mine)

Many have said that Jesus was a **false prophet** because he **did not** return for his disciples in that same generation. Some have said that Jesus **embarrassed himself** with this prophecy. Others have said that the disciples **misunderstood** this prophecy, and that even though these promises were made 2,000 years ago, his return is **still in the future.**

The study of the "Last Days" is derived from the Greek word εσχατος, eschatos, which is pronounced es-ka-taws). It is called eschatology, which means a study of last things. This study is also a part of God's promise of redemption, because within the bounds of these last things, Jesus died on the cross and took his perfect sacrifice into heaven to present to the Father.

As this volume unfolds before you, the truth of what happened as expected by his disciples and as recorded in the annals of history, will be exposed. Jesus told his disciples:

> Luk 21:28 "But when these things begin to take place, straighten up and lift up **your** heads, because **your** redemption is drawing near."

These words were **very specifically** spoken to his disciples. Did Jesus **mislead them** in that this prophecy was not for really for them as he said? Was this **really** a long range prophecy not to happen for thousands of years as many from the pulpits of America have preached?

The entire New Testament points to the supremacy and centrality of Christ and reveals these answers. Jesus the Messiah is **the only one** who will give you the strength and the joy to say, "I can absolutely trust him… because he is here… he speaks truth… he is good… he is risen!"

In showing you about **all** of his promises, **including** the promise of his return, it will show the status of the original promise of redemption spoken thousands of years ago and recorded for us in Genesis 3:15. Having said all of this, let us proceed.

NOTES

1. Sproul, R. C. (2013-07-01). The Promises of God: Discovering the One Who Keeps His Word (p. 30). David C. Cook. Kindle Edition.

Chapter 1

Last Things - Eschatology

A Brief Testimony

I need to give a brief testimony because it is relevant to my journey as a Christian, and the conclusions I have reached. I was raised to believe the theology of Jehovah's Witnesses. The training began at an early age. One day, my mother took me aside and told me some very scary words. She told me that someday soon in the "Last Days," Jehovah God was going to come down and destroy 99% of the population of the earth. The "Last Days" would be a horrible time for all of mankind. Then she told me that we were very fortunate that we were _mostly assured_ that it would not happen to us. You see, as she explained, we were a special people. We were blessed with great privilege. We were a part of _God's exclusive organization on earth_, and _as long as we practiced our faith_, and didn't displease Jehovah too much, we would be spared of this great disaster of the "Last Days," and would live in a Paradise earth.

She showed me graphic descriptions of what life would be like for us. It looked wonderful. People were playing with lions and tigers. Everyone had a beautiful home and plenty to eat. Wow! This was in the mid-nineteen fifties and I was only about eight years old at the time. This had a profound impact on me. Jehovah was a scary God! How did I know what to do in order to be "good enough" to get saved? Was Jehovah going to _destroy ME?_ To be honest, at that age, the prospect of this scared me to death. I had to learn what to do. I had to be good enough for God NOT to destroy me. Yes, even at this very tender age, my life had become affected deeply by what my mother referred to as "the Last Days." I did not even know of the word, but already the topic of eschatology or "last things" was affecting my life.

This idea that God was going to come down and destroy those who were not worthy always weighed heavy on my mind. I knew that I was not good enough. But I still believed that Armageddon was coming very, very soon. In fact, I knew that Armageddon was just around the corner. The Watchtower Society said that it was going to happen in 1975 and we would do well to sell all of our belongings and spend the "Last Days" telling others about what would happen soon. This type of activity was called "pioneering." This "pioneer" lived as simply as possible and spent at least 100 hours a month going from door to door witnessing to others about this great impending disaster in fulfillment of the "great commission" in Matthew chapter 24.

But after another twenty years or so of living this way, 1975 came and went by without any sign of a problem. Later I found out that this was just **one of many** failed dates given by this organization. I started having doubts about my beliefs. I remember going to a door of someone who actually knew the Bible and showed me a Scripture in John 20:28 which said that _the Apostle Thomas worshipped Jesus_. This shocked me. I was always taught that only Jehovah must be worshipped. The thought that any of the apostles worshipped Jesus was a faith shaker. Why would they do this? After all, **Jesus was just a man!!** When I got back to the car and spoke to the others about this, no one in the car could answer this question nor did they seem concerned about it. They all just blew it off. I went up the ladder and questioned the Elders. They all denied that this Scripture actually meant that Jesus received worship from Thomas, attaching some other silly meaning to it. Little did I know at that time, _but this one Scripture would actually change the course of my life_, and it began very soon.

My degradation into darkness began at that point. I knew that this man who witnessed to me at the door was correct in what he showed me. It even said Thomas worshipped Jesus _in my own_ Watchtower Society production of the Bible (the New World Translation of the Holy Scriptures, the only one which I believed was accurate). This one passage caused me to doubt everything. I knew that this actually meant that Jesus **was worshipped** by these men, and he did nothing to stop them from doing it! I felt so hypocritical because of my serious doubts which now crept into every aspect of my life as a Jehovah's Witness!

I had spent my life believing with all of my heart that I had _the exclusive truth_ of the Bible! What was going on here? To shore up my faith, I started having a debate with a Christian at work who knew his stuff, and I was losing, BIG! I knew deep down inside I had been lied to, but it was too late for me. I will spare you the details of what happened at this point in my life, except to say that I was so disillusioned that I was not even sure I believed in God for a while. Within five years of this event, and now in my early thirties, my wife and I got a divorce. My relationship with my ex-wife and my only daughter were devastated, and I was excommunicated from the Jehovah's Witnesses.

If there was one good thing about my life at that point it was this; now that I was out of the Watchtower organization, **I was free to do independent research!** My research showed me that my beliefs were wrong. As I began studying about Christ, everything changed. **God is good.** He forgave me! Now it was up to me to rely on that forgiveness to make the decision to turn my life around. In the distant past, I had left behind the beliefs of the Watchtower Society, but the effects it had on my early life and the consequences will be with me to the grave. That is why God's grace is so amazing. Not only has he actually forgiven me, he has given me eternal life! Jesus said: John 5:24 "Truly, truly, I say to you, he who hears My word, and **believes** Him who sent Me, has eternal life, and does not come into judgment, but has passed out of death into life." This belief is not just an intellectual belief, but is bound up in trust. This is ***the promise of redemption,*** and I knew I needed to **surrender my life** and trust the Lord Jesus completely. It had to be deeply heartfelt if it was going to be real. The fact that God would accept me in this way is one of the most **amazing promises** in the Word of God!

As I began my life as a Christian, I still wondered about this Armageddon scenario. Was this **completely false?** What about all of that bad stuff I read in the book of Revelation? If the Bible was true, this had to mean something. So I bought a series on the book of Revelation from one of my favorite preachers. I listened to every word and believed it all. Although the details were different, there still was going to be a visit from God and a battle of Armageddon. But we Christians were going to be rescued! We were going to be raptured! We were going to be changed in the twinkling of an eye! We wouldn't even have to die! Wow! This was comforting. Now all I had to do was wait for it to happen.

So for the next fifteen years I kept waiting, and waiting. But nothing happened. My commitment to God grew, and I decided to get more training in theology. Since I already had a Master's degree, I looked for a Seminary that would allow me to get my Doctorate. I enrolled in Trinity College and Seminary, and five years later I had my Doctorate. I did this because I felt like the Apostle Paul did when he wrote in 1 Timothy chapter one the following:

> 1Tim 1:15 It is a trustworthy statement, deserving full acceptance, that Christ Jesus came into the world to save sinners, among whom I am foremost *of all.*
> 1Tim 1:16 Yet for this reason I found mercy, so that in me as the foremost, Jesus Christ might demonstrate His perfect patience as an example for those who would believe in Him for eternal life.
> 1Tim 1:17 Now to the King eternal, immortal, invisible, the only God, *be* honor and glory forever and ever. Amen.

Yes, this took up five years of my life, but after all of this, I realized that this degree _only showed me how little I actually knew about the Scriptures_. I actually **did not need this degree to be approved by God, but I was compelled to do it.** Yes, my childhood fears of not being good enough were still working here. Even after all of those years, I was still fighting the feeling that I was not good enough to be accepted by God! I almost gave up in the process, but my wife and step sons drove me to complete it. But now that I was long since finished, and time continued to march on, I suddenly realized that I was over 60 years old and still waiting for something that my mother told me would happen "soon.".... and she told me this over 50 years ago! Oh well, I kept thinking "it must be soon in God's eyes, not mine."

I was attending a weekly Bible study where we began to explore the book of Revelation. I was excited. I wanted to confirm my earlier study of this in a set of tapes from one of my favorite preachers. I was convinced that this view, which was called premillennial dispensationalism, was correct. After all, most of the best known preachers in the Christian community were on the same page with this view of end times. There was no way it could be wrong, I thought. Then the Bible study began. There were several men there who seemed very good at expounding on the Bible and the discussions started. But the deeper we got into the book of Revelation, _the more confused I became._ The timelines were all mixed up. We were taught that this book was not in chronological order, and I found it to be very confusing. Additionally, there were several views of certain passages in this book. In fact there was no one there who agreed totally on anything that we studied!

It was at this point that I realized that even though I had gone to Seminary and spent 5 years studying, I had no clue what was going on with this book of Revelation. I realized that the only eschatological training I had was the dispensational view of theology. I knew there were other views, but being smug in once again thinking I had the truth under my belt, I had not even considered looking into any of them. It was finally at this point I determined that I would look into other scenarios of what was meant by the "Last Days." What did Jesus mean in Matthew 24 when he said:

> Mat 24:32 "Now learn the parable from the fig tree: when its branch has already become tender and puts forth its leaves, you know that summer is near;
> Mat 24:33 so, you too, when you see all these things, recognize that He is near, *right* at the door.
> Mat 24:34 "Truly I say to you, **this generation will not pass away until all these things take place.**
> Mat 24:35 "Heaven and earth will pass away, but My words will not pass away.
> Mat 24:36 "But of that day and hour no one knows, not even the angels of heaven, nor the Son, but the Father alone.

I was confused, and I was going to get to the bottom of it. Thus, I was once again on a mission. I would learn these other eschatological positions, and test them against my current position and see what would happen.

A Brief Description of Classical Dispensationalism

So for me, the hope of redemption was all caught up in what was going to happen in the future. I still believed that there was going to be an Armageddon scenario in my future. This is the teaching of dispensationalism, and here I was a dispensationalist. Your question is: uh…what? Yes, it is a big confusing term. So what is dispensationalism? It is beyond the scope of this work to delve into all of the components of this eschatalogical system as there are several versions within it. Although it can be hard to summarize dispensational eschatology, due to recent changes in certain aspects of the position, I will endeavor to give it a try. I will describe the most popular version which is called "classical dispensationalism." In general, there are three main aspects.

First, dispensationalism approaches the relationship with God in the following manner. God has set up his relationship with man through several stages which are divided into different dispensations (or periods of time). Each dispensation is a sort of "test" of mankind to be faithful to that particular set of commands given at that time. Generally, there are seven or eight of these dispensations. In the case of eight dispensations they are distinguished as: innocence (before the fall), conscience (Adam to Noah), government (Noah to Babel), promise (Abraham to Moses), law (Moses to Christ), grace (Pentecost to the rapture), tribulation (7 years), and the millennium (one thousand years).

Next, dispensationalism purports to hold to a literal interpretation of Scripture. This does not deny the existence of any of the non-literal language in the Bible, but rather means that there is a literal meaning behind those passages that appear to be figurative. If someone does not take a passage literally, many times they are accused of "spiritualizing" the passage. However, no one "spiritualized" passages any more than Jesus. For example: The book of Malachi states:

> Mal 4:5 "Behold, I am going to send you Elijah the prophet before the coming of the great and terrible day of the LORD."

Dispensationalists say that this must be fulfilled literally. In other words, before the great and terrible day of the Lord, Elijah the prophet must literally appear. Sounds logical doesn't it? However, here is Jesus' account of the meaning of this passage:

> Mat 11:11 "Truly I say to you, among those born of women there has not arisen *anyone* greater than John the Baptist! Yet the one who is least in the kingdom of heaven is greater than he.
> Mat 11:12 "From the days of John the Baptist until now the kingdom of heaven suffers violence, and violent men take it by force.
> Mat 11:13 "For all the prophets and the Law prophesied until John.
> Mat 11:14 "And if you are willing to accept *it,* John himself is Elijah who was to come.

Then later on in the book of Matthew, Jesus says:

> Mat 17:9 As they were coming down from the mountain, Jesus commanded them, saying, "Tell the vision to no one until the Son of Man has risen from the dead."
> Mat 17:10 And His disciples asked Him, "Why then do the scribes say that Elijah must come first?"
> Mat 17:11 And He answered and said, "Elijah is coming and will restore all things;
> Mat 17:12 but I say to you that Elijah **already came**, and they did not recognize him, but did to him whatever they wished. So also the Son of Man is going to suffer at their hands."
> Mat 17:13 Then the disciples understood that He had spoken to them about John the Baptist.

Yes, this is recorded twice! Jesus **unequivocally states** that this passage in Malachi is a reference to John the Baptist. Yet, I have had dispensationalists tell me that this **still** has a literal fulfillment that must come "before the great and terrible day of the lord." **And that "day of the lord" is yet to come.** But, I am compelled to ask the question: If Elijah was going to **literally appear**, don't you think Jesus would have clarified this?

Now, as I conclude my description of this view, I would like to add that finally, as a result of the foregoing information, dispensationalism holds to a distinction between Israel and the church. Accordingly, this means that the promises made to Israel in the Old Testament were literally to be fulfilled by Israel itself (largely in the coming millennium). This means the church was not intended as the recipient of such prophecies about what God would do for them. For example, there is the promise of the actual land given to Israel called the "promised land" in the Scriptures. Under this proposed scenario, God will someday return all of the land of promise to Israel. This is opposed to the view of others in the Christian faith that God would bring all those of faith in Christ together as the Israel of God (Romans 9:6).

Thus, we might say that according to the dispensational view, there are "two peoples of God." Although they believe both Jews and Gentiles are saved by Christ through faith, they believe natural or ethnic Israel will be the recipient of additional "earthly" promises. Additionally Israel may have to exercise certain rituals not required of believing Gentiles whose primary inheritance is heavenly (at least for a while). So now you are probably thinking: "Where did all of this come from?"

This form of eschatology is largely credited to the early-mid 19th century interpretation of John Nelson Darby. Darby is generally recognized as "the father of Classical Dispensationalism." Darby was a Bible teacher who began as one of the Plymouth Brethren and eventually became an influential figure among them. Subsequently, he founded a group called the Exclusive Brethren. After Darby promulgated his theories, a man by the name of Cyrus Scofield made this eschatalogical theme popular through a Bible which he produced called the Scofield Reference Bible. Unique to this eschatology is a "pre-tribulation rapture", in which born again believers are to be removed from the world, prior to a seven-year period of great tribulation that is to beset the rest of humanity. Futurism is also pre-millennial, expecting that Christ will return to rule and reign on earth for a period of a thousand years in a temple that is to be built on the temple mount in Jerusalem.

So now your question is: How did you come to believe this, Rob?

My answer is this: Since I was previously one of Jehovah's Witnesses, and they believed an eschatological view that is somewhat similar, it was a natural progression. This is especially true since most of the evangelical preachers of our time promulgate such a theory as Darby's. Jehovah's Witnesses, however, believe a little bit different version of this. First of all, they believe they are _absolutely the exclusive recipients_ of God's "undeserved kindness" because they are the only ones diligent enough to have found the truth of Scripture. Additionally, they are the only ones on the earth who have the guidance of Jehovah God's _exclusive_ channel of communication, and that channel is "The Watchtower Bible and Tract Society."

They believe that Jesus' second coming was an invisible return in AD 1914. Just to give a quick overview, they got this from their application of Daniel's prophecy. First of all they said that the Babylonians came and destroyed Jerusalem and the temple in 607 BC (the actual date was 586 BC). Using Daniel's prophecy in chapter 4 verse 16 they say that the seven times equaled 2520 years, thus bringing them to AD 1914. They said 1914 was the beginning of the "Last Days." Their theology said the Battle of Armageddon could be any time after this. So with all of this background, my breaking free of this organization actually led me to accept **the dispensational** theory without question because it was very similar. At that time, I felt that I had finally found the truth of the "Last Days."

For further information on Jehovah's Witnesses 1914 belief, consult the JW website at:

_http://www.jw.org/en/publications/books/bible-teach/1914-significant-year-bible-prophecy/#?insight[search_id]=02c1d1fc-e001-442f-a8f5-5a8987998e4c&insight[search_result_index]=1_

My Search Begins – AGAIN!

With this background, I began searching again. There in my own library was a book that I bought years ago, but never read. It was entitled _**"Four Views on the Book of Revelation"**_[1] where we were told about the following views:

- Preterist
- Idealist
- Progressive Dispensationalist
- Classical Dispensationalist

Since I already knew the Classical Dispensationalist view, I was mainly interested in the other two views from this book. I read the Preterist view, and it was shockingly different from what I had heard. I also read the Idealist view. It too was totally different, but it sounded a little **too** idealistic to be believable to me. Of these two views, the Preterist (past fulfillment) view held some promise, and I will have much more to say on this later, but I knew there was one more view I wanted to seriously consider and that one was the Amillennial view.

Amillennialism

An online search led me to a document entitled "What's 1000 years between friends?" I read this article and it piqued my interest. The author was Kim Riddlebarger. His arguments seemed to make sense. One of the things he said in this was:

> Since premillennialism is so dominant in American church circles, many who encounter Reformed theology for the first time are quite surprised when they discover that all of the Protestant Reformers, as well as virtually the entire Reformed and Lutheran traditions (along with their confessions), with a few notable exceptions, are *amillennial*[2].

Wow! I didn't know that. Furthermore it said of dispensationalism:

> In addition, there is a very serious side-effect produced by this approach to Bible prophecy. The Bible no longer speaks for itself, since it is so easily twisted by each of its interpreters, doing their best to make sure that the upheaval of the nations described in the Book of Revelation **has nothing whatsoever to do with the original reader in the first century struggling under Roman persecution, but is instead somehow related to the morning headlines.** In the minds of the

> dispensational prophecy pundit, **the Book of Revelation speaks more to us living at the end of the age, than it did to those Christians in the seven churches to whom John's vision is actually addressed** (i.e., Revelation 1:3).[3] (emphasis mine)

This really made sense. The book of Revelation should absolutely make sense to those to whom it was written! **Why else would the Lord Jesus inspire John to write it!** I was onto something here. I wanted more than what this little 12 page article had to say, so I went to my local Christian bookstore and bought a copy of **"A Case for Amillennialism" by Kim Riddlebarger.** He is the Pastor of Christ Reformed Church in Anaheim, CA. and has a Ph.D. from Fuller Seminary. This book became a source of study for me because I thought his theological concepts made a lot of sense. For example he stated:

> Historically, Protestant interpreters have argued that the New Testament provides the controlling interpretation of the Old Testament. The goal of the interpreter of eschatology is to determine how prophecies made in the Old Testament are treated and applied by writers of the New. If the New Testament writers spiritualize Old Testament prophecies by applying them in a nonliteral sense, then the Old Testament passage must be seen in light of that New Testament interpretation, not vice versa. Moreover, a major step toward finding an answer to the millennial question is to develop a contextual framework of interpretation from the New Testament itself. [4]

This makes perfect sense. After all, we are Christians are we not? Why should interpretation of Scripture be based on the Old Testament? Our Lord and Savior always should have the last word in Scripture interpretation, should he not? Additionally he stated in this book a principle called the *analogia fidei* which is a Latin term meaning "the analogy of faith." Under this principle, unclear biblical texts are to be interpreted in the light of clear passages which speak to the same subject rather than taking the literal sense in isolation from the rest of the Scriptures.

Also, with regard to how dispensationalists interpret Scripture he said that they see Old Testament prophecy as the determinative category by which New Testament prophecy is interpreted. This was interesting. I never considered that this is the dispensational way, but it made sense. There is indeed some truth to this idea, for we have to consider that many of the prophecies of the Old Testament were fulfilled in the New Testament.

Riddlebarger made another excellent point with regard to dispensational interpretation when he said:

> Although dispensationalists claim to interpret Scripture literally, in actuality, they often read a passage literalistically, meaning they downplay or ignore how Old Testament passages are interpreted by the authors of the New.[5]

For example, all of the prophecies of the Old Testament with regard to Christ were fulfilled in the New Testament. But if there is a question, the New Testament must always take precedence as in the case of the example stated earlier with the return of the prophet Elijah. **Jesus said** that what the prophet Malachi was referring to was the emergence of John the Baptist, and not a literal physical return of Elijah. Is not Jesus the last word on every subject? Of course!

All of this was in complete agreement with my Seminary textbook entitled "Interpreting the Bible" by A. Berkley Mickelsen. In his book, he states another principle in the start of this textbook which I thought was profound, and that thought was this:

> Simply stated, the task of the interpreters of the Bible is *to find out the meaning of a statement (command, question) for the author and for the first hearers or readers, and thereupon to transmit that meaning to modern readers.* The interpreter will observe whether a given

statement tends to be understood by a modern reader identically, similarly, or differently from the sense intended by the ancient writer, and will adjust his explanation accordingly.[6]

As I pursued the study of this book, Riddlebarger continued to make good points. He also was at one time a dispensationalist. He pointed out some things that were very valid. He showed how dispensationalists must insert gaps in many places throughout the Bible in order to make their theology work. And these gaps have no foundation in Scripture whatsoever.

It will help to give a few examples of these gaps:

1. Daniel 9:24-27. Daniel gives the prophecy of 70 weeks of years in this passage. Dispensationalists believe there is a gap in the prophecy of over 2000 years between week 69 and 70. **But where is the gap between week 69 and 70 in this passage?** Not only do they say that there is a gap here, but they maintain that God has put his prophecy on hold for two thousand years because the Jews did not accept Christ. God has always made clear through his prophets if these prophecies were conditional or not.

   To quote Riddlebarger:

   In order to make this fit into their interpretive scheme, dispensationalists insist that the Messiah is cut off after the sixty-two sevens. An indeterminate gap of time comes between the end of the sixty-nine sevens and the seventieth seven, they say, when the one who confirms a covenant with many (Israel) arrives on the scene to do his dastardly deed. The insertion of a gap of at least two thousand years between the sixty-ninth and the seventieth week is a self-contradictory violation of the dispensationalist's professed literal hermeneutic. **Where is the gap found in the text?** Dispensationalists must insert it. The failure to acknowledge the obvious covenantal context of the messianic covenant maker of verse 27, who confirms a covenant with many, leads dispensationalists **to confuse Christ with antichrist.** A more serious interpretive error is hard to imagine.[7] (emphasis mine)

2. John 5:28-29 states: "for the hour is coming in which all who are in the graves will hear his voice and come forth." This is a single event and not separated by 1000 years. In order for there to be a resurrection at the beginning and the end of the millennium, it is necessary to insert a gap in verse 29: "those who have done good, to the resurrection of life, (and 1000 years later) those who have done evil to the resurrection of condemnation". (NKJV parentheses mine)

To quote Riddlebarger:

After a time of unprecedented distress, there will be a resurrection of the righteous and the unrighteous, both groups receiving everlasting blessing or cursing. These words are echoed by our Lord himself in John's Gospel when Jesus spoke of a time to come when "all who are in their graves will hear his voice and come out— those who have done good will rise to live, and those who have done evil will rise to be condemned" (5: 28– 29). Both Daniel and Jesus spoke of one resurrection in which two distinct groups simultaneously participate— believers and unbelievers— each receiving the appropriate recompense. There is no hint anywhere in these two texts, implied or otherwise, that the resurrection of the righteous and the resurrection of the unrighteous are separated by a period of one thousand years, an essential feature of premillennialism. [1] Both Jesus and Daniel depicted the resurrection of the righteous and the unrighteous as occurring at the same time.[8]

3. 2 Peter 3:10 states: "But the day of the Lord will come like a thief, in which the heavens will pass away with a roar and the elements will be destroyed with intense heat, and

the earth and its works will be burned up." If the Lord comes as a thief in the night at the rapture of the church, is there a **gap** in this Scripture of 1,000 years before God performs this so-called Cosmic Renewal, in which the physical planet will be destroyed with fire, and re-created? **If dispensationalists hold to a literal hermeneutic, where is the gap in the text?**

The Two Age Model

One of the things that Riddlebarger emphasizes in his book is that the writers of the Bible believed that the current course and the future climax of human history included the progressive unfolding of two successive eschatological ages. He describes these as *"this age"* and *"the age to come."* He emphasizes that these two ages have a strong bearing on whether or not there will be an earthly millennium. His thinking is that these two ages provide an interpretive grid for eschatology in general and the millennial question in particular. He states that his book was based on an understanding of these two eschatological ages.

According to this theory, Christians live in the eschatological tension during a time when there is the partial overlap of the two ages as they await the arrival of the age to come in all of its fullness. Note what he says:

> The return of Christ in his second advent is the event that marks the end of this age as we know it (with all of its temporal qualities) and commences the age to come (with its eternal qualities). Following the historic Protestant hermeneutic, which utilizes the analogy of faith, instead of the dispensational hermeneutic, in which the Old Testament is allowed to interpret the New in matters related to eschatology, this model uses clear and unambiguous texts drawn from throughout the New Testament. In conclusion, the following points need to be made. First, both Jesus and Paul spoke of the present course of history as "this age" and the age of the consummation as "the age to come." Indeed, this was the basic eschatological understanding of history as set

forth in the New Testament. Second, the final judgment occurs when Christ returns. These texts give no hint of a delay in the judgment of unbelievers until after the thousand-year reign of Christ on the earth. The "white throne judgment" (Rev. 20: 11) occurs at Christ's return, not one thousand years later. This argument makes premillennialism in any form difficult to justify solely on the basis of a "literal" reading of the thousand years of Revelation 20: 1– 10. Third, since judgment occurs at the return of Christ, there can be only two categories of people after Christ's return: those who are righteous and participate in the blessings of the age to come and those who are not and are burned in the fire. This makes it difficult to argue that people are left on the earth in unresurrected bodies after Christ returns and after the judgment of all men and women.[9]

Thus, he makes it clear that we are still living in the first age of this two age model. _We are still waiting for Christ to return,_ and when he does return, then will be the final judgment.

But wait a minute....

From what I previously learned during this search, this seems to conflict with what our Lord said. Jesus said in Matt 24:34: "Truly I say to you, **this generation will not pass away until all these things take place.**" That is what he said. That is what he told his disciples. How can it be that we are still waiting for this to happen? Was Jesus wrong when he said this? Here is how Riddlebarger explains this:

> But what did Jesus mean when he said that "this generation," i.e., his contemporaries, would not pass away until all these things were fulfilled? Is this not an argument that this section of the discourse refers to the destruction of Jerusalem in AD 70, as preterists contend? [51] Jesus told his disciples that all the signs he had just described would be present and that the temple would be destroyed in a time of unprecedented tribulation. But those are "signs of the end," and even though the fig tree was ripe, the end was not yet. . . . . Let us also not overlook the following in verse 35. Only God in human flesh could predict the future of human

history, much less utter the following sentence: "Heaven and earth will pass away, but my words will never pass away." This was perhaps our Lord's strongest assertion of deity yet. His words will never pass away, though the heavens and earth will. The reason Jesus could speak of the future with such certainty is because his words are the words of God. **Yet, while the signs of the end can be known and to some degree understood, the timing of our Lord's return remains a mystery— intentionally so.** Jesus clearly said in verse 36, "No one knows about that day or hour, not even the angels in heaven, nor the Son, but only the Father."[10] (emphasis mine)

Is this true? _Did Jesus intentionally mislead his disciples_ by giving them a mysterious meaning to his words concerning "this generation?" This seems unlike our Lord. He was always straightforward with his disciples. What about the following verse: Did he also deliberately mislead the Pharisees when he said the following in Matt 23:33-36:

> Mat 23:33 "You serpents, you brood of vipers, how will you escape the sentence of hell?
> Mat 23:34 "Therefore, behold, I am sending you prophets and wise men and scribes; some of them you will kill and crucify, and some of them you will scourge in your synagogues, and persecute from city to city,
> Mat 23:35 so that upon you may fall _the guilt of_ all the righteous blood shed on earth, from the blood of righteous Abel to the blood of Zechariah, the son of Berechiah, whom you murdered between the temple and the altar.
> Mat 23:36 "Truly I say to you, all these things will come upon this generation.

To delay this does not seem consistent with the straightforwardness of our Lord. It sounded to me like the Lord was going to judge these hypocritical Pharisees in the present generation and not some future generation. Did he mean something different in each of these cases? Something is not adding up. Nonetheless, I continued my investigation.

The Kingdom of God

What is the Kingdom of God? If you ask this question you will probably get many different answers. Is it a physical kingdom as some will say, or is it a spiritual kingdom? Or is it still something else yet different than either of these? This was always a very confusing notion to me. Why? Because I was always taught that those kingdoms were somehow different. From the viewpoint of dispensationalism, what I had always learned is that the contrasting views between a physical and a spiritual kingdom were different for now, but will be the same later. I was told that because the Lord used the terms "Kingdom of Heaven" and "Kingdom of God" interchangeably in places in the four Gospels, most Christians think they are one and the same.

This teaching is that they will be, but not until the Second Coming of the Lord Jesus Christ when he rules the world for a thousand years while sitting on the throne of his father David. In other words, the Kingdom of God had a dual nature. This is sometimes called a dichotomy. In fact, I was further taught that Jesus took the Kingdom of God back to heaven with him. But is this actually true? If so, it seems confusing. But how does Jesus define the Kingdom of God? It is spoken of in all three of the synoptic Gospels. Let's look at them.

First, since Mark's Gospel was written first, let's look at it for the first hint :

> Mar 4:31 "*It is* like a mustard seed, which, when sown upon the soil, though it is smaller than all the seeds that are upon the soil, Mar 4:32 yet when it is sown, it grows up and becomes larger than all the garden plants and forms large branches; so that THE BIRDS OF THE AIR can NEST UNDER ITS SHADE."

Now let's look at Matthews Gospel for the second hint:

> Matt 13:33 He told them another parable. "The kingdom of heaven **is like leaven** that a woman took and hid in three measures of flour, till it was all leavened."

Now let's look at Luke's Gospel:

> Luk 13:18 So He was saying, "What is the kingdom of God like, and to what shall I compare it?
> Luk 13:19 "It is like a mustard seed, which a man took and threw into his own garden; and it grew and became a tree, and THE BIRDS OF THE AIR NESTED IN ITS BRANCHES."
> Luk 13:20 And again He said, "To what shall I compare the kingdom of God?
> Luk 13:21 **"It is like leaven,** which a woman took and hid in three pecks of flour until it was all leavened."

Now by a comparison of these Gospels, is there something that immediately jumps out at us? Both are likened to leaven. Yes! The Kingdom of God and the Kingdom of Heaven is the same Kingdom!! Why is this so hard to understand? What did Riddlebarger have to say on this subject? From my reading in his book, it was clear that he believed the Kingdom of God was a present reality, but had an "already, not yet" aspect to it. He gives 6 reasons for this.

1. Jesus cast out demons
2. Satan fell from heaven and was bound. This is based on Luke 10:17-19.

   The seventy returned with joy, saying, "Lord, even the demons are subject to us in Your name." And He said to them, "I was watching Satan fall from heaven like lightning. Behold, I have given you authority to tread on serpents and scorpions, and over all the power of the enemy, and nothing will injure you."

3. Jesus performed miracles, miracles unlike anyone had ever seen before.
4. The Gospel was preached to the poor.
5. Jesus forgave sins.
6. The kingdom was present because Jesus declared it to be a spiritual kingdom.

Note what he says regarding the fifth and sixth signs:

The fact that Jesus declared the forgiveness of sins was a sure sign that the kingdom was present. When seen against this backdrop, it is difficult to argue that Jesus took the kingdom back to heaven as dispensationalists claim.

Sixth, the kingdom was present because Jesus declared it was a spiritual kingdom. The Pharisees asked Jesus when the kingdom of God was coming. They knew what the prophets had written, and they saw that Jesus clearly connected himself and his ministry to this particular aspect of prophetic revelation. **Jesus responded by saying, "The kingdom of God does not come with your careful observation, nor will people say, 'Here it is,' or 'There it is,' because the kingdom of God is within you"** (Luke 17: 20– 21). When Pilate asked our Lord about the nature of this kingdom, Jesus said, "My kingdom is not of this world. . . . But now my kingdom is from another place" (John 18: 36). **Jesus' kingdom was a spiritual kingdom, completely unlike the nationalistic kingdom Israel expected.** This should also be a caution to those who would see Jesus's kingdom in terms of nationalism or secular progress in economics, politics, and culture. Many interpreters, accordingly, see the need to equate the present eschatological kingdom with the age to come. [28] In other words, when the kingdom came in the person of Jesus, the age to come also arrived, at least in some provisional sense. The consummation of that kingdom, when Jesus Christ returns to judge the world, raise the dead, and make all things new, coincides with the arrival of the age to come in all its fullness. This is why the two-age model depicts the presence of the age to come in a provisional sense during the course of this present evil age. It indicates that the presence of Jesus's spiritual kingdom, the "rule of Christ," is a reality that guarantees the consummation of the kingdom of God yet to come.[11] **(emphasis mine)**

What Riddlebarger says about the Kingdom of God makes sense, and seems thoroughly based on Scripture. Jesus said "The kingdom of God is within you" (or within your midst, as variously translated). But here once again, we see he makes reference to this two age model, that it has an already, not yet flavor to it. Still, I find this two age model a bit confusing.

But this did clear up the question: What is the kingdom of God? How much clearer could it be in the Bible? After all of the verses that are mentioned here, how is it that so many people have gotten it wrong?

These Scripture passages make it clear that the Kingdom of God _is present now among us!_ It is not something for which we have to wait for in a future cataclysmic event. We can experience the Kingdom of God right now in our present lives! This kingdom is not a physical kingdom. It is a spiritual kingdom (although it does have physical components) which is now within our midst, and it is alive through us who believe.

As Christ put it when speaking to Pilate:

> John 18:36 Jesus answered, "My kingdom is not of this world. If My kingdom were of this world, then My servants would be fighting so that I would not be handed over to the Jews; but as it is, My kingdom is not of this realm."

Yes, the Kingdom of God was introduced with the presence of Jesus on the earth. He described it as a "Mustard Seed" when planted, but grew steadily and eventually became huge in scope. This is in fact what is happening right before our eyes, and nothing can stop it! It is as described in the Old Testament book of Daniel:

> Dan 2:44 "In the days of those kings the God of heaven will set up a kingdom which will never be destroyed, and _that_ kingdom will not be left for another people; it will crush and put an end to all these kingdoms, but it will itself endure forever.

What Jesus was saying was that this Kingdom was at hand in his time. It was established when he came to earth and it is here right now in our midst, and it is staying forever! It is just as King Solomon said: "A generation goes, and a generation comes, but the earth remains forever."(Eccl 1:4).

But now that Riddlebarger made all of these good points, I still had to deal with his view of eschatology. The first was the two age model. It seemed to make sense. But at the same time it was somewhat confusing. He was an Amillennialist. So what is Amillennial eschatology? From Riddlebarger's book we read the following:

> My own position is Reformed amillennialism, which can also be called "present" or "realized" millennialism. Reformed eschatology argues for a present millennial age manifest in the present reign of Jesus Christ in heaven. [32] I stand in the Dutch Reformed school and redemptive-historical trajectory of Geerhardus Vos, Herman Ridderbos, Anthony Hoekema, Cornelis Venema, and Meredith Kline.
>
> Amillenarians hold that the promises made to Israel, David, and Abraham in the Old Testament are fulfilled by Jesus Christ and his church during this present age (see chart on page 45). The millennium is the period of time between the two advents of our Lord, with the thousand years of Revelation 20 being symbolic of the entire interadvental age. At the first advent of Jesus Christ, Satan was bound by Christ's victory over him at Calvary and the empty tomb. The effects of this victory continued because of the presence of the kingdom of God via the preaching of the Gospel and were evidenced by Jesus's miracles. Because of the spread of the Gospel, Satan is no longer free to deceive the nations. **Christ is presently reigning in heaven and will reign during the entire period between his first and second coming.** At the end of the millennial age, Satan is released, a great apostasy breaks out, the general resurrection occurs, Jesus Christ returns in final judgment for all people, and he establishes a new heaven and earth.[12] (emphasis mine)

However, as I continued reading this book, questions were raised in my mind.

Although it was now apparent to me that Jesus spoke to his disciples telling them what they should expect, it sounded like according to this amillennial view that much of this was still in our future. Note what he says:

> New Testament revelation opened with the strong sense that God was about to fulfill the promises anticipated under the old covenant. The promised Redeemer was about to come. As the New Testament writers unpacked this Old Testament expectation and its fulfillment in Jesus Christ, it soon became clear that the fulfillment of the Old Testament prophecies regarding the messianic age and the blessings Christians can enjoy in the present age were a major step toward a final and glorious fulfillment to come. This is known as the already, the "realized eschatology," or as George Ladd speaks of it, "the presence of the future." Because of Jesus Christ and his coming, the Christian possesses the complete fulfillment and blessings of all the promises of the messianic age made under the old covenant. But the arrival of the messianic age also brought with it a new series of promises to be fulfilled at the end of the age. The fulfilled promises pointed to a more glorious and future fulfillment. This is called the not yet or future eschatology. It is this already/not yet tension that serves as the basis for understanding much of New Testament eschatological expectation.[13]

What was this already/not yet tension? Did it make sense that God would have such conflicting information in a Bible that we are supposed to understand?

He stated further:

> Therefore, the New Testament contains a distinct and pronounced tension between what God has already done in fulfilling the promises of the Old Testament and what God will do yet in the future. This so-called already/ not yet tension characterizes much of New Testament theology.[14]

Where did he get this from Scripture? Is there any place in Scripture that really states that some of these promises will not be fulfilled for thousands of years? It seems to me that if we are going to apply the correct rules of interpretation, then should we not be trying to understand what the words written to specific groups in the Bible meant to them, and then search for application in our lives? After all, prophecies that applied to them, could not also apply to us, could they?

Furthermore, it became apparent to me that according to this eschatological view the term "Last Days" **was a misnomer.** Wouldn't it be reasonable to think that the "Last Days" was a short period of time? How is it possible that the "Last Days" could keep going for thousands of years? Yet this is exactly what is being stated in this book. Note what it says:

> Paul made it clear that Christians should expect something quite unlike postmillenarians would lead us to believe. This can be seen in two distinct lines of thinking in Paul's writings. One has to do with the characteristics of the last days. Throughout the New Testament, the last days constitute that period of time between the first and second advent of Jesus Christ. In his second pastoral letter to young Timothy, Paul gave this warning about the course of the age: But mark this: There will be terrible times in the last days. People will be lovers of themselves, lovers of money, boastful, proud, abusive, disobedient to their parents, ungrateful, unholy, without love, unforgiving, slanderous, without self-control, brutal, not lovers of the good, treacherous, rash, conceited, lovers of pleasure rather than lovers of God— having a form of godliness but denying its power. Have nothing to do with them. (2 Tim. 3: 1– 5) Although some postmillenarians say that the "last days" is a reference to that brief period of apostasy before Christ comes back, [32] Paul more likely referred to the course of the entire interadvental age.[15]

So much like what we hear from the dispensational camp, Riddlebarger is also saying that the "Last Days" is a period of time _which stretches for thousands of years!_ Why would it be labeled as the "Last Days?" Logically speaking, could this term, "Last Days" really mean thousands of years? Wouldn't another name be more appropriate? This just did not make sense.

Finally, there were too many passages that just did not fit. For example consider Isaiah 65:20 "No longer will there be in it an infant *who lives but a few* days, Or an old man who does not live out his days; For the youth will die at the age of one hundred and the one who does not reach the age of one hundred will be *thought* accursed."

When will this happen? If you say it will happen prior to the supposed cosmic renewal of 2 Peter 3, then this fits in with either Premillennialism or Postmillennialism. If you say it happens after the 2nd coming of Christ and (as labeled by Riddlebarger), the cosmic renewal, then we have death in eternity. If you say this is figurative language to indicate the time after Christ's Second Coming, according to dispensationalism or amillennialism then why would there be a reference to death at all? **There is no death in eternity.**

My question was this: This system certainly seems more accurate than dispensationalism, but are there holes like this in all of these eschatological systems? It seemed that this was what I was learning. My search would continue. Maybe I needed to get that book out again that I started with. There was a section that seemed interesting to me, but I put aside for the time.

NOTES

1. "Four Views on the Book of Revelation" – 1998, Zondervan Publishing, C. Marvin Pate, General Editor
    Preterist – Kennth L. Gentry Jr.
    Idealist – Sam Hamstra Jr.
    Progressive Dispensationalist – C. Marvin Pate
    Classical Dispensationalist – Robert L. Thomas

These are the four views and the authors that are the subject of this book.

2. "What's 1000 years between friends?" http://kimriddlebarger.squarespace.com/theological-essays/amilllecture%20revised.pdf
3. Ibid.
4. Riddlebarger, Kim (2013-08-15). A Case for Amillennialism: Understanding the End Times (pp. 50-51). Baker Publishing Group. Kindle Edition.
5. Ibid, (p. 52). Baker Publishing Group. Kindle Edition.
6. Interpreting the Bible, Mickelsen, 1981, A.B., Eerdmans Publishing Co., Grand Rapids MI. page 5
7. Riddlebarger, Kim (2013-08-15). A Case for Amillennialism: Understanding the End Times (p. 181). Baker Publishing Group. Kindle Edition.
8. Ibid, (pp. 160-161). Baker Publishing Group. Kindle Edition.
9. Ibid, (pp 104-105). Baker Publishing Group. Kindle Edition.
10. Ibid, (p. 204). Baker Publishing Group. Kindle Edition.
11. Ibid, (pp. 123-124). Baker Publishing Group. Kindle Edition.
12. Ibid, (p. 40). Baker Publishing Group. Kindle Edition.
13. Ibid, (p. 76). Baker Publishing Group. Kindle Edition.
14. Ibid, (p. 76). Baker Publishing Group. Kindle Edition.
15. Ibid, (p. 139). Baker Publishing Group. Kindle Edition.

Chapter 2

Prophecy Revisited

Equipped with the information I now had learned, I got that book out again (Four Views on the Book of Revelation, Marvin Pate General Editor)[1] to examine it more closely. After reading some more in Ken Gentry's section on Preterism, I realized that there were words of truth in what he wrote. I went back to that section entitled "The Temporal Expectation (Rev. 1:1-3)." Gentry pointed out something very important here that I had never actually realized before. The opening of the book of Revelation reads like this:

> Rev 1:1 The Revelation of Jesus Christ, which God gave Him to show to His bond-servants, the things which **must soon take place**; and He sent and communicated *it* by His angel to His bond-servant John,
> Rev 1:2 who testified to the word of God and to the testimony of Jesus Christ, *even* to all that he saw.
> Rev 1:3 Blessed is he who reads and those who hear the words of the prophecy, and heed the things which are written in it; for **the time is near.**

This is the very opening of the book! These are the first words written by John! Why is it that no one has ever pointed this out to me before? And how could I have been so stupid not to have seen it myself? The Apostle John laid out the time expectation of all of his visions before he ever mentioned any of them! These were all to **happen soon,** not thousands of years later. Even if I got nothing else from this discussion, that point became crystal clear in my mind. Gentry went on to point out that this idea was also in several other places in the book of Revelation, including the end of the book, where it says:

> Rev 22:7 "And behold, I am coming **quickly.** Blessed is he who heeds the words of the prophecy of this book."
> Rev 22:10 And he *said to me, "**Do not seal up the words** of the prophecy of this book, for the **time is near.**

The New Testament was written in Koine Greek. Therefore, when we have questions about the meaning of certain words and passages, we must go back to this ancient Greek language. Gentry pointed out that Greek lexicons and modern translations agree that these terms indicate what he called "temporal proximity." In other words, it meant exactly what it said. Near means near; shortly means shortly; soon means soon. There is no hidden meaning here. It reads in the English exactly as it means in the Greek.

Yes, even at the very end of the book of Revelation, we are told the same words by John! Why would he say these words unless he meant them? Why is this so obvious to me now, and why did I not see them before? What did he mean when he said not to seal up the book?

I did a little research on this last point and found out something which I had read earlier in my daily Bible readings, but had forgotten. In the book of Daniel, God told him:

> Dan 12:4 But you, Daniel, shut up the words and **seal the book, until the time of the end.** Many shall run to and fro, and knowledge shall increase." (ESV)

This told me that there must be a link between the words of Daniel and the words of John. God inspired both of these prophets, and there was an obvious link. What was it? I made a note that this must be explored further. As I continued reading what Gentry wrote here, he noted that this book, _The Revelation of Jesus Christ_ was written to give attention to the fact that since first century Israel had rejected the Messiah, its judgments applied to them.

After all, they were the ones who cried out to Pilate, "Crucify him!....Let his blood be on us and our children!" This made sense. The opening and closing words of this book made it clear that this was written to the first century people and the judgments that could be expected in the very near future. This had a ring of truth. It made sense. The puzzle pieces looked like they fit together. I remembered reading the account of Matthew 26 where Jesus was bound and questioned by the high priest in front of the members of the Jewish Sanhedrin. He was accused of blasphemy for claiming to be the Son of God, thus making himself equal to God. The account of this in Matthew's Gospel said:

> Matt 26:63 But Jesus remained silent. And the high priest said to him, "I adjure you by the living God, tell us if you are the Christ, the Son of God."
> Matt 26:64 Jesus said to him, "You have said so. But I tell you, from now on _YOU will see_ the Son of Man seated at the right hand of Power and coming on the clouds of heaven."
> Matt 26:65 Then the high priest tore his robes and said, "He has uttered blasphemy. What further witnesses do we need? You have now heard his blasphemy.

This answered the question, what did Jesus mean with these words? This was not a reference to some far distant event. Jesus was very specific. He said "**YOU will see** the Son of Man seated at the right hand of Power and coming on the clouds of heaven." Yes, he was speaking **directly** to the high priest. He told him that **he and the other members of the Sanhedrin would see** the Son of Man "seated at the right hand of power and coming on the clouds of heaven." Now, this passage made sense. Jesus **was telling them specifically** that he would return while they were still alive.

Now I had the answer to another question that had always bothered me. Why did Jesus tell them that he was going to return in that generation? What I had always been told was that the real meaning of this passage is that the generation which saw the signs he spoke of would also see the return of Christ, and those signs have not been present until now. The problem is that people who promulgate this view have been stating this **for the better part of four generations!** Yes, that's right. Since this concept was introduced by John Darby in the 1870's, there have been over 3.5 generations that have passed. Doesn't this speak to the fact that there is a problem with this eschatalogical position?

In the 1970's Hal Lindsey made his case for the premillennial rapture of the church based on the fact that Israel became a Nation in 1948. Considering that a generation in the Bible is 40 years, if you add one generation to this, you come up with 1988. He and several others expected the church to be raptured within that generation, but nothing happened! Now, as of the writing of this book, another 27 years has passed since this date of 1988, and we are still hearing the same old story! Doesn't anyone recognize a false doctrine when they hear it? The words spoken in Deuteronomy chapter 18 are still true! Note the words:

> Deut 18:22 "When a prophet speaks in the name of the LORD, if the thing does not come about or come true, that is the thing which the LORD has not spoken. **The prophet has spoken it presumptuously;** you shall not be afraid of him.

And speaking strictly from a logical perspective about that generation to which Jesus uttered the words from Matthew 24, Mark 13, and Luke 21, we have to ask the question: Why would he elaborate details to his disciples about something which would not happen for thousands of years? This would be of no concern to them. But actually, Jesus was telling them things that would happen **in their generation.** This was what they wanted to know!

This was the crux of their question. Note how it is worded in the opening of Matthew 24:

> Mat 24:1 Jesus came out from the temple and was going away when His disciples came up to point out the temple buildings to Him.
> Mat 24:2 And He said to them, "Do you not see all these things? Truly I say to you, not one stone here will be left upon another, which will not be torn down."
> Mat 24:3 As He was sitting on the Mount of Olives, the disciples came to Him privately, saying, "Tell us, when **will these things** happen, and what *will be* the sign of Your coming, and of the end of the age?"

Do you see it? They asked: "When will **these** things happen?" Their questions were about **that** period of time in which they were living. The above mentioned passage is the beginning of what is sometimes called the Olivet Discourse because it was given to his disciples while Jesus was sitting on the Mount of Olives. Church historian Eusebius points out that Jesus' words in this prophecy were fulfilled at the destruction of Jerusalem. That was less than 40 years later, and in the generation of which Jesus spoke. Eusebius recorded the following:

> But the number of calamities which everywhere fell upon the nation at that time; the extreme misfortunes to which the inhabitants of Judea were especially subjected, the thousands of men, as well as women and children, that perished by the sword, by famine, and by other forms of death innumerable—all these things, as well as the many great sieges which were carried on against the cities of Judea, and the excessive sufferings endured by those that fled to Jerusalem itself, as to a city of perfect safety, and finally the general course of the whole war, as well as its particular occurrences in detail, and **how at last the abomination of desolation, proclaimed by the prophets, Daniel 9:27 stood in the very temple of God,** so celebrated of old, the temple which was now awaiting its total and final destruction by fire — all these things any one that wishes may find accurately described in the history written by Josephus.[1]

And then later on in Chapter 7 he states:

> Verse 1: It is fitting to add to these accounts the <u>true</u> prediction of <u>our Saviour</u> in which he foretold these very events.....Verse 4: These things took place in this manner in the second year of the reign of <u>Vespasian,</u> in accordance with the prophecies of <u>our Lord and Saviour Jesus Christ,</u> who by divine power saw them beforehand as if they were already present, and wept and mourned according to the statement of the <u>holy</u> <u>evangelists,</u> who give the very words which he uttered, when, as if addressing Jerusalem herself, he said: 5. If you had <u>known,</u> even you, in this day, the things which belong unto your peace! But now they are hid from your eyes. For the days shall come upon you, that your enemies shall cast a rampart about you, and compass you round, and keep you in on every side, and shall lay you and your children even with the ground. 6. And then, as if speaking concerning the people, he says, For there shall be great distress in the land, and <u>wrath</u> upon this people. And they shall fall by the edge of the sword, and shall be led away captive into all nations. And Jerusalem shall be trodden down of the <u>Gentiles,</u> until the times of the <u>Gentiles</u> be fulfilled. And again: When you shall see Jerusalem compassed with armies, then <u>know</u> that the desolation thereof is near. 7. **If any one compares the words of <u>our Saviour</u> with the other accounts of the historian concerning the whole <u>war,</u> how can one fail to wonder, and to admit that the foreknowledge and the <u>prophecy</u> of <u>our Saviour</u> were <u>truly</u> divine and marvelously strange.**[2]

We will examine the details of this prophecy and its fulfillment in the material ahead. But here in this passage written by Eusebius we find that one of the chief historians of the Christian Church acknowledged the fulfillment of Jesus prophecy in AD 70. It is from this passage that I came to realize that in order to understand the meaning of Jesus "Last Days," I needed to understand the meaning of the 70 weeks of years in Daniel 9: 24-27, and the meaning of the Olivet discourse. Both of these are essential components of this issue.

Why is Daniel's Prophecy important?

So your question is: What does Daniel's prophecy have to do with all of this? The short answer is that Daniel would be given a prophetic timeline that would predict the coming events of the next 490 years of human history and would lead all the way to the Messiah and beyond. It would play a significant role in what would happen in the future of the disciples to whom Christ uttered his prophecy.

The Babylonian captivity was God's judgment on Israel's sin, and it lasted for 70 years. Second Chronicles 36:21 tells us why it was a 70 year exile:

> 2Ch 36:20 Those who had escaped from the sword he carried away to Babylon; and they were servants to him and to his sons until the rule of the kingdom of Persia,
> 2Ch 36:21 to fulfill the word of the LORD by the mouth of Jeremiah, until the land had enjoyed its sabbaths. All the days of its desolation it kept sabbath until seventy years were complete.

One of the primary aspects of the law was the Sabbath. In fact it was even written in the 10 commandments. Violating the Sabbath day was a very serious sin for ancient Israel. One of the reasons God gave it to them was so they would recognize his sovereignty. Under this arrangement from God, every seventh year, the land was to be given a rest, and not be cultivated. Whatever grew up on its own could be eaten, but the land was not to be farmed. Under God's law, the land was to have its rest (Lev. 25:1-7). To make up for this, God promised an abundant crop in the sixth year, so no one would go hungry during the following Sabbath year (Lev. 25:20-22). Then the 50th year was called the jubilee year. God would provide for them **during this two year period** in the same manner. He would provide an abundant crop in the 48th year that would last them for 2 years.

God warned Israel in Leviticus 26 that if they did not keep this Sabbath by following his Sabbath law in this manner, they would have to forfeit their land for the entire period of the Sabbath's that they stole from God:

Lev 26:32 'I will make the land desolate so that your enemies who settle in it will be appalled over it.

Lev 26:33 'You, however, I will scatter among the nations and will draw out a sword after you, as your land becomes desolate and your cities become waste.

Lev 26:34 'Then the land will enjoy its Sabbaths all the days of the desolation, while you are in your enemies' land; then the land will rest and enjoy its Sabbaths.

Lev 26:35 'All the days of *its* desolation it will observe the rest which it did not observe on your Sabbaths, while you were living on it.

Since Israel blatantly ignored God's Sabbath laws, the prophet Jeremiah told them that they would soon see God's wrath. This is found in Jeremiah 25:

Jer 25:11 'This whole land will be a desolation and a horror, and these nations will serve the king of Babylon seventy years.

Jer 25:12 'Then it will be when seventy years are completed I will punish the king of Babylon and that nation,' declares the LORD, 'for their iniquity, and the land of the Chaldeans; and I will make it an everlasting desolation.

Jer 25:13 'I will bring upon that land all My words which I have pronounced against it, all that is written in this book which Jeremiah has prophesied against all the nations.

Jer 25:14 '(For many nations and great kings will make slaves of them, even them; and I will recompense them according to their deeds and according to the work of their hands.)'"

Just exactly as prophesied, Nebuchadnezzar and his armies came in and destroyed Jerusalem in its entirety, including the once magnificent temple that King Solomon built. Subsequently, the inhabitants of the city were taken captive. Note the account of this in 2 Kings:

> 2Ki 24:11 And Nebuchadnezzar the king of Babylon came to the city, while his servants were besieging it.
> 2Ki 24:12 Jehoiachin the king of Judah went out to the king of Babylon, he and his mother and his servants and his captains and his officials. So the king of Babylon took him captive in the eighth year of his reign.
> 2Ki 24:13 He carried out from there all the treasures of the house of the LORD, and the treasures of the king's house, and cut in pieces all the vessels of gold which Solomon king of Israel had made in the temple of the LORD, just as the LORD had said.
> 2Ki 24:14 Then he led away into exile all Jerusalem and all the captains and all the mighty men of valor, ten thousand captives, and all the craftsmen and the smiths. None remained except the poorest people of the land.

The prophet Daniel lived during the time of this exile. He was well aware of the prophecy of Jeremiah. He also realized that Jeremiah predicted an end to the Babylonian exile after 70 years. Daniel *was* living in obedience to the commands of God. As a result of this, God had shown him great favor. The first six chapters of the book of Daniel are a testimony to this. At the start of chapter 7 we find the beginning of Daniel's prophecy. But now as we look at chapter 9, we find that Daniel is very concerned. He knew the seventy year period was coming to an end, and as the chapter opens we find Daniel getting ready to pray for the restoration of Jerusalem and its temple. Here, Daniel prays that Yahweh, a keeper of covenants and merciful God to those who love him, would turn his anger away from them. His plea with God was to act without delay for his own sake, and so that the people called by his name could be restored. His prayer was a desperate plea because he realized that by their repeated disobedience, Israel broke the covenant given through Moses. Notice the extreme humility of Daniel's prayer in the chapter's opening:

Dan 9:1 In the first year of Darius the son of Ahasuerus, of Median descent, who was made king over the kingdom of the Chaldeans--

Dan 9:2 in the first year of his reign, I, Daniel, observed in the books the number of the years which was *revealed as* the word of the LORD to Jeremiah the prophet for the completion of the desolations of Jerusalem, *namely,* seventy years.

Daniel made reference to a prophecy the Lord spoke through the prophet Jeremiah years earlier:

Jer 29:10 "For thus says the LORD, 'When seventy years have been completed for Babylon, I will visit you and fulfill My good word to you, to bring you back to this place.

Although no one listened to him at the time, there is no question that Jeremiah the prophet was now respected by the people, for his prophecies were accurate. And it appears that Daniel also had easy access to the words of the prophet.

Dan 9:3 So I gave my attention to the Lord God to seek *Him by* prayer and supplications, with fasting, sackcloth and ashes.

Dan 9:4 I prayed to the LORD my God and confessed and said, "Alas, O Lord, the great and awesome God, who keeps His covenant and lovingkindness for those who love Him and keep His commandments,

Dan 9:5 we have sinned, committed iniquity, acted wickedly and rebelled, even turning aside from Your commandments and ordinances.

It is apparent that Daniel was deeply concerned. As he looked around, even though he could see the words of Jeremiah before him, he did not see anything that would indicate that this was about to happen. Therefore, as was typical in times of public mourning, he prayed, fasted, dressed in sackcloth, and put ashes upon his head. His prayer was not for him alone, but was a corporate prayer on behalf of all of those in exile.

Dan 9:6 "Moreover, we have not listened to Your servants the prophets, who spoke in Your name to our kings, our princes, our fathers and all the people of the land.

Dan 9:7 "Righteousness belongs to You, O Lord, but to us open shame, as it is this day--to the men of Judah, the inhabitants of Jerusalem and all Israel, those who are nearby and those who are far away in all the countries to which You have driven them, because of their unfaithful deeds which they have committed against You.

You can hear the profound sincerity of Daniel's heart in this prayer. He was _pleading_ with God on behalf of this sinful nation.

Dan 9:8 Open shame belongs to us, O Lord, to our kings, our princes and our fathers, because we have sinned against You.

Dan 9:9 To the Lord our God _belong_ compassion and forgiveness, for we have rebelled against Him;

Dan 9:10 nor have we obeyed the voice of the LORD our God, to walk in His teachings which He set before us through His servants the prophets.

Dan 9:11 Indeed all Israel has transgressed Your law and turned aside, not obeying Your voice; so the curse has been poured out on us, along with the oath which is written in the law of Moses the servant of God, for we have sinned against Him.

Dan 9:12 Thus He has confirmed His words which He had spoken against us and against our rulers who ruled us, to bring on us great calamity; for under the whole heaven there has not been done _anything_ like what was done to Jerusalem.

Without question, Daniel correctly declared the sins of the people as he made supplication in their behalf. The history of this people is replete with total rebellion against God. The prophet Jeremiah, tabbed as the weeping prophet, preached to this stubborn people for over 50 years without a single sign of repentance on their part, and Daniel saw nothing that would indicate a change of heart in them.

Dan 9:13 As it is written in the law of Moses, all this calamity has come on us; yet we have not sought the favor of the LORD our

God by turning from our iniquity and giving attention to Your truth.

Dan 9:14 Therefore the LORD has kept the calamity in store and brought it on us; for the LORD our God is righteous with respect to all His deeds which He has done, but we have not obeyed His voice.

Dan 9:15 And now, O Lord our God, who have brought Your people out of the land of Egypt with a mighty hand and have made a name for Yourself, as it is this day--we have sinned, we have been wicked.

Dan 9:16 O Lord, in accordance with all Your righteous acts, let now Your anger and Your wrath turn away from Your city Jerusalem, Your holy mountain; for because of our sins and the iniquities of our fathers, Jerusalem and Your people *have become* a reproach to all those around us.

Yes, Daniel's pleading was **not** due to the repentance of the people, but his prayer was fixed on **the character of God!** For it was based on **God's** justice, **God's** mercy, and **God's** goodness. It was based on the **faithfulness of God** to his people. So in view of all of these character traits, he pleaded that God would intervene and turn away his anger from his people now. After continuing to elaborate on this sin, and acknowledging that the seventy year period is about to end, notice how Daniel concluded his prayer:

Dan 9:17 So now, our God, listen to the prayer of Your servant and to his supplications, and for Your sake, O Lord, let Your face shine on Your desolate sanctuary.

Dan 9:18 O my God, incline Your ear and hear! Open Your eyes and see our desolations and the city which is called by Your name; for we are not presenting our supplications before You on account of any merits of our own, but on account of Your great compassion.

Dan 9:19 O Lord, hear! O Lord, forgive! O Lord, listen and take action! For Your own sake, O my God, do not delay, because Your city and Your people are called by Your name."

But Daniel did not even get to complete his prayer before God provided a response. The God who searches hearts saw the heart of this faithful loyal servant, and immediately the angel Gabriel appears in response that God would indeed renew this covenant.

> Dan 9:20 Now while I was speaking and praying, and confessing my sin and the sin of my people Israel, and presenting my supplication before the LORD my God in behalf of the holy mountain of my God,
> Dan 9:21 while I was still speaking in prayer, then the man Gabriel, whom I had seen in the vision previously, came to me in *my* extreme weariness about the time of the evening offering.
> Dan 9:22 He gave *me* instruction and talked with me and said, "O Daniel, I have now come forth to give you insight with understanding.

It is quite clear that when Daniel kneeled for this period for prayer, it was not to inquire into the ultimate events which would occur in Jerusalem, but merely to pray that the purpose of God, as predicted by Jeremiah, might be accomplished. There is no indication here as to what time Daniel began to pray, but it is quite possible that after reading the words of Jeremiah, he devoted a considerable portion of the day to this prayer.

> Dan 9:23 "At the beginning of your supplications the command was issued, and I have come to tell *you,* for you are highly esteemed; so give heed to the message and gain understanding of the vision.

However, God gave Daniel not only an implied assurance about the accomplishment of these purposes, **but also stated something far more profound.** He gave him a remarkable prophecy concerning events that would consume the next 490 years of human history. In the following chapter we will look at this prophecy in detail.

NOTES

1. Church History (Eusebius), Book 3, Chapter 5, verse 4.
   From http://www.newadvent.org/fathers/250103.htm)
2. Church History (Eusebius), Book 3, Chapter 7, verses 1, 4-7.
   http://www.newadvent.org/fathers/250103.htm)

Chapter 3

A Consideration of Daniel 9:24-27

This will be a lengthy and somewhat complicated chapter. If you get bogged down in the details, read the conclusion in the form of a summary first, then go back and look at the details of this prophecy. I have gone to great lengths to detail this as much as possible because getting the proper understanding of this passage *is key* to understanding the meaning of the "Last Days" of which our Lord spoke. There are some very specific things that are revealed in this prophecy that are crucial to understand. One of the things that truly puzzled me enough to look so closely at this passage is that some believe that parts of this passage are a **reference to Christ**, and others believe that those references are a **reference to antichrist**! *How is it possible that there could be these two beliefs???* This alone should be enough to make us want to examine this prophecy closely. But since this passage *gives the timeline for the next 490 years*, and since it leads to the life of our beloved Savior and beyond, we must examine it closely. When I looked at this a few years ago, I went into much more detail, including an analysis of the key words in Hebrew. This document is available on my website at www.truthinliving.net. In this rendition of these verses I will provide a condensed version of what I originally wrote.

I have selected this passage to be read from J.P. Green's Literal Translation (**LITV**). This is because it appears to be the closest to the original text, and appears to have no translator bias. However, since I am making reference to much of what Albert Barnes wrote in his commentary on this passage, the details written by him and others of the 19th century will reflect the writings of the King James Version.

> Dan 9:24 Seventy weeks are decreed as to your people, and as to your holy city, to finish the transgression, and to make an end of sins, and to make atonement for iniquity, and to bring in everlasting righteousness, and to seal up the vision and prophecy, and to anoint the Most Holy.
>
> Dan 9:25 Know, then, and understand *that* from the going out of a word to restore and to rebuild Jerusalem, to Messiah *the* Prince, *shall be* seven weeks and sixty two weeks. The street shall be built again, and the wall, even in times of affliction.
>
> Dan 9:26 And after sixty two weeks, Messiah shall be cut off, but not *for* Himself. And the people of a coming ruler shall destroy the city and the sanctuary. And its end *shall be* with the flood, and ruins are determined, and war *shall be* until *the* end.
>
> Dan 9:27 And he shall confirm a covenant with the many *for* one week. And in the middle of the week he shall cause the sacrifice and the offering to cease. And on a corner *of the altar will be* abominations *that* desolate, even until *the* end. And that which was decreed shall pour out on the desolator. (LITV)

As I mentioned in the previous chapter, we must therefore begin by looking at the first part of the chapter (vs 1-19), wherein we find its context. Daniel was praying a prayer of intercession to God for restoration of Jerusalem and its temple. Afterward, the angel Gabriel sent him a message concerning the exile (vs 20-27). Here, Daniel prays that God, a keeper of covenants, a merciful God to those who love him, would turn his anger away from them. He asked God to act without delay for his own sake, and so that the people called by his name could be restored. His prayer was a desperate plea because he realized that Israel shattered the covenant given to Moses by their repeated disobedience. Gabriel provided a message in response that God would indeed renew this covenant. The details of this he laid out in verses 24-27 as quoted above.

This passage may be properly divided into two parts. First, in 9:24, was a statement of what would occur in the time specified - the seventy weeks, (we will see that this was a reference to 70 weeks of years). Next, in 9:25, was a statement of the way it would be accomplished. Here we see the whole time of the seventy weeks broken up into three smaller portions of seven, sixty-two, and one. These were given to designate some important periods of time. The last week was again subdivided to show that something would happen that would take up the entire week, but in the middle of that week a significant event would occur.

Daniel was looking at the close of the seventy "years" of Hebrew exile. But the angel Gabriel _disclosed_ to him a _new period of "seventy times seven,"_ in which still more important events took place, a period spoken of in the Greek as seventy "heptades", meaning weeks. Thus, Daniel was informed of this **_new period of seventy weeks of years, or 490 years._** We can get a picture of what was meant here by a comparison of Matt 8:21, 22 when Jesus spoke to Peter about forgiveness. Jesus told Peter that we should forgive up to seventy seven times. In such a connection, nothing but seventy "heptades" of years could be reasonably supposed to have been meant by the angel Gabriel in this passage. Gabriel was trying to console Daniel and to assure him about the rebuilding of the city, and to inform him of the great events that were to occur there.

So the passage begins with "Seventy weeks are decreed as to your people, and as to your holy city." Nineteenth century American theologian Albert Barnes analyzed this phrase. I will be quoting Barnes a lot in this section, because his analysis is very thorough. Note his words:

> The meaning would seem to be, that this portion of time - the seventy weeks - was "cut off" from the whole of duration, or cut

<u>out of it, as it were, and set by itself for a definite purpose</u>. It does not mean that it was cut off from the time which the city would naturally stand, or that this time was "abbreviated," but that a portion of time - to wit, **four hundred and ninety years** - was designated or appointed with reference to the city, to accomplish the great and important object which is immediately specified.

A certain, definite period was fixed on, and when this was past, the promised Messiah would come. . . . .The true meaning seems to be, that the seventy weeks are spoken of "collectively," as denoting a period of time; that is, a period of seventy weeks is determined. <u>The prophet, in the use of *the singular verb*, seems to have contemplated the time, not as separate weeks, or as particular portions, but as one period</u>. (emphasis mine)

Barnes made some important points here with regard to this period of time. It was to be set *by itself* for a definite purpose. Thus, the seventy weeks of years was to be a *continuous period of time with no separation*. **This point is crucial** to understanding this passage. Daniel was here making special inquiry respecting his people and the holy city which was the capital of the nation. The purpose respecting the seventy weeks was in reference to "**your** people, and as to **your** holy city." It was not written to some far distant culture.

Now the angel Gabriel tells Daniel that there are 6 things to be accomplished during this period of time spanning 490 years:

1. To finish the transgression
2. To make an end of sins
3. To make reconciliation for iniquity
4. To bring in everlasting righteousness
5. To seal up vision and prophecy
6. To anoint the Most Holy

Many scholars have pointed out that what is unique about Daniel's prayer is the repeated use of the covenant name of God (YHWH) which is translated as "Yahweh" or "Jehovah" in English. J.P. Green's Literal Translation uses this name a total of 5 times in these 19 verses. This is covenant language. The entire ninth chapter of Daniel *follows the pattern set forth in Leviticus 26*. Daniel used this name because the theme of his prayer was about this covenant between God and Israel. It is about how Israel had broken the covenant, but that God in his mercy and grace promised to restore the nation to the holy city. Gabriel came to Daniel to show him that there is much more to be accomplished with the fulfillment of the seventy years given to the prophet Jeremiah. *Israel also **had to pay the "seventy sevens"** before the complete fulfillment of this prophecy could be reached.* During that period of time the six things outlined above would be accomplished.

1. To finish the transgression

Of this, Barnes notes the following:

> According to Hengstenberg, the sense here of "shutting up" is derived from the general notion of "restraining" or "hindering," belonging to the word; and he supposes that this will best accord with the other words in this member of the verse - "to cover," and "to seal up."

> The idea according to him is, that "sin, which hitherto lay naked and open before the eyes of a righteous God, is now by his mercy shut up, sealed, and covered, so that it can no more be regarded as existing - a figurative description of the forgiveness of sin.". . . The effect would be that which occurs when one is shut up in prison, and no longer goes at large. There would be a restraining power and influence which would check the progress of sin.

Thus, the meaning can be deduced as "restrain or covering up the sins of the world." This was what Christ did when he came to the earth. Thus we are led to a much more meaningful interpretation; a work which Christ would do to ultimately cover up, restrain and hinder sin. Yes, there was indeed victory planned through a coming Messiah! His work, through the sacrifice made on the cross, was such that it covered up and worked to restrain sin altogether!

2. To make an end to sins

Note the words of Barnes:

> The true rendering is, doubtless, "to seal sin;" and the idea is that of removing it from sight; to remove it from view.

Thus, the idea to be conveyed here is that sin was to be sealed up, or closed, or hidden, so that it will not be seen. It can be compared to a _sealed book, or a lock box_, the contents of which cannot be seen. It should be pointed out that Daniel had no idea of the meaning of this at the time. But since **we have Christ revealed**, we can understand how this was to be accomplished. It was accomplished by the blood of the atonement, through which sin has been forgiven. It is as if it were hidden from the view, sealed with a seal that cannot be broken.

3. To make reconciliation for iniquity

Notice here that this is different from the second purpose in that reconciliation is the word which is commonly used with reference to atonement. As Luther understood it, it meant "to reconcile for transgression." Its bearing would be on human iniquity; on the way by which it might be pardoned and removed from view, and never be a factor again. This would point forward to a method whereby sin could be taken care of, once and forever more.

4. To bring in everlasting righteousness

Again we have two key words, everlasting and righteousness.

The phrase "to bring in" - refers to the truth spoken of here by Gabriel that there would be some way in which righteousness would be brought into the world. Again, Daniel was not given the meaning of this, but today, through "Christ revealed," we understand that it has been brought in by the Messiah. As Barnes notes in his commentary:

> The word "everlasting" is used here to denote that the righteousness would be permanent and perpetual. In reference to the method of becoming righteous, it would be unchanging - the standing method ever onward by which men would become holy; in reference to the individuals who should become righteous

under this system, it would be a righteousness which would continue forever.

What a glorious promise we have as revealed in Christ. It is a permanent and enduring foundation on which we can base our faith. If we believe in Christ, we are a new creation, justified and declared righteous forever!

5. To seal up vision and prophecy

Here we have one key phrase "seal up," and two key words, "vision" and "prophecy."

Thus, we could rightly interpret this to mean "To authenticate or close up vision and prophecy." Once a scroll was sealed, it would be imprinted with a specific seal mark. The purpose was that it would be authentic until it was opened. If opened, it would need to be sealed again and authenticated by the mark.

Concerning this, note what Barnes says:

> To seal, says he, has also the idea of confirming, since the contents of a writing are secured or made fast by a seal. .... It would be, as it were, locking it up, or sealing it, forever. It would determine all that seemed to be undetermined about it; settle all that seemed to be indefinite, and leave it no longer uncertain what was meant. According to this interpretation the meaning would be, that the prophecies would be sealed up or settled by the coming of the Messiah. (underline mine).

Christ would settle this matter once and for all. Only Christ could authenticate this prophecy, for only Christ could provide the answers to the other parts of this prophecy.

6. To anoint the Most Holy

Here we have one key word, and one key phrase. The key word is anoint. The key phrase is Most Holy. As has already been noted, the entire chapter of Daniel chapter 9 is covenant language. The entire ninth chapter of Daniel follows the pattern set forth in Leviticus 26.

Although the term "Most Holy" does not appear in Leviticus 26, it is important to point out something *quite profound* with regard to the phrase "Most Holy." The term "Most Holy" appeared 44 times in the Bible. **Of these 44 times it appeared in Leviticus _only_ in reference to a sacrifice.** In most of the other instances it refers to the "Most Holy Place" or the Holy of Holies in the temple. Please notice again; in _every instance_ in which this term is found in the book of Leviticus, **it is in reference to _a sacrifice_.** And in Leviticus we find a reference to the lamb as follows:

> Lev 14:13 "Next he shall _slaughter the male lamb_ in the place where they slaughter the sin offering and the burnt offering, at the place of the sanctuary--for the guilt offering, like the sin offering, belongs to the priest; _it is most holy_. (underline italic mine)

This tied all of the verses together as one unit referring to the Christ! For _he was the lamb of God_ who took away the sin of the world (John 1:29).

Regarding this passage Barnes notes:

> The word would then denote a setting apart to a sacred use, or _consecrating a person or place as holy._ Oil, or an unguent, prepared according to a specified rule, was commonly employed for this purpose, but the word may be used in a figurative sense - as denoting to set apart or consecrate in any way "without" the use of oil - as in the case of the Messiah. So far as this word, therefore, is concerned, what is here referred to may have occurred without the literal use of oil, by any act of consecration or dedication to a holy use.

It must be pointed out here that there is much controversy surrounding the interpretation of this last phrase in Daniel 9:24. The phrase, "the Most Holy" has been interpreted many different ways. By the dispensationalist it has been understood to apply literally to the most holy place - the holy of holies, in the temple. Some have referred to it as the whole temple, which is regarded as holy. Some have even referred to it as Jerusalem or the Christian Church.

Adam Clarke, in his commentary makes this comment regarding the "anointing of the Most Holy" in Daniel 9:24:

And to anoint the Most Holy, קדש קדשים kodesh kodashim, "the Holy of holies." משיח mashach, to anoint, (from which comes משיח mashiach, the Messiah, the anointed one), signifies in general, to consecrate or appoint to some special office. <u>Here it means the consecration or appointment of our blessed Lord, the Holy One of Israel, to be the Prophet, Priest, and King of mankind.</u> (emphasis mine)

Once again as confirmed by Clarke, the most holy spoken of here is the coming Messiah. This agrees with the context of Daniel 9.

Moving on to verse 25 we find:

Dan 9:25 Know, then, and understand *that* from the going out of a word to restore and to rebuild Jerusalem, to Messiah *the* Prince, *shall be* seven weeks and sixty two weeks. The street shall be built again, and the wall, even in times of affliction.

Next Gabriel laid out the timeframe of the prophecy. It appears that Gabriel gave Daniel the assurance that the promise of the walls and streets of Jerusalem, now desolate, would be built again. His mind was particularly anxious respecting the desolate condition of the city, and the declaration is here made that it would be restored. But when does it start? One of the key words here is "commandment." In Hebrew this word is: דבר *dâbâr*. The expression "gone forth" (מצא *môtsâ'*) would therefore indicate the "issuing" of an order or decree. The problem is - which of the several decrees that were issued, was the decree spoken of here?

A study of the books of Ezra and Nehemiah show that there were 4 decrees that went forth. The first was the decree in 538 BC. But upon examination of that decree, it was given to rebuild <u>only</u> the temple. The prophecy was clear that it was to be a decree to rebuild the <u>city</u> of Jerusalem. This is what is indicated by the term "the street and the wall" in the verse. The subsequent decrees of Darius and Artaxerxes I were issued because of all the trouble encountered by opposers of this rebuilding plan.

It wasn't until the 20th year of the reign of Artaxerxes that a different decree was issued and delivered by the hand of Nehemiah that also outlined the rebuilding of the city wall of Jerusalem. Therefore most Bible scholars agree that ___the issuing of the decree in 457 BC would be the correct one___ to be used in the dating of this seventy weeks of years.

Let's look back at Daniel 9:25. We see that we have two periods mentioned. First there was a period of seven weeks, and then a period of 62 weeks, equaling 69 weeks (of years). Therefore, we see the first seven weeks as a 49-year period. The Scripture tells us that it would be in troublous times. If you study the book of Nehemiah, you see that they had a lot of trouble building the city, due to the opposing efforts of Sanballat the Horonite, and Tobiah the Ammonite. ___So calculating from 457 BC___ we see that 49 years later puts us at about 408 BC. Thus, we begin the timeline as follows:

The Decree to   Jerusalem
rebuild the City   and Temple
and Temple   rebuild finished
457 BC   408 BC

O---------------------------O
seven weeks
of years = 49 years

Now adding another 62 weeks of years, the total is 62 x 7 = 434 more years. Taking into account the difference of the Jewish calendar being 5 days shorter per year, and leap years, and no year zero, this would bring us to somewhere around AD 27. Of course these calculations may vary slightly, but it gives us valid assurance that this prophecy is referring to Messiah the Prince spoken of in Daniel 9:25.

The Decree to rebuild the City and Temple 457 BC	Jerusalem and Temple rebuild finished 408 BC	Jesus begins his ministry after 483 years AD 27
O-----------------------	O-----------------------------------	-------O
seven weeks of years = 49 years	sixty-two weeks of years = 434 years	

Now, moving on to verse 26 we read:

> Dan 9:26 And after sixty two weeks, Messiah shall be cut off, but not *for* Himself. And the people of a coming ruler shall destroy the city and the sanctuary. And its end *shall be* with the flood, and ruins are determined, and war *shall be* until *the* end.

Spoken of here is the period of four hundred and thirty-four years. Gabriel has shown in the previous verse that during the first period of "seven weeks" the wall and the street would be built, in essence, the city. This would be during turbulent times. In this period of time the particular characteristic would be that the Messiah would be cut off, and that a series of events would commence which would be completed in the destruction of the city and the temple. **He does not say that this would happen immediately**, but it would be an event which would _follow_ the close of that period. The word does not mean necessarily immediately, but it denotes what is to succeed - to follow. So with this it is referring to the "next event" in the order of events to occur.

As Albert Barnes notes in his commentary:

> There are two circumstances in the prophecy itself which go to show that it is not meant that this would immediately follow:

> (a) One is, that in the previous verse it is said that the "sixty-two weeks" would extend "unto the Messiah;" that is, either to his birth or to his manifestation as such; and it is not implied anywhere that he would be "cut off" at once on his appearing, nor is such a supposition reasonable, or one that would have been embraced by an ancient student of the prophecies;

(b) the other is, that, in the subsequent verse, it is expressly said that what he would accomplish in causing the oblation to cease would occur "in the midst of the week;" that is, of the remaining one week that would complete the seventy. This could not occur if he were to be "cut off" immediately at the close of the sixty-two weeks.

The careful student of this prophecy, therefore, would anticipate that **the Messiah would appear at the close of the sixty-two weeks,** and that he would continue during a part, at least, of the remaining one week before he would be cut off. This point could have been clearly made out from the prophecy before the Messiah came. (emphasis mine)

But not for himself – Our Lord Jesus the Messiah did not die for himself. His life was given as a ransom for others. His human life would cease, and from a human standpoint his dominion would cease. What the passage says after this is that "the people of the prince that shall come shall destroy the city and the sanctuary; and the end thereof *shall be* with a flood, and unto the end of the war desolations are determined." Thus, the Messiah would come as a "Prince." Most everyone who knew him expected that he would come to rule and set up a kingdom. But he would be suddenly cut off by a violent death. The anticipated Kingdom of David would not be set up on earth as expected with the Messiah on the throne. He would have no successor; and soon the people of a foreign prince would come and would sweep all away. This is not to say that the real object of his coming would be thwarted, or that he would not set up a kingdom in accordance with the prediction properly explained, but that such a kingdom as expected by the people would not be set up. Thus, there would be nothing from a human perspective.

Putting it all together, Adam Clarke notes in his commentary of this verse:

> **And the people of the prince that shall come shall destroy the city and the sanctuary** - By the "prince" **Titus, the son of Vespasian, is plainly intended**; and "the people of that prince"

are no other than the Romans, who, according to the prophecy, destroyed the sanctuary, הקדש hakkodesh, the holy place or temple, and, as a flood, swept away all, till the total destruction of that obstinate people finished the war. (emphasis mine)

Thus we see that *after* the 62 weeks there would be a prince who would destroy the city and the sanctuary. This rightly refers to the Roman prince Titus who destroyed the city and *fulfilled the prophecy given by Jesus* concerning the temple in Matt 24:2: "Do you not see all these things? Truly I say to you, not one stone here will be left upon another, which will not be torn down." This prophecy would have been thought impossible 40 years prior. The temple was amazing. It was the pride of the Jewish nation.

In the opening of Book 7 Chapter 1 of Josephus' Wars of the Jews we note:

Now as soon as the army had no more people to slay or to plunder, because there remained none to be the objects of their fury, (for they would not have spared any, had there remained any other work to be done,) Caesar gave orders that they should now demolish the entire city and temple, but should leave as many of the towers standing as were of the greatest eminency; that is, Phasaelus, and Hippicus, and Mariamne; and so much of the wall as enclosed the city on the west side. This wall was spared, in order to afford a camp for such as were to lie in garrison, as were the towers also spared, in order to demonstrate to posterity what kind of city it was, and how well fortified, which the Roman valor had subdued; but for all the rest of the wall, *it was so thoroughly laid even with the ground by those that dug it up to the foundation, that **there was left nothing** to make those that came thither believe it had ever been inhabited*. This was the end which Jerusalem came to by the madness of those that were for innovations; a city otherwise of great magnificence, and of mighty fame among all mankind.[4]

Under the command of Titus, in AD 70 there was complete destruction. Everything spoken of above was reduced to rubble.

The account of the siege and destruction of the city is left to us by Josephus, a historian who later became known as Flavius Josephus, being named such by Roman Emperor Vespasian.

Now, as we move to verse 27 we see:

> Dan 9:27 And he shall **confirm** a covenant with the many *for* one week. And in the middle of the week he shall cause the sacrifice and the offering to cease. And on a corner *of the altar will be* abominations *that* desolate, even until *the* end. And that which was decreed shall pour out on the desolator.

This **does not say** he shall _make_ a covenant. The first key word is _confirm_, literally in Hebrew means:

Confirm - a form of the word gâbar gaw-bar'; a primitive root; to be strong; by implication, to prevail, act insolently:—exceed, confirm, be great, be mighty, prevail, put to more (strength), strengthen, be stronger, be valiant.

And he shall confirm the covenant - literally, "he shall make strong" - The idea is that of strengthening, or giving stability; of making firm and sure. This was a reference to the "covenant" _which God had already established_ with his people. It denoted promises and laws in a relationship between God and man. According to this, _**he would confirm**_ that which was understood. There has been some controversy, however, as to the proper nominative to the verb "confirm" whether it is a reference to the Messiah, or to the foreign prince, or to the "one week" here mentioned.

Concerning this Barnes notes:

> There has been a difference of opinion, however, as to the proper nominative to the verb "confirm" - הגביר _higᵉbiyr_ - whether it is the Messiah, or the foreign prince, or the "one week."

Hengstenberg prefers the latter, and renders it, "And one week shall confirm the covenant; with many."

These two agents are the "Messiah," and the "prince that should come."

But it is not reasonable to suppose that the latter is referred to, because it is said in <u>Dan 9:26</u> that the effect and the purpose of his coming would be to "destroy the city and the sanctuary." He was to come "with a flood," and the effect of his coming would be only desolation. <u>The more correct interpretation, therefore, **is to refer it to the Messiah, who is the principal subject of the prophecy; and the work which, according to this, he was to perform was, during that "one week,"** to exert such an influence as would tend to establish a covenant between the people and God.</u> The effect of his work during that one week would be to secure their adhesion to the "true religion;" to confirm to them the Divine promises, and to establish the principles of that religion which would lead them to God. Nothing is said of the mode by which that would be done; and anything, therefore, which would secure this would be a fulfillment of the prophecy. As a matter of fact, if it refers to the Lord Jesus, this was done by his personal instructions, his example, his sufferings and death, and the arrangements which he made to secure the proper effect of his work on the minds of the people - all designed to procure for them the friendship and favor of God, and to unite them to him in the bonds of an enduring covenant. (emphasis mine).

Continuing verse 27, it says:

With many – once again, Barnes notes it refers to Christ:

He would perform a work which would pertain to many, or which would bear on many, leading them to God. There is nothing in the word here which would indicate who they were, whether his own immediate followers, or those who already were in the covenant. The simple idea is, that this would pertain to "many" persons, and it would be fulfilled if the effect of his work were to confirm "many" who were already in the covenant, or if he should bring "many" others into a covenant relation with God. Nothing could be determined from the meaning of the word used here as to which of these things was designed, and consequently a fair fulfillment would be found if either of them occurred. **If it refers to the Messiah, it would be fulfilled if in fact the effect of his coming should be either by statute or by instructions to confirm and establish those who already sustained this relation to God, or if he gathered other followers, and confirmed them in their allegiance to God.** (emphasis mine).

Now we continue:

For one week – Simply within the space of seven years. But what would occur within this period that would confirm the covenant? This raises two questions. 1. What was the meaning of the week? And what occurred during that week? Barnes comments at length regarding the week. Some of this is quoted below:

(a) that the "one week," would comprise seven years, immediately succeeding the appearance of the Messiah, or the sixty-two weeks, and that there was something which he would do in "confirming the covenant," . . .

(b) That in the middle of that period of seven years, another important event would occur, serving to divide that time into two portions, and especially to be known as causing the sacrifice and oblation to cease; in some way affecting the public offering of sacrifice, so that from that time there would be in fact a cessation.

(c) And that this would be succeeded by the consummation of the whole matter expressed in the words, "and for the overspreading of abomination he shall make it desolate," etc. It is not said, however, that this latter would immediately occur, but this would be one of the events that would pertain to the fulfillment of the prophecy. There is nothing, indeed, in the prediction to forbid the expectation that this would occur at once, nor is there anything in the words which makes it imperative that we should so understand it. . . . When the Messiah should have come, and should have made an atonement for sin, the great design of rebuilding Jerusalem and the temple would have been accomplished, and both might pass away. Whether that would occur immediately or not might be in itself a matter of indifference; but it was important to state here that it would occur, for that was properly a completion of the design of rebuilding the city, and of the purpose for which it had ever been set apart as a holy city.

(2) The other inquiry is whether there was that in what is regarded as the fulfillment of this, which fairly corresponds with the prediction. <u>I have attempted above (on Dan 9:25) to show that this refers to the Messiah properly so called - the Lord Jesus Christ.</u> (emphasis mine)

Barnes established many points for his reference to Christ here. For Barnes' complete comment with regard to this, please consult his commentary.

Continuing on it says: **And in the midst of the week –**

Once again we note Barnes' reference to the work of Christ in the midst of the week:

> The meaning of the passage is fully met by the supposition that it refers to the Lord Jesus and his work, and that the exact thing that was intended by the prophecy was his death, or his being "cut off," and thus causing the sacrifice and oblation to cease.

> Whatever difficulties there may be about the "precise" time of our Lord's ministry, and whether he celebrated three passovers or four after he entered on his public work, **it is agreed on all hands that it lasted about three years and a half - the time referred to here.** _Though a few have supposed that a longer period was occupied, yet the general belief of the church has coincided in that, and there are few points in history better settled_. On the supposition that this pertains to the death of the Lord Jesus, and that it was the design of the prophecy here to refer to the effects of that death, this is the very language which would have been used. If the period of "a week" were for any purpose mentioned, then it would be indispensable to suppose that there would be an allusion to the important event - in fact, the great event which was to occur in the middle of that period, when the ends of the types and ceremonies of the Hebrew people would be accomplished, and a sacrifice made for the sins of the whole world. (emphasis mine).

Thus, as Barnes confirmed, few points in history are better confirmed than that the work of Christ lasted about three and a half years.

This brings our timeline to:

The Decree to rebuild the City and Temple 457 BC	Jerusalem and Temple rebuild finished 408 BC		Jesus begins his ministry after 483 years AD 27	Jesus Crucified at Calvary AD 30
O-----------------------	O---		-----------O-----------------	-----------O
seven weeks of years = 49 years	sixty-two weeks of years = 434 years		3 ½ years	

Yes, as Barnes pointed out, this was undoubtedly the most important event in the history of mankind, and **it was right on schedule!**

He shall cause the sacrifice and the oblation to cease –

As Barnes notes:

> The word "he," in this place, **refers to the Messiah,** if the interpretation of the former part of the verse is correct, for there can be no doubt that it is the same person who is mentioned in the phrase "he shall confirm the covenant with many." **The words "sacrifice" and "oblation" refer to the offerings made in the temple.** The former word more properly denotes "bloody" offerings; the latter "offerings" of any kind - whether of flour, fruits, grain, etc. See these words explained in the notes at Isa_1:11, Isa_1:13. . . . .The literal signification here would be met by the supposition that an end would be made of these sacrifices, and this would occur either by their being made wholly to cease to be offered at that time, or by the fact that the object of their appointment was accomplished, and that henceforward they would be useless and would die away. (emphasis mine).

Thus we see that it was a reference to Christ. In fact he would cause the eventual end of the sacrifices. There would no longer be any need of them. **God's promise of redemption was happening!**

And for the overspreading of abominations he shall make it desolate –

There are many renderings of this. This is a difficult passage as Barnes examines:

> These different translations show that there is great obscurity in the original, and perhaps exclude the hope of being able entirely to free the passage from all difficulties. An examination of the words, however, may perhaps enable us to form a judgment of its meaning. The "literal" and "obvious" sense of the original, as I understand it, is, "And upon the wing of the abominations one causing desolation" - ועל כנף שקיצים משמם *veʿal kenap shiqqytsiym meshomēm*. The word rendered "overspreading" (כנף *kânâp*) means, properly, a "wing;" so called as "covering," or because it "covers" - from כנף *kânap*), to cover, to hide. . . . . Nothing certain can be determined about the allusion here from the use of this word, but the connection would lead us to suppose that the reference was to something pertaining to the city or temple, for the whole prophecy has a reference to the city and temple, and it is natural to suppose that in its close there would be an allusion to it. (emphasis mine).

Here Barnes shows agreement by pointing out that it will likely be impossible to obtain a rendering free of all difficulties. Nonetheless, there is agreement that this is most likely a reference to some part of the temple.

As already mentioned, this did occur as a matter of historical record from the writings of Josephus. (see my quote from "The Wars of the Jews" Book 7:1:1 on page 77)

Finally, we come to the end of the passage which reads as follows:

even until the consummation, and that determined shall be poured upon the desolate.

Barnes brings up an interesting point here:

> Though it would be rebuilt, yet it would be again reduced to desolation, for the purpose of the rebuilding - the coming of the Messiah - would be accomplished. As the prophecy finds Jerusalem a scene of ruins, so it leaves it, and the last word in the prophecy, therefore, is appropriately the word "desolate." The

intermediate state indeed between the condition of the city as seen at first and at the close is glorious - for it embraces the whole work of the Messiah; but the beginning is a scene of ruins, and so is the close. The sum of the whole in the latter part of the verse may be expressed in a free paraphrase: "He, the Messiah, shall cause the sacrifice and oblation to cease," by having **fulfilled in his own death** the design of the ancient offerings, **thus rendering them now useless**, and upon the outspreading - upon the temple regarded as spread out, or some wing or portico, there are seen abominable things - idolatrous ensigns, and the worship of foreigners. A desolator is there, also, come to spread destruction - a foreign army or leader. And this shall continue even to the end of the whole matter - the end of the events contemplated by the prophecy - the end of the city and the temple. And what is determined on - the destruction decreed - shall be poured out like a tempest on the city doomed to desolation - desolate as surveyed at the beginning of the prophecy - desolate at the close, and therefore appropriately called "the desolate." (emphasis mine).

Barnes concluded his case here by paraphrasing the end of Daniel 9:27. Here he emphasized that this prophecy **was fulfilled as prophesied**, and as we have seen by the words of Josephus, history confirms it. In what amounts to a closing series of questions below, Barnes in effect made a powerful argument with respect to this prophecy. When compiled together, these questions having been answered by the fulfillment of this prophecy compose a great truth. Note Barnes closing words:

After this protracted examination of the meaning of this prophecy, all the remark which it seems proper to make is, that this prediction could have been the result only of inspiration. There is the clearest evidence that the prophecy was recorded long before the time of the Messiah, and it is manifest that it could not have been the result of any natural sagacity. There is not the slightest proof that it was uttered as late as the coming of Christ, and there is nothing better determined in relation to any ancient matter than that it was recorded long before the birth of the Lord Jesus. But it is equally clear that it could have been the result of no mere natural sagacity. **How could such events have been foreseen** except by Him who knows all things? How could the order have been determined? How could the time have been fixed? **How could it have been anticipated that the Messiah, the Prince, would be cut off?** How could it have been known that he would cause the sacrifice and oblation to cease? How could it have been ascertained that the period during which he would be engaged in this would be **one week - or about seven years?** How could it be predicted that a remarkable event would occur in the middle of that period that would in fact cause the sacrifice and oblation ultimately to cease? And how could it be conjectured that a foreign prince would come, and plant the standard of abomination in the holy city, and sweep all away - laying the city and the temple in ruins, and bringing the whole polity to an end? _These things lie beyond the range of natural sagacity, and if they are fairly implied in this prophecy, they demonstrate that **this portion of the book is from God.**_ (emphasis mine).

What a powerful argument in favor of the truth of God's word and the prophecies fulfilled! The sum of these questions makes it impossible that this prophecy could have been contrived, but attest to the power of God's Word. Barnes comes down on this prophecy **as being fulfilled entirely in Christ,** who through his own death made abominable the offerings made in the temple after his death. These offerings would be abominable, idolatrous offerings as in the worship of foreigners. This later would be exemplified in Roman General Titus bringing the Roman ensigns to the temple and making sacrifices to them, as recorded by Jewish historian Josephus. Finally, Jesus uses this desolator (Roman General Titus) to make desolate the city of Jerusalem.

In Conclusion of this passage...

In conclusion of this magnificent prophecy, first we must ask the question, what was this intended to mean to those to whom it was written? What was the background of the passage? In this case, why was Daniel praying? He prayed knowing that the 70 years of exile was nearing an end. But the angel Gabriel gave him new information, information that was intended to encourage Daniel that **Yahweh is a God who keeps his promises.** He presented a unit of time, a new period of "seventy times seven," in which still more important events were to take place, a period spoken of in the Greek as seventy "heptades," meaning weeks. This was important in this revelation to Daniel to bring him consolation, and to assure him about the rebuilding of the city, and the great events that were to occur there. The angel Gabriel brought him a message that the coming of the Messiah was to accomplish 6 things. These were as follows:

- **To finish the transgression** - The coming of the Messiah was to restrain or cover up the sin of the world. His work, **through the sacrifice made on the cross,** is such that it covered up the sin of the elect, and would **eventually** succeed in atoning for sin altogether! This did not refer to the particular transgressions for which the Jewish people had suffered in their long captivity, but sin (הפשע *hapesha'*) in general - the sin of the world.

- **To make an end of sins** – This is normally understood as חתם *châthēm* - from חתם *châtham* - "to seal, to seal up." The idea to be conveyed here is that sin was to be sealed up, or closed, or hidden, so that they will not be seen. It can be compared to a sealed book, or a lock box, the contents of which cannot be seen. And although Daniel had no idea of the meaning of this at the time, we can. Since we have Christ revealed, _we can_ understand how this was to be accomplished. It was **accomplished by the blood of the atonement,** by which sin is now forgiven. It is as if it were hidden from the view, sealed with a seal that cannot be broken.

- **To make reconciliation for iniquity** – This he did by the once offering up of himself. This is different from the second purpose in that reconciliation is the word which is commonly used with reference to atonement. As Luther understood it, it meant "to reconcile for transgression." Its bearing would be on human iniquity; on the way **by which it might be pardoned and removed.**

- **To bring in everlasting righteousness** - Everlasting used here denotes that the righteousness would be permanent and perpetual. In reference to the method of becoming righteous, it would become the *only method* by which men would become holy. In this way, it would be a righteousness which would continue forever.

- **To seal up vision and prophecy** - The idea seems to be sealed in the sense that they would be closed or shut up - no longer open matters. Also, sealing up can carry the meaning of authentication. Thus, we could rightly interpret this to mean "To authenticate or close up vision and prophecy." Once a scroll was sealed, It would be marked with a seal mark. The purpose was that it would be authentic until it was opened. If opened, it would need to be sealed and authenticated again by the mark. Christ would settle this matter **once and for all.** Only Christ could authenticate this prophecy, for only Christ could provide the answers to the other parts of this prophecy.

- **To anoint the Most Holy** – This is **the most important point**. The entire ninth chapter of Daniel follows the pattern set forth in Leviticus 26. Although the term "most holy" does not appear in Leviticus 26, it is important to point out that it appears in Leviticus **only** in reference to a sacrifice. In **every instance** in which this term is found in the book of Leviticus, it is in reference to **a sacrifice.** And in Leviticus we find a reference to the lamb in Leviticus 14:13. Here the slain lamb is referred to as **most holy.**

This ties this time frame together as one unit of time in which the coming of the Messiah will accomplish these 6 things! As the Scripture says: "He is the Lamb of God who takes away the sin of the world" (John 1:29). The angel Gabriel was giving Daniel a message showing that within the 490 years, these 6 items would lead to and be fulfilled in the promised Messiah.

Next the angel Gabriel gives the time frame. He gives it in 3 periods of time. The three periods are:

1. Seven weeks, that is, forty-nine years.

2. Sixty-two weeks, that is, four hundred and thirty-four years.

3. One week, that is, seven years.

The first period of time refers to the rebuilding of Jerusalem. As previously mentioned, this was from the 2nd decree given king Artaxerxes. It had to be this decree because it was the first of the four decrees that included rebuilding the wall of Jerusalem. There is considerable debate among historians regarding this date, and this is tied into the calendar corrections made by historians. However, Sir Isaac Newton established the Julian date of 4257 which corresponds to 457 BC. (This was added as a footnote in the 1701 KJV):

> *Seventy weeks are cut out upon thy people, and upon thy holy city, to finish transgression,* &c. Here, by putting a week for seven years, are reckoned 490 years from the time that the dispersed *Jews* should be re-incorporated into [7] a people and a holy city, until the death and resurrection of *Christ;* whereby *transgression should be finished, and sins ended, iniquity be expiated, and everlasting righteousness brought in, and this Vision be accomplished, and the Prophet consummated,* that Prophet whom the *Jews* expected; and whereby *the most Holy* should be *anointed,* he who is therefore in the next words called the *Anointed,* that is, the *Messiah,* or the *Christ.*

For by joining the accomplishment of the vision with the expiation of sins, the 490 years are ended with the death of *Christ.* Now the dispersed *Jews* became a people and city when they first returned into a polity or body politick; and this was in the seventh year of *Artaxerxes Longimanus,* when *Ezra* returned with a body of *Jews* from captivity, and revived the *Jewish* worship; and by the King's commission created Magistrates in all the land, to judge and govern the people according to the laws of God and the King, *Ezra* vii. 25.

There were but two returns from captivity, *Zerubbabel's* and *Ezra's;* in *Zerubbabel's* they had only commission to build the Temple, in *Ezra's* they first became a polity or city by a government of their own. Now the years of this *Artaxerxes* began about two or three months after the summer solstice, and his seventh year fell in with the third year of the eightieth *Olympiad*; and the latter part thereof, wherein *Ezra* went up to *Jerusalem*, was in the year of the *Julian Period* 4257. Count the time from thence to the death of *Christ*, and you will find it just 490 years.

If you count in *Judaic* years commencing in autumn, and date the reckoning from the first autumn after *Ezra*'s coming to *Jerusalem*, when he put the King's decree in execution; the death of *Christ* will fall on the year of the *Julian Period* 4747, *Anno Domini* 34; and the weeks will be *Judaic* weeks, ending with sabbatical years; and this I take to be the truth: but if you had rather place the death of *Christ* in the year before, as is commonly done, you may take the year of *Ezra*'s journey into the reckoning.[1]

Thus, Newton's timeline is similar, but not exact. Since the Jews used a lunar calendar, determining with exact precision these dates is a challenge. But using this beginning date, and subtracting the first 7 weeks of years or 49 years, we come to 408 BC. Now if we add another 62 weeks of years (434years), this would bring us to somewhere around AD 27. This was the beginning of Christ's ministry. After approximately 3 ½ years he was crucified or "cut off" (Dan 9:26, See Barnes explanation as previously noted). Adding another 3 ½ years we come to AD 34 for the end of Daniel's 70 weeks of years. This was very likely at the stoning of Stephen. It was absolutely **apparent that the Jews present DETESTED even the mention of the name of the Lord Jesus.** Acts 7:57 tells that they hated this name so much that **they cried out with a loud voice and covered their ears** as they **rushed to murder** that precious saint in cold blood. It only served to reinforce what Jesus told them in Matt 23:

Mat 23:34 Because of this, behold, I send to you prophets and wise ones and scribes. **And *some* of them you will kill and crucify**, and some of them you will flog in your synagogues and will persecute from city to city;

Mat 23:35 so that should come on **YOU** all *the* righteous blood poured out on the earth, from the blood of righteous Abel to the blood of Zechariah the son of Berechiah **whom you murdered** between the Holy Place and the altar.

Mat 23:36 Truly I say to you, All these things will come on this generation. (LITV)

These Jews were pronounced guilty! And their future actions **included more murdering** of the Lord's sheep. Their sentence was given, and now the Lord's prophecy of Matt. 24:34 was left to be fulfilled when he said:

Mat 24:34 Truly I say to you, this generation will not pass away until all these things take place.

That is also when the disciples **started their ministry outside of the Jewish community.** From this point forward, the message started going to the Gentiles in the Roman world.

Of course these calculations may vary slightly, but it gives us valid assurance that this prophecy is a reference to Messiah the Prince spoken of in Daniel 9:25.[4] The Scripture tells us that it would be in troublous times. If you study the book of Nehemiah, you see a similar pattern that they also had a lot of trouble building the city, due to the opposing efforts of Sanballat the Horonite, and Tobiah the Ammonite.

Next we see that _**after**_ the 62 weeks there would appear a prince who would destroy the city and the sanctuary (although nothing in this text says it would happen immediately). The Roman prince Titus did appear soon after this, and he did destroy the city, thus fulfilling the prophecy given by Jesus concerning the temple in Matt 24:2: "And Jesus said unto them, See ye not all these things? Verily I say unto you, there shall not be left here one stone upon another, that shall not be thrown down." This prophecy would have been thought impossible 40 years prior. The temple was an amazing architectural structure. It was the pride of the Jewish nation. _Under the command of Titus, in AD 70 there was complete destruction._ **_As Jesus said, not one stone was left upon another!_**

The biggest controversy of this entire passage is contained in the 27th verse. Is this the Christ, or is it the Antichrist? This **_must refer to Christ_** for the following reasons:

- It says "he shall confirm a covenant" not _make_ a covenant. **Christ, the Messiah, _confirmed_ the covenant which _Yahweh_** made. The confirmation of the covenant is assigned to him by the prophet Isaiah. This is from Isaiah 42: 1-9. In Isa 42:6, "I will give thee for a _covenant_ of the people" (that is, he in whom the covenant between Israel and God is personally expressed). The Messiah confirmed it by his death on the cross and the subsequent work of the apostles in evangelizing the Jews. There was **no covenant** to confirm with an antichrist figure.

- In the middle of the last week, that is 3 ½ years after the start of his ministry, he was cut off. At that time, the veil of the temple was torn in two. Thus the seventy weeks extend to AD 34, and although Jerusalem was not actually destroyed until AD 70, it was rendered invalid symbolized by the tearing of the veil and by the preaching of the Gospel which for the next 3 ½ years was preached exclusively to the Jews. When the Jews continued persecuting the Church and stoned Stephen, it was over for them. Israel, having rejected Christ, was now under judgment even though individual Jews were still accepting Christ. Its actual destruction by Titus and the "people of the prince" **was now set in stone.**

- At this point, the 490 years of the prophecy are now complete. When Titus came to the temple to destroy it, they brought their religious artifacts into the temple, and made sacrifices to them.

- Jerusalem was destroyed completely after the end of the prophecy, confirming the judgment which was represented by the tearing of the veil of the Most Holy. Thus, as shown by the Hebrew word "shaw-mame" (ruined, desolate), it **was** ruined or desolate. The reference is to Jerusalem which was completely destroyed and reduced to rubble by Titus and his armies. The angel Gabriel could have been indicating this outcome and therefore spoke of Jerusalem as "the desolate."

Additionally, speaking strictly from a logical perspective, how is it even possible that the angel Gabriel would give this wonderful promise, and then all of a sudden switch subjects and start talking about an antichrist figure as some have said? There was no reason for such a thing. It doesn't make any sense!

This wonderful prophecy of Daniel was a promise to the nation of Israel. There would be a Messiah who would come, in whom six wonderful things **would be fulfilled.** The writer of Hebrews notes in chapter 9 that Christ came as high priest with a greater and more perfect tabernacle, not made with hands, **to offer the perfect sacrifice** and mediate **a new covenant** (Heb 9:11-16). Later we read of God's final answer for sin in Hebrews 9:24-28. This time quoting from the English Standard Version:

> "For Christ has entered, not into holy places made with hands, which are copies of the true things, but into heaven itself, now to appear in the presence of God on our behalf. Nor was it to offer himself repeatedly, as the high priest enters the holy places every year with blood not his own, for then he would have had to suffer repeatedly since the foundation of the world. But as it is, he has appeared **once for all** _at the end of the ages_ to put away sin by the sacrifice of himself. And just as it is appointed for man to die once, and after that comes judgment, so Christ, having been offered once to bear the sins of many, will appear a second time, not to deal with sin _but to save those who are eagerly waiting for him."_

Praise God that he allowed his Son to fulfill Daniel 9:27, to be "cut off" after 3 ½ years of ministry, and "to bring an end to sacrifice and offering." For he has given us such a precious promise, of this we can be eternally grateful, for *it is the key to our redemption!*

Now we can see why this prophecy is so important to an understanding of "The Last Days," that is, the "Last Days" of which Jesus spoke. Now we see the timeline as follows:

					o----(This generation 40 years)-----o
The Decree to	Jerusalem		Jesus begins	Jesus	Stephen	AD 70
rebuild the City	and Temple		his ministry	Crucified	stoned	Jerusalem
and Temple	rebuild finished		after 483 years	at Calvary	by Jews	destroyed
457 BC	408 BC		AD 27		AD 34	

o-------------------------o---o-------------------o-------------------o

seven weeks	sixty-two weeks	3 ½ years	3 ½ years
of years = 49 years	of years = 434 years		seven years

o--o

Daniel's seventy weeks = 490 years — Preaching to Gentiles begins

But there is still more from the prophet Daniel. Let us continue!

NOTES

1. (from "Observations upon the Prophecies of Daniel and the Apocalypse of St. John (Chapter 10), by Sir Isaac Newton) http://www.gutenberg.org/files/16878/16878-h/16878-h.htm#DanX

2. Albert Barnes Notes on the Bible, taken from e-Sword, Version 10.2.1, 2013, Rick Meyers (Free download at www.e-sword.net)

3. Adam Clarke's Commentary on the Bible, taken from e-Sword, Version 10.2.1, 2013, Rick Meyers (Free download at www.e-sword.net)

4. Josephus The Complete Works, Translated by William Whiston, A.M., 1988 Thomas Nelson Publishers, p.900.

5. The exact precision of these dates is next to impossible to determine. If you study the recorded words of the scholars on these verses, you see numerous variances in these dates among the commentaries they have written. **The most important point** concerning this prophecy is that the specific dates are not as important as the fact that the overall timeframe of prophecy is valid in proving that the seventy weeks of years brings us to the "generation" which Jesus prophesied would see the end of the Jewish political and religious system.

Chapter 4

The Problem of Sin and Death
More on Daniel's Prophecy

While we are discussing Daniel's prophecy, there is another point which must be considered. There are those who would say that Daniel's prophecy cannot be fulfilled because there is still sin on the earth. They say that if this was to be fulfilled in Jesus that either it is not yet fulfilled, or Jesus was a failure. They argue this way: Daniel 9:24 says that the seventy weeks at its completion would put an end to sin. Therefore, many of these even go so far as to state that the seventieth week of Daniel's prophecy is now on hold because of this. But there are many New Testament passages that show explicitly that sin **was** conquered by our Lord when he came to earth. For example, to confirm the prophecy of Daniel, John the Baptist prophesied concerning Jesus when he said:

> John 1:29 . . . . , "Behold, the Lamb of God, who takes away the sin of the world!"

The writer of Hebrews also confirmed the prophecy when he said of Jesus who is the Christ:

> Heb 9:26 ....But as it is, he has appeared once for all at the end of the ages to put away sin by the sacrifice of himself.

This verse very clearly states that his sacrifice put an end to sin. Yes, it is true that after Jesus died on the cross, and within a period of forty years, the entire Jewish economy, both political and religious, came to an end. Thus, the typical sin-offerings of the law ceased. This was the essence of what was expressly foretold in Daniel 9:24.

Paul's letter to Titus reveals:

> Titus 2:11 For the grace of God has appeared, bringing salvation for all people,
> Titus 2:12 training us to renounce ungodliness and worldly passions, and to live self-controlled, upright, and godly lives in the present age,
> Titus 2:13 waiting for our blessed hope, the appearing of the glory of our great God and Savior Jesus Christ,
> Titus 2:14 who gave himself for us to redeem us from all lawlessness and to purify for himself a people for his own possession who are zealous for good works.

Did you notice that last verse? It says that he would redeem believers from all lawlessness and purify them. This, in effect put an end to sin. And also in this verse, wouldn't you agree that there are few passages in the Bible that set out in such a vivid manner the power of God's grace? In this letter to Titus, he reiterated that because of what Christ has done, and our response to it, we **can** live upright lives. Jesus **has** redeemed us from lawlessness, and through the process of sanctification, we become purified. Thus Christ not only liberated us from the penalty of past sin, but he enables us to be a people of good works.

Considering this, there seems to be a misunderstanding about the meaning of the words of Daniel 9 where the angel told him that the savior would "put an end to sin." The fact is that Jesus **CONQUERED** sin. He has redeemed us! In so doing, he has *fulfilled* God's promise of redemption!

Yes, sin does continue to exist, but if we have put our trust in Christ, it has no mastery over us. Paul pointed this out to the Roman Church in Romans 6:6-11:

> Rom 6:6 We know that our old self was crucified with him in order that the body of sin might be brought to nothing, so that we would no longer be enslaved to sin.
> Rom 6:7 For one who has died has been set free from sin.
> Rom 6:8 Now if we have died with Christ, we believe that we will also live with him.
> Rom 6:9 We know that Christ, being raised from the dead, will never die again; death no longer has dominion over him.
> Rom 6:10 For the death he died he died to sin, once for all, but the life he lives he lives to God.
> Rom 6:11 So you also must consider yourselves dead to sin and alive to God in Christ Jesus.

So even though those Roman Christians Paul was speaking to did still sin, the point Paul was making here was that sin no longer has any power over the believer. This is also true today. Sin still does exist. Those who claim that someday sin will be abolished do not understand the nature of man, or the **nature of the redemption.** As such, it is very doubtful that they understand the nature of death. Jesus repeatedly told his disciples that if they trusted him, they would not die at all! (John 5:24; John 8:51; John 11:26) Does this mean that they would never leave their physical bodies? Of course not! But it does mean that they would immediately be in the presence of the Lord. This is where we as Christians will spend eternity. The Apostle Paul clearly stated:

> Phil 3:20 But our citizenship is in heaven, and from it we await a Savior, the Lord Jesus Christ,
> Phil 3:21 who will transform our lowly body to be like his glorious body, by the power that enables him even to subject all things to himself.

Thus, we who live in the present time are not waiting for some cataclysmic event to come to this earth, after which there will be no sin on the earth. This is not what the Bible teaches. But it does teach us that Jesus conquered death. It has no power over us who believe in him who conquered death once and for all time. We are redeemed by the power of his precious blood!

But what about death?

So then what is death? Your question probably sounds something like this: "Are you telling me that most people _do not even understand the meaning of death?_" Yes, that's right. What did God mean in the book of Genesis when he told Adam that he would die in the very day that he ate of the fruit? Did they die that day? Or did God lie about this? Of course God did not lie! And yes, **they did die that very day.** But their death, and the death God was speaking about was not a physical death of the body. _It was spiritual death._ Let's look at one of the passages cited earlier, words spoken by our Lord when he was on the earth -- John 11:25,26. I would like to examine this passage in three different translations here:

> John 11:25 Jesus said to her, "I am the resurrection and the life. The one who believes in me, even if he dies, will live,
> John 11:26 and everyone who lives and believes in me will never die [forever]. Do you believe this?" (LEB)

> John 11:25 Jesus said to her, "I am the resurrection and the life. Whoever believes in me, though he die, yet shall he live,
> Joh 11:26 and everyone who lives and believes in me shall never die. Do you believe this?"(ESV)

> John 11:25 Jesus said to her, "I am the resurrection and the life; he who believes in Me will live even if he dies,
> John 11:26 and everyone who lives and believes in Me will never die. Do you believe this?" (NASB)

This passage makes it crystal clear that when Jesus said everyone who believes in him would never die, he was **not** speaking of the physical death of the body. Physical death for the believer is just a step into the life that Jesus promised to those who have been redeemed. This is confirmed by his earlier statements in the book of John:

Joh 5:24 "Truly, truly, I say to you, he who hears My word, and believes Him who sent Me, has eternal life, and does not come into judgment, but has passed out of death into life.
Joh 8:51 "Truly, truly, I say to you, if anyone keeps My word he will never see death."

So we see that in conquering death for us, and making these promises, our Lord not only promised us that we who put our trust in him would never die spiritually, but that the physical death which we experience will have absolutely no power over us. This physical death is just a passing from the realm of the physical to another realm of the spiritual. *What a blessing to those recipients of the promise of redemption!*

Now back to Daniel. . . .

How Daniel's prophecies fit together

When considering the book of Daniel it is important to remember that the first 6 chapters of Daniel's book is history, and the second 6 chapters are prophecy. We also must remember that the purpose of Daniel's prophecy was to encourage the Jews in exile. This would be done by revealing to them God's program for them, both in the short term, and in the long term.

Daniel has been reputed to have descended from the royal family of David. After the Babylonian siege, he appears to have been carried into Babylon when very young. He and his three younger associates, Hananiah, Mishael, and Azariah, (who eventually became Shadrach, Meshach and Abednego) were chosen because of their abilities. These three would be trained to have an education which would suit them for what the king had determined.

Thus, Daniel was instructed in all the wisdom of the Chaldeans, which was at that time considered to be greatly superior to the learning of the other cultures; but we also see that he was soon distinguished for his divinely appointed wisdom and devotion to his God.

When he told Nebuchadnezzar exactly what his dream was, and then gave him the exact interpretation of the metallic image, he was given the title of governor of the province of Babylon. Nebuchadnezzar made him chief of all the magicians, or wise men in that country. Even in Babylon, Daniel was considered to be one of the wisest and most noble men of his time. God ranks him among the most holy and exemplary of men. Ezekiel 14 ranks him with Noah and Job (Ezekiel 14:14, 20).

In chapter seven of Daniel's prophecy verses 1-9, we see the prophet's visions is that of the four beasts, which arose out of the sea. Then we see one like the Son of man who destroyed the dominion of the fourth beast. Next we see the following:

> Dan 7:13 I kept looking in the night visions, And behold, with the clouds of heaven One like a Son of Man was coming, And He came up to the Ancient of Days And was presented before Him.
> Dan 7:14 And to Him was given dominion, Glory and a kingdom, That all the peoples, nations and men of every language Might serve Him. His dominion is an everlasting dominion Which will not pass away; And His kingdom is one Which will not be destroyed.

An angel declares that there are four beasts, diverse one from another, and these represent four world powers that will succeed each other. But he makes a distinction in the fourth beast. Notice what he says:

> Dan 7:23 Thus he said: 'The fourth beast will be a fourth kingdom on the earth, which will be different from all the other kingdoms and will devour the whole earth and tread it down and crush it.'

From this would arise 10 kings including one which would subdue three of these kings. In Daniel 7:24 and 25 we find a description of one called the "little horn." It arises out from among the fourth beast, and, "will wear down the saints of the

Highest one." Nowhere in Scripture is this "little horn" specifically identified. But we do know that the timing of this "little horn" relates to the time of the Roman Empire. Don Preston notes of this one:

> The prophet of the exile was given a vision during the night. He saw the coming of four kingdoms, and in the days of the fourth, a small horn was manifested as the enemy of God's saints (Daniel 7: 8). The little horn persecuted the saints until the time of the judgment (v. 8f). Daniel described the judgment scene, "I beheld till the thrones were cast down and the Ancient of Days did sit... and the judgment was set and the books were opened" (Daniel 7: 9-10).
>
> As the judgment scene unfolded, Daniel gave one of the great prophecies of the Old Testament, "I saw in the night vision and behold, one like the Son of man came with the clouds of heaven, and came to the Ancient of Days and they brought him near to Him. And there was given to Him dominion and glory, and a kingdom, that all people, nations and languages, should served Him, His dominion is an everlasting dominion which shall everlasting dominion . . . . It is widely held that Daniel 7: 13-14 was fulfilled on the day of Pentecost, with the establishment of the church. **This is patently false.** Daniel 7 is a vision of the judgment of the "little horn" that was guilty of persecuting the saints! If the day of Pentecost was the fulfillment of Daniel 7: 13-14, it follows that for some time before Pentecost, the Lord's saints had been persecuted (a time, times, and half time , Daniel 7: 25). Regardless of whether one identifies "the saints" as Old Covenant Israel, or the church, it is impossible to find a time of persecution prior to Pentecost.
>
> The posit that Pentecost was the fulfillment of Daniel 7: 13-14 is a miscarriage of exegesis. But if Daniel 7 was not fulfilled on Pentecost, _when was/ will it be fulfilled?_ _In Matthew 24: 30, Jesus predicted his judgment coming against Jerusalem,_ and cites Daniel 7: 13-14 about the Son of Man coming on the clouds of heaven. Thus, Jesus applied the time of judgment of the little horn to the judgment of Israel.[1] (emphasis mine)

Preston's point is well taken. Jesus made it clear that judgment was coming to Israel:

> Mat 23:34 "Therefore, behold, I am sending you prophets and wise men and scribes; some of them you will kill and crucify, and some of them you will scourge in your synagogues, and persecute from city to city,
> Mat 23:35 so that **UPON YOU** may fall *the guilt of* all the righteous blood shed on earth, from the blood of righteous Abel to the blood of Zechariah, the son of Berechiah, whom you murdered between the temple and the altar.
> Mat 23:36 "Truly I say to you, **all these things will come upon this generation.**
> Mat 23:37 "Jerusalem, Jerusalem, who kills the prophets and stones those who are sent to her! How often I wanted to gather your children together, the way a hen gathers her chicks under her wings, and you were unwilling.
> Mat 23:38 "Behold, **your house is being left to you desolate!** (emphasis mine)

Yes! This generation would experience an overwhelming judgment which would include their house (the temple) being left desolate! In fact, it was also a self-proclaimed judgment when the crowd said before Pilate in Matt 27:25: "His blood shall be on us and our children!"

The eventual end of this would be:

> Dan 7:26 'But the court will sit *for judgment,* and his dominion will be taken away, annihilated and destroyed forever.
> Dan 7:27 'Then the sovereignty, the dominion and the greatness of *all* the kingdoms under the whole heaven will be given to the people of the saints of the Highest One; His kingdom *will be* an everlasting kingdom, and all the dominions will serve and obey Him.'

This directly ties with Daniel's prophecy in the ninth chapter. It also ties directly with Daniel's prophecy in chapter 12. In the first three verses we see a great tribulation as referred to in Daniel 9:26, we see a rescue, and a resurrection, in which certain ones would shine brightly forever. Reading from Daniel 12 we see:

Dan 12:1 And at that time, Michael shall stand up, the great ruler who stands for the sons of your people. And there shall be a time of distress, such as has not been from the being of a nation until that time. And at that time, your people shall be delivered, everyone that shall be found written in the Book.
Dan 12:2 And many of those sleeping in the earth's dust shall awake, some to everlasting life, and some to reproaches *and* to everlasting abhorrence.
Dan 12:3 And those who act wisely shall shine as the brightness of the firmament, and those turning many to righteousness as the stars forever and ever.

Notice how verse one makes it clear that this time of distress is specifically pointed to the nation of Israel, that it would be the greatest time of distress ever for that nation. But it also pointed out that there would be deliverance for the true people of God. This is a reference to the true believers of the Lord Jesus!

In the next verse we see that Daniel is told to seal up the book until the *time of the end*. Although some versions translate this "end of time," this is inaccurate. The Bible **never speaks** of the end of time. God has determined that this earth will stand forever:

Ecc 1:4 A generation goes and a generation comes, But **the earth remains forever**. (emphasis mine, See also Psalm 78:69; 104:5)

In verse four he writes:

Dan 12:4 But you, Daniel, shut up the words and seal the book, until the time of the end. Many shall run to and fro, and knowledge shall increase." (ESV)

As we shall see in future chapters, the "Last Days" is a reference to the generation alive when Jesus was crucified. Thus, Daniel was instructed to seal up the words of this prophecy for the next 490+ years until the judgment of those spoken of by our Lord would come to pass.

There is also a tie directly to the events of the book of Revelation. As Don Preston notes in his book "Who is this Babylon:"

> Now, unless there are two different "time, times and half a time" periods for the consummation of Biblical eschatology, then this means that Daniel 12 ties in directly with the little horn prophecy of Daniel 7, the persecution of the saints by the beast in Revelation, the testimony of the two witnesses and the fate of the two cities in Revelation, i.e. the holy city and the harlot city. Since it is agreed by virtually all commentators that all of these referents are to the same time, i.e. the time of the end, then this much should be clear: First , _we are dealing with the same time period as Daniel 9_, i.e. the fulfillment of the Seventy Weeks, since Daniel 9 and Daniel 12 both deal with the fate of Daniel's people (Daniel 9: 24; Daniel 12: 1). Thus, all of these referents must be viewed within the confines of God's dealings with Israel. Second _If in fact Daniel 9 and Daniel 12 are dealing with the same time subject, then there is simply no way to posit either text into a far distant future and "end of time" application._, if Daniel 9 and Daniel 12 are parallel texts, then since the seventy weeks of Daniel 9 consummate in the "overwhelming flood" of the time of the end against "your people and your holy city" (Daniel 9 :24), then this means that Daniel 12 must consummate at that same time. .... Third , if Daniel 9 and Daniel 12 are parallel, then since the "time, times and half a time" of Daniel 12 are also the ground for Revelation 11-13, then _this means that the "time, times and half a time" of Revelation is inextricably bound up with the fulfillment of the seventy weeks and the fate of "your people and your holy city."_ [2] (emphasis mine)

Yes, without question these time periods mentioned in Daniel chapter nine and twelve are parallel time frames. This ties together the prophecy of the seventy weeks of years, and the judgment that our Lord spoke of when he pronounced judgment on Israel in Matthew 23 as mentioned above.

In his book "Unravelling the End," John Noe compares the prophecies of Daniel 9 and Daniel 12 to the front and rear bookends. I believe this is a good analogy. The front bookend was the prophecy of the seventy weeks of Daniel and came about perfectly as written with the 490 years commencing in the year 457 BC, and ending in the year AD 34. This timeline also agrees with the one outlined in the previous chapter. The back bookend is outlined in Daniel's prophecy of chapter 12 which speaks of a time period of 1335 days (which includes a period of 1290 days). (Daniel 12:9-13). (ref: Unraveling the End, pp229-236)

So here is how these two prophecies work together. In Daniel 9:24-27 we have outlined the events that would take place over the next 490 years. As previously stated, this would take us up to the year AD 34. In Daniel 12:6 we see two angels standing on the banks of the river talking to one another:

> Dan 12:5 And I, Daniel, looked. And, behold! Another two stood there, the one on this *side*, and one on that *side* of the river's edge.
> Dan 12:6 And *one* said to the man clothed in linen, who *was* on the waters of the river, Until when *is* the end of the wonders?

However, this time we hear the angel using a different time analogy.

> Dan 12:7 And I heard the man clothed in linen, who *was* on the waters of the river, when he held up his right and his left *hand* to the heavens and swore by Him who lives forever, that it *shall be* for *a time, times, and a half*. And when they have made an end of scattering the power of the holy people, all these *things* shall be finished.
> Dan 12:8 And I heard, but I did not understand. And I said, O my lord, what *shall be* the end of these *things*?
> Dan 12:9 And He said, Go, Daniel! For the words *are* closed up and sealed until the end time.
> Dan 12:10 Many shall be purified and made white and tested. But the wicked shall do wickedly. And not one of the wicked shall understand, but the wise shall understand.
> Dan 12:11 And from the time the regular *sacrifice* shall be taken away, and the abomination that desolates set up, a thousand, two hundred and ninety days *shall occur*.
> Dan 12:12 Blessed *is* he who waits and comes to the thousand, three hundred and thirty five days.

Dan 12:13 But you go on to the end, for you shall rest and stand for your lot at the end of the days.

At first he refers to "time, times, and a half." But later he clarifies this. This time he is speaking in terms of days. He mentions a period of time of 1290 days, but later mentions another time of 1335 days. Note: _These are not two separate time periods._ This 1335 days includes the 1290 days. This is the same period of time spoken of in Daniel 7:23-28, which is a description of the Roman empire of the first century. _Yes, this would happen in the first century._ It would tie several prophecies of the Bible together. And as we shall see in a later chapter, the Lord Jesus will also make reference to this in the "Olivet Discourse" of Matthew 24, Mark 13, and Luke 21. As to why there are two periods of time listed here, it is because the events of that period of time show it, although it is impossible to pin this down to exact dates. Let me be more specific.

As outlined in Josephus' "Wars of the Jews" Book 2, Chapter 17, we see a description of how the war started. This was in July of AD 66. The zealots were fervently trying to excite the Jewish people to revolt against the Roman authorities. King Agrippa tried to get the rebellion under control, but failed. Upon this failure, he sent word to the Roman authorities that things were getting out of control. But the zealots were determined and they made a treacherous assault on Masada, killing the Romans that were there and taking control of this fortress. Also, Eleazar, the son of the high priest, who was the governor of the temple made an edict that no gift or sacrifice would be received from any foreigner. They even rejected the continuation of the sacrifice of Caesar, which was always to take place twice daily.

This infuriated the Roman authorities, and was taken by them to be a formal declaration of war against Rome. Roman procurator Flores was glad to see this rebellion occur. He _wanted_ to see a war started. Eventually, the Jewish zealots set fire to the houses of Annanias the high priest, and to the palaces of Agrippa and

Bernice. Then they burned the financial records, which included all the debts of the people, thus hoping for support from the poorer members of the Jewish community for their insurrection.

With this, the devastation started, and all of this continued until approximately 3 and one half years later when the final end of the city commenced. Book 6 of the Wars of the Jews states that it covers a period of about one month, but a lot happened in that period of time. The Tower of Antonia was demolished. The famine got so bad that mothers were eating their own children. The temple was destroyed. From a distance, the smoke was so great, that it was thought that the entire city was on fire. Josephus reports that there was a vision in the sky where many people saw chariots and troops of soldiers running about in the sky, among the clouds and surrounding cities. Titus brought his ensigns to the temple and set them over against its eastern gate; and there did they offer sacrifices to them. During that 3 and one-half year period, 1.1 million Jews were killed, and ninety-seven thousand were taken captive from the city of Jerusalem. But even this number did not tell the whole story of the destruction. There were still more casualties. The footnote from Book 6, chapter 9 states:

> The whole multitude of the Jews that were destroyed during the entire seven years before this time, in all the countries of and bordering on Judea, is summed up by Archbishop Usher, from Lipsius, out of Josephus, at the year of Christ 70, and amounts to 1,337,490. Nor could there have been that number of Jews in Jerusalem to be destroyed in this siege, as will be presently set down by Josephus, but that both Jews and proselytes of justice were just then come up out of the other countries of Galilee, Samaria, Judea, and Perea and other remoter regions, to the passover, in vast numbers, and therein cooped up, as in a prison, by the Roman army, as Josephus himself well observes in this and the next section, and as is exactly related elsewhere, B. V. ch. 3. sect. 1 and ch. 13. sect. 7.[3]

But none of this touched the Christians. Why? It was because Jesus told them to flee prior to all of these final developments. All of this was predicted by Christ. In Matthew 24 notice the words of

Jesus:

> Mat 24:15 "Therefore when you see the ABOMINATION OF DESOLATION which was spoken of through Daniel the prophet, standing in the holy place (let the reader understand),
> Mat 24:16 then those who are in Judea must flee to the mountains.

Also similar words recorded by Luke show the timing of their exit.

> Luk 21:20 "But when you see Jerusalem surrounded by armies, then recognize that her desolation is near.
> Luk 21:21 "Then those who are in Judea must flee to the mountains, and those who are in the midst of the city must leave, and those who are in the country must not enter the city;

So your question is: When did the Christians leave Jerusalem?

There were 2 sieges of Jerusalem. The first was under Vespasian. Under this siege, no one was allowed out of the city. But during this siege, the emperor Nero dies. As previously stated, the entire Roman Empire was in trouble and was on the verge of collapse. Vespasian withdrew his forces, most likely so he could go back to Rome and protect his interests as well as that of the entire empire. In fact history records that this was so unsettling to the empire that during that very year four different emperors were in power, with Vespasian eventually winning out. After settling this and putting the Roman Empire back on solid footing, he sent Titus to finish the job he started in Jerusalem. It was _during this withdrawal period_ that the Christians had the opportunity to "flee to the mountains." Eusebius records that _they did_ flee in his account:

> But the people of the church in Jerusalem had been commanded by a revelation, vouchsafed to approved men there before the war, to leave the city and to dwell in a certain town of Perea called Pella. And when those that believed in Christ had come there from Jerusalem, then, as if the royal city of the Jews and the whole land of Judea were entirely destitute of holy men, the judgment of God at length overtook those who had committed such outrages against Christ and his apostles, and totally destroyed that generation of impious men.[4]

With this, we have the words of Jesus fulfilled concerning the Christians. Now we need to look at the Olivet Discourse to see Jesus' most famous prophecy. In this prophecy, Jesus would reveal to his disciples that they were about to see the "Last Days" of the Jewish system of worship!

But wait a minute....Aren't we living in the Last Days now?

Now you may be saying to yourself, but wait a minute! I thought we were living in the "Last Days" now! Isn't this what the prophecy pundits have been telling us for years?

It is true that we are continually hearing that we are on the verge of a time of complete and utter chaos that will be brought about by God. We are told that this will be so bad, that God is going to remove his people from the earth by means of an event called the rapture of the church, in which they will all at once disappear from the earth causing even greater chaos. This scenario is being touted by many of the world's most famous preachers. The sad part is that many who are touting this are men whom I have admired for years....men of integrity, good and honorable men, who I believe would absolutely give their lives for the message of Christ.

Most of the men I have just spoken of here are purveyors of dispensational theology. We described it in a previous chapter. One of the reasons these men have been preaching that we are still in the Last Days is because of their interpretation of Daniel's prophecy in chapter 9, as we have just examined. Their interpretation of Daniel's 70th week is that it has been postponed, because the Jews rejected Jesus as their King and Messiah. Under this scenario, the sixty-nine weeks ran consecutively, but the seventieth week has been projected ahead for thousands of years and is yet in our future. And just prior to the resumption of the seventieth week, the believers would all leave the planet in an event called the rapture of the church. Then, somewhere near the end of the seventieth week, the antichrist would appear, and this would lead the world into the battle of Armageddon. Thus, there is a **HUGE gap** between the sixty-ninth and seventieth week.

We discussed this gap in an earlier chapter. The problem with this system is that the **_only ones who are on board_** with this are dispensationalists. The presence of the gap in the prophecy is **_absolutely crucial_** to this system of theology, otherwise it completely falls apart, and none of the things they say about anything that happens surrounding this event makes any sense. This includes the rapture, the tribulation, and the rebuilt temple. But as we said in an earlier chapter **nowhere** in this passage is there even the **slightest indication** that there would be a gap. Where is their **scriptural support** for this view? Answer: **There is none.** This gap was added in order to make the theology work. It is just that simple.

But now we have seen this scenario being spoken of and being shouted by our religious leaders **over and over again for several generations**. Although this idea was started almost 200 years ago by a man named John Darby, the really big push started in 1969 and gained a huge amount of followers when a book came out called "The Late Great Planet Earth" by Hal Lindsey. It became a bestseller, and took the world of Christendom by a storm. Lindsey's original view was that the end times events would take place in the 1980s. When this didn't happen as predicted, more books came out which were sequels or revisions and extensions of his first book. Others jumped on the bandwagon with their own predictions, all of which proved to be wrong.

Let me give you just a few examples of this as mentioned in Gary Demar's book, "Last Days Madness:"

> The most notorious was Edgar C. Whisenant's 88 Reasons Why the Rapture Is in 1988. Upon the release of his calculations, Whisenant remarked, "Only if the Bible is in error am I wrong, and I say that unequivocally. There is no way Biblically that I can be wrong; and I say that to every preacher in town." When the author's intricate system of predicting the end failed, he went on

undaunted with a new book called "The Final Shout: Rapture Report 1989."

Next came Grant R. Jeffrey's book, "*Armageddon: Appointment with Destiny.*" Jeffrey writes that through his own research into biblical prophecies he has discovered a number of indications "which suggest that the year A.D. 2000 is a probable termination date for the 'last days.'"

Lester Sumrall wrote in his book I Predict 2000 A.D.: "I predict the absolute fullness of man's operation on planet Earth by the year 2000 A.D. Then Jesus Christ shall reign from Jerusalem for 1000 years."

Following this, Iraq invaded Kuwait, and this caused another round of speculation as the prophecy books once again emerged. Hal Lindsey's Late Great Planet Earth started selling again. John F. Walvoord reissued a revised edition of Armageddon, Oil and the Middle East Crisis to fit new developments in the Mideast. Walvoord claimed that Saddam Hussein's "move into Kuwait was motivated by a desire to 'set up a power base from which to attack Israel.'

Charles R. Taylor wrote in Bible Prophecy News in the summer of 1992 that Jesus' return would occur in the fall of the same year: "What you are starting to read probably is my final issue of Bible Prophecy News, for Bible prophecy fulfillments indicate that Jesus Christ our Lord will most likely return for us at the rapture of the Church before the Fall 1992 issue can be printed." [5]

All of this was a total and complete embarrassment to the Christian community. How many people do you think were so discouraged by these predictions that they actually walked away from the Christian faith?

I have to admit to you that ___I myself believed these guys were right!___ After all, isn't there an old saying that there is safety in numbers? And when these predictions failed, one after another, I just thought that their only error was that they were too specific and should not have gotten into the date setting trap. But then came the Gulf war, and more of the same predictions, and this was followed by the horrible events of 9/11/2001, and I was sure that this was it....The end was here and everything that these guys were predicting was just about to happen. I thought the war in Iraq would begin this chain of events that would bring about this very scenario that these prophecy pundits kept proclaiming...but after years of this going on, *nothing happened.*

But a few years ago, I decided that it was time for me to look at this system of theology very closely. Maybe these men whom I had admired for so many years *were actually wrong* about what they were teaching. I was shocked at what I learned from a very close examination of the facts. For example, when I read Gary Demar's book "Last Days Madness" I found that not only was this a scenario that played out in my lifetime, but one *which goes back for centuries.* Listen to this quote from his book:

> "As the last day of 999 approached, "the old basilica of St. Peter's at Rome was thronged with a mass of weeping and trembling worshipers awaiting the end of the world," believing that they were on the eve of the Millennium. Land, homes, and household goods were given to the poor as a final act of contrition to absolve the hopeless from sins of a lifetime. Some Europeans sold their goods before traveling to Palestine to await the Second Coming. This mistaken application of biblical prophecy **happened again in 1100, 1200, and 1245.** Prophetic speculation continued. "In 1531, Melchior Hofmann announced that the second coming would take place in the year 1533.... Nicholas Cusa held that the world would not last past 1734."[6]

Yes, that's right! This same scenario was being played out *a thousand years ago!!* Let me repeat that: **A THOUSAND YEARS AGO!!!** This got my attention in a big way.

I had to ask myself, what makes us think that this is any more likely to happen now than at this event that occurred over a thousand years ago? I realized that it was now time to go back to the basics and look at what our Lord Jesus actually said. The place to start in this journey is with what Jesus said in the passage of

Scripture that started all of this. It is a passage known as the "Olivet Discourse" because it was given to his disciples on the Mount of Olives.

So now in the light of what I just read, perhaps we need to ask: **Is this really what Jesus meant when he said he was coming soon?** RC Sproul wrote an entire book on this subject entitled, "The Last Days according to Jesus." Sproul admits that he doesn't have all of it figured out, and may never do so. **But we must ask the question;** by crying wolf and being wrong each time, is the Christian church being perceived as foolish and unreliable? Will skeptics of the Christian faith conclude that since these self-proclaimed prophets were wrong on the timing of Jesus' return when they seemed so certain, then maybe they are wrong on other issues which they teach with equal certainty? Will people say, "Maybe the entire Christian message is a sham." Recently, my 92 year old mother-in-law who has been a follower of John Hagee for over 20 years has expressed such a concern.

But before we look at what Jesus actually said in this "Olivet Discourse" we need to **review** our method of interpreting what is said in the Bible. In his book titled "Interpreting the Bible," Professor A. Berkley Mickelson gives the basic objective of anyone who wants to render an accurate interpretation of a Bible passage by stating:

> Simply stated, the task of interpreters of the Bible is to find out the meaning of a statement for the author and _**for the first hearers or readers,**_ and thereupon to transmit that meaning to modern readers.[7] (emphasis mine)

In other words, the job of the interpreter is _to make an interpretation based on what the writer wanted the hearers to hear and understand, and thereby to draw application for the modern readers._ This is in line with what Paul said in Romans 15:4 "For whatever was written in former days was written for our instruction, that through endurance and through the encouragement of the Scriptures we might have hope." With this precept in mind, I would like to reiterate that in order to understand the prophecies of the aforementioned books, or for that matter, any passage of Scripture, we need to first of all understand 3 things:

- When it was written?
- To whom it was written?
- What was the purpose for writing it?

Now as we finish this chapter, I would like to ask you a question, which contains a challenge. Do you want to go on believing that we are on the verge of a cataclysmic end of this world as the prophecy pundits keep telling us, or do you want to take a close look at what Jesus **REALLY** said about the Last Days? We will begin looking at this in the next chapter.

NOTES

1. D. Div., Don K. Preston (2012-06-17). Who Is This Babylon? (Kindle Locations 2448-2494). JaDon Management Inc.. Kindle Edition.
2. D. Div., Don K. Preston (2012-06-17). Who Is This Babylon? (Kindle Locations 946-958). JaDon Management Inc.. Kindle Edition.
3. The Works of Josephus, Translated by William Whiston, AM, Hendrickson Publishers, Peabody, Mass. 1987, page 749
4. http://www.newadvent.org/fathers/250103.htm (Eccl. Hist. Book 3:Chapter 5: verse 3)
5. Last Days Madness, by Gary DeMar, 1999 American Vision, Chapter one "The Dating Game" pages 23-25
6. Last Days Madness, by Gary DeMar, 1999 American Vision, Chapter one "The Dating Game" pages 23-25
7. "Interpreting the Bible" A.B Mickelsen, Eerdmans Publishing 1981, Grand Rapids MI, page 5

Chapter 5

Matthew 24 & 25: The Olivet Discourse - Part 1

At the end of the last chapter, I asked you to embark upon a journey to examine what Jesus said about the Last Days. I said that we needed to understand 3 things when we examine a passage of Scripture. These are:

- When was it written?
- To whom was it written?
- What was the purpose for which it was written?

Throughout this book, I have been quoting from some excellent commentaries. First is that of Albert Barnes, an American Theologian who lived from 1798-1870. He graduated from Princeton Theological seminary in 1823 and was a Presbyterian Minister in Philadelphia. Another resource I have used is Adam Clarke's commentary. He was a British Methodist Theologian and Bible Scholar who compiled his commentary over a period of 40 years. He lived from 1762-1832. Additionally, I have utilized information from some excellent writers on this subject, as you will see in the following pages.

One of my goals with this work is to present my findings in such a way as to encourage others who believe as I did to look into this matter further. The information I am about to present was overwhelming to me upon first hearing it, and it has deeply challenged beliefs which I have held for years. It is with a humble heart and an open mind that I present this material.

In this chapter, we will begin our examination of what **Jesus said** concerning the Last Days by looking at the Gospel of Matthew. Why did I choose the book of Matthew when there are three accounts of this passage? I chose it because it is the most detailed, and the longest of the three accounts. As previously mentioned, I would like for you to get used to the term, **"the Olivet Discourse."** This term is a description of the discourse Jesus gave his disciples while on the Mount of Olives. It is in all three Synoptic Gospels. The accounts are Matthew 24, Mark 13, and Luke 21. These are parallel accounts of the same event. It is noteworthy to consider that in the Olivet discourse we find our Lord Jesus giving a prophecy containing several very specific items.

- He speaks of a time of big trouble in the future.
- A _definite, specific_ period of time is stated: "**This** generation will not pass away"
  - o Let me stop right here. Our Lord did not say that this would be something that would happen thousands of years later. He was very specific when he said the events he was about to explain would happen within the time frame of **the generation being addressed.**
- I want you to carefully notice the questions that are asked by the disciples, and how **directly** and explicitly Jesus answered them.
- I want you to notice the audience to whom Jesus is speaking. Once again, this is **distinctly** given to the generation Jesus said would see all of these things.
- _Detailed_ instructions are given by Jesus as to _what_ the disciples should do and _when_ they should do it. These

instructions were so detailed, that they **would not fit any other time period** than the time period of the current generation.

Just prior to chapter 24 of Matthew's account, at the end of chapter 23, we find Jesus speaking boldly to the scribes and Pharisees, excoriating their hypocritical religious practices. He prophesies against them in Matt 23:31-36 as follows:

> Mat 23:31 Thus you witness against yourselves that you are sons of those who murdered the prophets.
>
> Mat 23:32 Fill up, then, the measure of your fathers.
>
> Mat 23:33 You serpents, you brood of vipers, how are you to escape being sentenced to hell?
>
> Mat 23:34 Therefore I send you prophets and wise men and scribes, some of whom you will kill and crucify, and some you will flog in your synagogues and persecute from town to town,
>
> Mat 23:35 so that on **YOU** may come all the righteous blood shed on earth, from the blood of righteous Abel to the blood of Zechariah the son of Barachiah, whom **YOU** murdered between the sanctuary and the altar.
>
> Mat 23:36 Truly, I say to you, all these things will come upon *__this generation__*. (ESV)(emphasis mine)

Notice that Jesus pronounces judgment on *"__this generation__."* There is no question that he was referring to the generation to whom he was speaking. He pronounced judgment on these hypocritical religious leaders, and told them they were murderers. He expressed great sorrow that his own people would reject him and told them in Matt 23:38 "See, your house is left to you desolate."

Now as we begin reading Matthew 24, I want to encourage you to watch closely for these specific items. And as we begin going through them, I will be asking you questions to make you think about what is being said here in these verses, and to find out if you think it makes sense for some future generation. Beginning in Matthew 24:1, we read:

> Mat 24:1 Jesus came out from the temple and was going away when His disciples came up to point out the temple buildings to Him.
>
> **Mat 24:2** And He said to them, "Do you not see all these things? Truly I say to you, not one stone here will be left upon another, which will not be torn down."

Here in the second verse is the prophecy which sets the timeline for the entire chapter. The timeline will come to pass exactly as Jesus predicted. We will discuss more on this later.

> Mat 24:3 As He was sitting on the Mount of Olives, the disciples came to Him privately, saying, "Tell us, when will these things happen, and what *will be* the sign of Your coming, and of the end of the age?"

So here we find the four apostles closest to Jesus getting very specific with Jesus and asking him 2 questions: When will this happen? And what will be the sign that will let us know it is about to take place at the end of the age? Many have said that this is actually 3 questions, but the logic of this is faulty. The phrase "and of the end of the age" actually would be better translated as "and the end of the age." It is translated as such in the Good News Bible:

> Mat 24:3 As Jesus sat on the Mount of Olives, the disciples came to him in private. "Tell us when all this will be," they asked, "and what will happen to show that it is the time for your coming and the end of the age."

The reason this is a better translation is because the Greek word και (and) shows a cumulative force from the previous phrase. It is not introducing a separate subject. Commentator John Gill makes a good point concerning this phrase in Matthew 24:3 when he says:

> **And what shall be the sign of thy coming, and of the end of the world?** Which two are put together, as what they supposed would be at the same time, and immediately follow the destruction of the temple. That he was come in the flesh, and was the true Messiah, they firmly believed: he was with them, and they expected he

would continue with them, for **they had no notion of his leaving them, and coming again.** (emphasis mine)

Without question, this must be correct. Gill has made a **very notable observation.** There is no way the disciples would be asking about some other far distant future event, because they thought Jesus **would become their King, and always be** with them! This erases any idea of it being three questions. It was a continuation of the second question. If this phrase is translated properly it is understood.

Jesus elaborates on the second question first, as we continue. Now keep in mind that we now know the time frame he is talking about here, because as I said previously, history has recorded it for us. We will see this a little later in the discussion. I would also like you to notice as we read through verse 23 how many times he specifically tells these four disciples that this would happen to **THEM**....not some future generation.

> Mat 24:4 And Jesus answered and said to them, "See to it that no one misleads *you*.

While reading this sentence, I have to ask, why would he say this to them if the meaning of what he was saying was for some future generation? Wouldn't he say something like "pray that **THEY** will not be led astray?"

> Mat 24:5 "For many will come in My name, saying, 'I am the Christ,' and will mislead many.
> Mat 24:6 "You will be hearing of wars and rumors of wars. See that you are not frightened, for *those things* must take place, but *that* is not yet the end.
> Mat 24:7 "For nation will rise against nation, and kingdom against kingdom, and in various places there will be famines and earthquakes.
> Mat 24:8 "But all these things are *merely* the beginning of birth pangs.

Jesus was describing a time of trouble in the near future which they would see. This included wars, earthquakes, and famines. Now notice in the next verse, Jesus uses the word *"you" 3 times*.

> Mat 24:9 "Then they will deliver **you** to tribulation, and will kill **you**, and **you** will be hated by all nations because of My name.
> Mat 24:10 "At that time many will fall away and will betray one another and hate one another.
> Mat 24:11 "Many false prophets will arise and will mislead many.
> Mat 24:12 "Because lawlessness is increased, most people's love will grow cold.
> Mat 24:13 "But the one who endures to the end, he will be saved.

It is abundantly clear here that Jesus was speaking to these four disciples, and **what THEY** would experience.

> Mat 24:14 "This gospel of the kingdom shall be preached in the whole world as a testimony to all the nations, and then the end will come.

What did Jesus mean by "the whole world?" Upon an examination of the Greek we find this. The word "world" here is the Greek word οικουμενη (oikoumene.) Note Strong's Greek dictionary:

> οἰκουμένη oikouménē oy-kou-men'-ay feminine participle present passive of 3611 (as noun, by implication, of 1093); land, i.e. the (terrene part of the) globe; especially, the Roman empire:--earth, world. [1] (underline mine).

Note here as pointed out by Strong, that this word can be translated land, and is *specifically* directed at the Roman Empire. The apostles did in fact preach the Gospel to the entire Roman Empire prior to the destruction of Jerusalem. This is the only place in Matthew that this word is used. It is elsewhere used in Luke 2:1:

> "In those days a decree went out from Caesar Augustus that all the world (oikouménē) should be registered."

Certainly there could be no one claiming that all of the inhabited earth needed to come to be registered by Caesar Augustus. In agreement with this idea was the Apostle Paul. He noted in Romans 1:8: "First, I thank my God through Jesus Christ for all of you, because your faith is proclaimed in all the world."(ESV)

The Greek word for world here is **κοσμος**:

κόσμος kósmos kos'-mos probably from the base of 2865; orderly arrangement, i.e. decoration; by implication, the world (in a wide or narrow sense, including its inhabitants, literally or figuratively (morally)):--adorning, world. [2]

Albert Barnes notes in his commentary regarding this:

The evidence that this was done is to be chiefly derived from the New Testament, and there it is clear. Thus Paul declares that it was preached to **every creature under heaven** Col 1:6, Col 1:23; that the faith of the Romans was spoken of throughout the whole world Rom_1:8; that he preached **in Arabia** Gal_1:17, and **at Jerusalem**, and round about **unto Illyricum** Rom_15:19. We know also that He traveled through **Asia Minor, Greece, and Crete**; that he was in **Italy**, and probably in **Spain and Gaul**, Rom_15:24-28. At the same time, the other apostles were not idle; and there is full proof that within thirty years after this prophecy was spoken, churches were established in all these regions. (emphasis mine)

The implication here is clear. The Roman Empire was the "whole world" unto which Jesus was referring. And this was accomplished prior to AD 70.

Now as we continue with the following verses, notice the reference to the prophet Daniel. This is the tie in with Daniel's prophecy we spoke of in an earlier chapter.

Mat 24:15 "Therefore when you see the ABOMINATION OF DESOLATION which was spoken of through Daniel the prophet, standing in the holy place (let the reader understand),
Mat 24:16 then those who are in Judea must flee to the mountains.

As noted in a previous chapter, similar words recorded by Luke show the timing of their exit.

> Luk 21:20 "But when you see Jerusalem surrounded by armies, then recognize that her desolation is near.
> Luk 21:21 "Then those who are in Judea must flee to the mountains, and those who are in the midst of the city must leave, and those who are in the country must not enter the city;

There were 2 sieges of Jerusalem. The first was under Vespasian. Under this siege, _no one was allowed out of the city_. But during this siege, the emperor Nero dies. With the entire Roman Empire in trouble and on the verge of collapse, Vespasian withdraws his forces, most likely so he could go back to Rome and protect his interests as well as that of the entire empire. In fact history records that this was so unsettling to the empire that during that very year _four different emperors were in power_, with Vespasian eventually winning out. After settling this and putting the Roman Empire back on solid footing, he sent Titus to finish the job he started in Jerusalem. It was _during this withdrawal period_ that the Christians had the opportunity to "flee to the mountains." Eusebius records that _they did_ flee in his account:

> But the people of the church in Jerusalem had been commanded by a revelation, vouchsafed to approved men there before the war, to leave the city and to dwell in a certain town of Perea called Pella. And when those that believed in Christ had come there from Jerusalem, then, as if the royal city of the Jews and the whole land of Judea were entirely destitute of holy men, the judgment of God at length overtook those who had committed such outrages against Christ and his apostles, and totally destroyed that generation of impious men. [3]

Then, looking back at Matt. 24:16 we see that clearly, this would not apply to any future generation. The context would not fit. If this is a futurist passage, _would that future generation be required to come back to Judea, so they could flee to the mountains?_ If not, then what about those who do not live in Judea? What should they do? Is there any indication of any instructions for them? This makes it clear that Jesus' words were only for this specific audience.

Moving on to verse 17 we read:

Mat 24:17 "Whoever is on the housetop must not go down to get the things out that are in his house.

Notice the wording of the above passage. Do you see how Jesus describes the architecture of **his** day? How many of us have a flat roof on our house with an outside stairway? But this was a typical house in Jesus' day. If Jesus was speaking to our generation or beyond, would he have said it this way?

Now as we continue:

Mat 24:18 "Whoever is in the field must not turn back to get his cloak.
Mat 24:19 "But woe to those who are pregnant and to those who are nursing babies in those days!

Jesus gave them this instruction for a good reason. For Jewish Historian Josephus documents in detail the fact that when Jerusalem was under siege from the Roman armies, that mothers of infants trapped inside Jerusalem were so desperate that they had nothing with which to feed their children, and some of them committed **unspeakable atrocities**, such as **cooking and eating their own children!**

Then we note in this passage:

Mat 24:20 "But pray that your flight will not be in the winter, or on a Sabbath.
Mat 24:21 "For then there will be a great tribulation, such as has not occurred since the beginning of the world until now, nor ever will.
Mat 24:22 "Unless those days had been cut short, no life would have been saved; but for the sake of the elect those days will be cut short.

Yes, it is true, Jesus used some very strong language here. He said that this would be the greatest tribulation that would ever be. But did he mean that literally? One could argue that it was. Josephus notes that there were 1.1 million Jews killed! Bodies were piled upon bodies. This was a horrific scene as noted later in his writings:

> 3. Now the number (32) of those that were carried captive during this whole war was collected to be ninety-seven thousand; *as was the number of those that perished during the whole siege eleven hundred thousand,* the greater part of whom were indeed of the same nation [with the citizens of Jerusalem], but not belonging to the city itself; for they were come up from all the country to the feast of unleavened bread, *and were on a sudden shut up by an army,* which, at the very first, occasioned so great a straitness among them, that there came a pestilential destruction upon them, and soon afterward such a famine, as destroyed them more suddenly. And that this city could contain so many people in it, is manifest by that number of them which was taken under Cestius, who being desirous of informing Nero of the power of the city, who otherwise was disposed to contemn that nation, entreated the high priests, if the thing were possible, to take the number of their whole multitude. [4](emphasis mine.)

But as we look at Matthew's account in verse 21, we find this type of expression commonly referred to as hyperbolic language. I will expound on this in a few more verses. Continuing on.....

Mat 24:23 "Then if anyone says to you, 'Behold, here is the Christ,' or 'There *He is,*' do not believe *him.*
Mat 24:24 "For false Christs and false prophets will arise and will show great signs and wonders, so as to mislead, if possible, even the elect.
Mat 24:25 "Behold, I have told you in advance.
Mat 24:26 "So if they say to you, 'Behold, He is in the wilderness,' do not go out, *or,* 'Behold, He is in the inner rooms,' do not believe *them.*
Mat 24:27 "For just as the lightning comes from the east and flashes even to the west, so will the coming of the Son of Man be.

Mat 24:28 "Wherever the corpse is, there the vultures will gather.

Were there false Christs and false prophets in the days following this? Yes! This is documented in "The History of the Christian Church" as follows:

> Under the last governors, Felix, Festus, Albinus, and Florus, moral corruption and the dissolution of all social ties, but at the same time the oppressiveness of the Roman yoke, increased every year. After the accession of Felix, assassins, called "Sicarians" (from *sica*, a dagger), armed with daggers and purchasable for any crime, endangering safety in city and country, roamed over Palestine. Besides this, the party spirit among the Jews themselves, and their hatred of their heathen oppressors, rose to the most insolent political and religious fanaticism, **and was continually inflamed by false prophets and Messiahs,** one of whom, for example, according to Josephus, drew after him thirty thousand men. Thus came to pass what our Lord had predicted: "There shall arise **false Christs,** and false prophets, and shall lead many astray."[5](emphasis mine.)

Also, as recorded in the writings of Josephus:

> But there was an Egyptian false prophet that did the Jews more mischief than the former; for he was a cheat, and pretended to be a prophet also, and got together thirty thousand men that were deluded by him; these he led round about from the wilderness to the mount which was called the Mount of Olives, and was ready to break into Jerusalem by force from that place; and if he could but once conquer the Roman garrison and the people, he intended to domineer over them by the assistance of those guards of his that were to break into the city with him. [6]

Now as we return to Matthew 24, notice the extreme emphasis Jesus puts on the following verse:

> Mat 24:29 "But immediately after the tribulation of those days THE SUN WILL BE DARKENED, AND THE MOON WILL NOT GIVE ITS LIGHT, AND THE STARS WILL FALL from the sky, and the powers of the heavens will be shaken.

Is what Jesus saying to be taken literally? Was the sun to be literally darkened? Was the moon literally said not to give its light? Were there literally to be stars falling from the sky, and were the powers of the heavens literally to be shaken?

My answer to these questions is a resounding **NO.**

This is not literal. So now you ask, "How can you say this with so much certainty? What makes you so sure? After all, this is one of the reasons that everyone is saying this still has not happened. Most people are waiting for such a sign to occur to know that the end is near."

I can tell you that I am so sure of this because **we have a precedent** in the Old Testament for such a thing. Listen to what Albert Barnes says about this in his commentary written over a hundred and fifty years ago. Commenting on Matthew's exact account of this, Barnes notes about this extreme verbiage:

> The images used here are _not to be taken literally_. They are _often employed_ by the sacred writers to denote "any great calamities." As the darkening of the sun and moon, and the falling of the stars, would be an inexpressible calamity, so any great catastrophe - any overturning of kingdoms or cities, or dethroning of kings and princes is represented by the darkening of the sun and moon, and by some terrible convulsion in the elements. Thus the destruction of Babylon is foretold in similar terms Isa_13:10, and of Tyre Isa_24:23. The slaughter in Bozrah and Idumea is predicted in the same language, Isa_34:4. See also Isa_50:3; Isa_60:19-20; Eze_32:7; Joe_3:15. (emphasis mine.)

So then, considering what Barnes said, let's look for ourselves. Let's read what the prophet Isaiah says in Isaiah 13:10:

> For the stars of the heavens and their constellations will not give their light; the sun will be dark at its rising, and the moon will not shed its light.

Continuing on in verse 13 we read:

> Therefore I will make the heavens tremble, and the earth will be shaken out of its place, at the wrath of the LORD of hosts in the day of his fierce anger.

Was this a prediction **of some future event? NO!!** For in verse one of this chapter we read:

> The oracle concerning Babylon which Isaiah the son of Amoz saw.

That's right! This was a prophecy concerning **the destruction of Babylon.** A prophecy which came about exactly as foretold. The language which was used here is commonly referred to as hyperbole. It is a statement which contains verbiage which is extreme in order to make a point. We do this all the time, don't we, by saying such things as: It's colder than blue ice out there, or I'm so hungry I could eat a horse.

So, now as we look at this prophecy in Isaiah 13 concerning Babylon, we have to ask: Did the sun, moon, and stars **actually go dark?** Did the heavens **actually tremble**, and was the earth **actually shaken** out of its place? Of course not!! This was merely a common way of expressing judgment upon a nation or nations, and is frequently used in the Old Testament.

And in Matthew 24:29, we have Jesus using the same type of language to describe the destruction of Jerusalem as it occurred in AD 70. The apostles understood this and were used to hearing this type of verbiage. As I pointed out earlier, Jesus told the four disciples he was closest to that they would have to suffer many things, and that this instruction was **specifically given to them.** However, I would like to add that there is no question that we also can _draw an application_ from this today. Speaking of the Old Testament, Paul wrote in Romans 15:4:

> For whatever was written in former days was written for our instruction, that through endurance and through the encouragement of the Scriptures we might have hope. (ESV)

There is no question that Christians today are still undergoing persecution, some of it even to the point of death. Yes, we can draw application from this, but nonetheless, this passage was given **_TO_** the four disciples to whom Jesus was speaking, and the prophecy was given to let **_them_** know the terrible things that were going to happen within their lifetime.

Just to make my point, consider the following events which happened to the disciples of Jesus in their generation. After Jesus' death, Stephen was the first Christian martyr recorded in the Bible, and as it is recorded, he was stoned to death while speaking to the Jewish religious leaders. As for the apostles, Fox's Book of Martyrs records that:

- The apostle James was beheaded in AD 44. Philip was scourged, thrown into prison and crucified.
- Matthew was slain with a halberd, a sort of a sword and ax combination.
- James, the overseer of the Church in Jerusalem and half brother of Jesus had his brains dashed out with a fullers club.
- The apostle Andrew was crucified on an x shaped cross which later became known as St. Andrew's cross.
- Mark, who wrote the book of Mark, was dragged to pieces by the people of Alexandria. Peter was crucified upside down on a cross in Rome.
- Paul was led out of Rome by the soldiers and gave his neck to the sword.
- Jude was crucified.
- Thomas was thrust through by a spear. Simon was crucified.
- The only apostle who survived was John, who was said to be boiled in oil, although reportedly he miraculously escaped without injury. [7]

It is exactly as the Apostle Paul said in 1 Cor. 4:9:

For I think that God set us out last, the apostles, as appointed to death, because we became a spectacle to the world, even to angels and to men.

As for the Jews who suffered in the siege of Jerusalem by the Roman armies, people were ruthlessly murdered and tortured in unspeakable ways for the tiniest morsels of food. _Mothers killed and sometimes **ate** their children. Up to **500 people a day** were crucified by the Roman soldiers._ Yes, no wonder Jesus used such strong language to say what would happen during that period of time.

But now as we read Matthew's account in verse 30, we notice something different:

> Mat 24:30 "And then the sign of the Son of Man will appear in the sky, and then all the tribes of the earth will mourn, **_and they_** will see the SON OF MAN COMING ON THE CLOUDS OF THE SKY with power and great glory.
> Mat 24:31 "And He will send forth His angels with A GREAT TRUMPET and THEY WILL GATHER TOGETHER His elect from the four winds, from one end of the sky to the other.

Now, for the first time in this account, we hear the word **they.** This solidifies the point I have been making. Previously, everything was **_directed to_** the four disciples. And now Jesus is saying "**they** will see the Son of Man coming in clouds with power and great glory." So now who is Jesus referring to? For a clue, we can look at the parallel account of Matthew from J. P. Green's Literal Translation.

> Mat 24:30 And then the sign of the Son of Man will appear in the heavens. And then all the tribes **of the land** will wail. And they will see the Son of Man coming on the clouds of heaven with power and much glory. (LITV)(emphasis mine)

Yes, the word translated as **earth** in most translations is more accurately translated as **land** by Green. So Jesus is referring to the Jewish nation who rejected and crucified him. For the first time in this chapter, we see a reference to someone outside of the circle of the apostles who would see these things. Once again, this is not a reference to some far distant future event, but a reference to something which would happen during the lifetime of the disciples to whom he was speaking. Did this occur? Was there a sign? Was there a presence of power and great glory seen in the heavens? Listen to what Josephus records in his account in the Wars of the Jews.

> Thus there was a star resembling a sword, which stood over the city, and *a comet, that continued a whole year.* Thus also, before the Jews rebellion, and before those commotions which preceded the war, when the people were come in great crowds on the feast of unleavened bread....so great a light shone that it appeared to be bright daytime; which light lasted for half and hour. This light seemed to be a good sign to the unskillful, but was so interpreted by the sacred scribes, as to portend those events that followed immediately upon it. At that same festival also, *a heifer, as she was led by the high priest to be sacrificed, brought forth a lamb in the midst of the temple.*[8] (emphasis mine)

Can there be any question, that this was a sign from heaven? It is completely impossible that these events were some natural occurring thing. You talk about a sign? **Wow!** A star resembling a sword that stood over the city, and a comet lasting a whole year!...A bright light shining on the holy house in the dark of night...**A heifer giving birth to a lamb** at the very time that it was brought into the temple to be sacrificed...**Yes, the Jews always wanted a sign....Jesus delivered it to them in a mighty way.** But there is more. Listen as Josephus continues:

> Moreover, the eastern gate of the inner court of the temple, which was brass, and vastly heavy, and had been with difficulty shut by twenty men, and rested upon a basis armed with Iron, and had bolts fastened very deep into the firm floor which was made of entire stone, was seen to be opened of its own accord about the sixth hour of the night...But the men of learning **understood it,** that the security of their holy house was dissolved of its own accord, and that the gate was opened for the advantage of their

enemies. So these publicly declared that this signal foreshadowed the desolation that was coming upon them. [9](emphasis mine)

Yes, no question, that gate was opened by the Lord Jesus as part of the sign he promised, and those religious leaders knew it. But there is still more. Listen to this as recorded by Josephus:

> Besides these, a few days after the feast, on the twenty-first day of the month Artemisius [Jyar], a certain prodigious and incredible phenomenon appeared; I suppose the account of it would seem to be a fable, were it not related by those who saw it, and were not the events that followed it of so considerable a nature as to deserve such signals; for, before the sunsetting, **chariots and troops of soldiers were seen running about among the clouds**, and surrounding cities. Moreover at that feast which we call Pentecost, as the priests going by night into the inner [court of the] temple, as their custom was, to perform their sacred ministrations, they said that, in the first place, they felt a quaking, and heard a great noise, and after that they heard a sound of a great multitude saying, "Let us remove hence." [10](emphasis mine)

Now I have to ask you, have you ever heard of anything like this being documented by a notable historian, one whose credibility is undeniable? Isn't it extremely noteworthy to see that Almighty God would use a Jewish historian to record such events? By using a notable historian to record this, there is no space here to ridicule the Scriptures as many liberal college professors tend to do. This is recorded by one who is highly considered by those in positions of authority in the educational ranks. Regarding the credibility of Flavius Josephus, look at this quotation.

> Our knowledge of the last two centuries of the Second Commonwealth depends very substantially on the writings of Josephus. Matters such as his credibility, accuracy and sources are therefore foremost among the topics which should occupy scholarship. The most obvious data for examination, it would seem to us, is *archaeological* material. In many instances, numerous details provided by Josephus can be checked, including architectural data, and their accuracy confirmed. Such precision, where it can be established, is surprising, especially since the

information was set down in writing years after Josephus had left Palestine. [11]

Having established this now, let's return to the subject at hand. But now you ask the question, but what about Jesus coming in the clouds? Are you saying that this judgment described in detail in the writings of Josephus is what Jesus was speaking of here?

Well let's determine this from the scriptural evidence.

Once again, the term coming in the clouds was not something new to the disciples to whom Jesus was speaking. Having an understanding of the Old Testament, as taught by Jesus, they knew what this meant. Let's look at some examples:

Exo 19:9 And the LORD said to Moses, "Behold, I am coming to you in a thick cloud, that the people may hear when I speak with you, and may also believe you forever."

Exo 34:5 The LORD descended in the cloud and stood with him there, and proclaimed the name of the LORD.

Now let's look at how Isaiah worded it in this prophecy against Egypt.

Isa 19:1 An oracle concerning Egypt. Behold, the LORD is riding on a swift cloud and comes to Egypt; and the idols of Egypt will tremble at his presence, and the heart of the Egyptians will melt within them.

Again, I have to ask: In this judgment of Egypt, did the Lord **ride on a literal cloud?** Did the idols **literally** tremble? Did the hearts of the Egyptians **literally melt** in their chests? NO! It was just the way the prophet described it, using extreme language to make his point, and the cloud reference is quite common in the Old Testament. In fact, in Exodus alone we find over 15 examples of the Lord appearing to Israel in the clouds, and over 70 such references throughout the Old Testament.

But now, once again, let's go back to Matt. 24:30, because we still have to finish one item in this verse. Who is the **THEY** that is spoken of in this verse where it says: "**they** will see the Son of Man coming in clouds with power and great glory?"

We touched on this earlier, but let's look at it closer. We find it documented in Matthew chapters 26 and 27. Yes, it is those who, instead of embracing Jesus as Lord and savior, **actually decided to murder him**…. And not only to put him to death, but to torture him, and lead him to a disgraceful death as a criminal, nailing him to the cross.

This included two groups of people. First we have the religious leaders that Jesus spoke to directly in Matt. 26. Let's listen to this account of Jesus standing before the high priest, and the scribes, and Pharisees of the Jewish Sanhedrin:

> Mat 26:63 But Jesus remained silent. And the high priest said to him, "I adjure you by the living God, tell us if you are the Christ, the Son of God."
> Mat 26:64 Jesus said to him, "You have said so. But I tell **YOU**, from now on **YOU** will see the Son of Man seated at the right hand of Power and coming on the clouds of heaven."
> Mat 26:65 Then the high priest tore his robes and said, "He has uttered blasphemy. What further witnesses do we need? You have now heard his blasphemy.
> Mat 26:66 What is your judgment?" They answered, "He deserves death."
> Mat 26:67 Then they spit in his face and struck him. And some slapped him, (emphasis mine)

….how despicable!

Also included in this judgment were those whom Pilate addressed in Matthew 27:

> Mat 27:22 Pilate said to them, "Then what shall I do with Jesus who is called Christ?" They all said, "Let him be crucified!"

Mat 27:23 And he said, "Why, what evil has he done?" But they shouted all the more, "Let him be crucified!"

Mat 27:24 So when Pilate saw that he was gaining nothing, but rather that a riot was beginning, he took water and washed his hands before the crowd, saying, "I am innocent of this man's blood; see to it yourselves."

Mat 27:25 And all the people answered, "His blood be on us and on our children!"

Yes, these people created their own indictment! They **did** have the innocent blood of Jesus on their hands! And all of them were pronounced guilty by Jesus, and were to be **judged shortly.** Now I think it is important for you to understand that the Wars of the Jews which lasted from AD 66 through about AD 73 was **not** just some small skirmish in the Middle East. Before we finish this segment, once again, let's just look at the statistics. During the final siege of Jerusalem in AD 70, Josephus reports that there were **1.1 million Jews killed.** But from Book 2 through Book 7 of the Wars of the Jews, Josephus reports that the total killed in all of this was over 1.3 million Jews which includes over 200,000 that were killed in over 20 cities and regions throughout all of Judea. He reports that in Jerusalem the bodies were piled so high in what was left of the city that the soldiers had to walk over them as they lay in big heaps everywhere. Additionally, Josephus reports that 97,000 were taken captive.

And in fulfillment of verse 27 of Mark chapter 13, the Christians did flee the city as instructed by Jesus. In fact, Eusebius reports in his Ecclesiastical History that not a single Christian was killed during the destruction of Jerusalem.

So from all of this we see that this evil that those Jews did on that occasion by rejecting the savior, and nailing him to that cross **came back on them** in one of the **most powerful ways** ever recorded in the annals of history. For in doing this, our Lord Jesus fulfilled the prophecy of John the Baptist in John 1:29: "Behold, the Lamb of God, who takes away the sin of the world!

And aren't we thankful that our Lord Jesus became that Lamb, shedding his precious blood for us, and thus giving us the promise of life eternal for those of faith! These disciples gave their lives for Jesus because of this.

So as we have noted, Jesus said that there would be certain ones who would see him coming in the clouds of glory. Now we have identified who these people were. It is very important that you notice that when Jesus spoke to these disciples, he changed from saying "**you will see**" to "**they will see**." This is **consistent in all 3** Gospel accounts. We also looked at the testimony of Josephus, and how he said that there were many who had reported to him that they had seen chariots of troops and soldiers running about in the sky. This does not directly say that they saw Jesus, but Josephus was not a part of the audience Jesus mentioned, and was merely recording what was told to him. Also, keep in mind that the book of Acts records that Stephen looked into heaven and saw Jesus standing at the right hand of God when he said:

> Acts 7:55 But he, full of the Holy Spirit, gazed into heaven and saw the glory of God, and Jesus standing at the right hand of God. Acts 7:56 And he said, "Behold, I see the heavens opened, and the Son of Man standing at the right hand of God."

Why did this enrage the council so much that they wanted to kill him? It was because **he was confirming** the very words that they heard our Lord tell them. And believe me, _**they never forgot those words,**_ especially when at the moment that he died on the cross, there was a great earthquake and the veil of the temple was torn in two. They were probably scared to death at these events happening.

So we actually see that there is precedence in this account for someone seeing Jesus in the heavens during that generation. Therefore I ask you in all sincerity, is it so hard to believe that these ones spoken to by Jesus when he was on trial **actually saw**

Jesus just as Stephen had done? Now we turn back to the Gospel of Matthew to continue reading:

> Mat 24:32 "Now learn the parable from the fig tree: when its branch has already become tender and puts forth its leaves, you know that summer is near;
>
> Mat 24:33 so, you too, when you see all these things, recognize that He is near, *right* at the door.
>
> Mat 24:34 "Truly I say to you, this generation will not pass away until all these things take place.

Notice here that Jesus **_did not say "that generation"_** in reference to some different generation. No, Jesus makes it plain here that this would happen within the generation **_in which the apostles were living._** But there has been considerable controversy regarding this passage. Some notable atheists have said Jesus was a false prophet. Some have **even said** that Jesus was wrong, **because he didn't return at all.**

Notable among these doubters is the beloved C.S. Lewis who once said:

> Say what you like, we shall be told, the apocalyptic beliefs of the first Christians proved to be false. It is clear from the New Testament that they all expected the Second coming in their lifetime. And worse still, they had a reason, and one which you will find very embarrassing, Their Master told them so. He shared, and indeed created their delusion. He said in so many words 'this generation will not pass until all these things are done.' And he was wrong. He clearly knew no more about the end of the world than anyone else. It is certainly the most embarrassing verse in the Bible. [12]

Yes, as much as we all love C.S. Lewis, and all he has done for the Christian Faith, he was wrong about this, and one of the purposes of this book has been to dispel mistaken theories such as he said here. Jesus **did return** in that generation, and I have shown the evidence here. And even though Lewis was wrong, it is clear from his statement, that he **knew** that Jesus meant the generation in which he was living.

Some have said that Jesus did not return in that generation, but what this really means is that "the generation that would see all these signs would also see the end of the ages." But I ask you, is that really what Jesus said? Why is this so complicated? It was a simple statement.

Others have said that the term "this generation" actually meant "this race will not pass away." Why would they try to put such a meaning on this, when it seems so clear? It's because they too, want to say that that Jesus didn't really mean the generation he was living in. He meant it for a future time, most likely ours. Therefore, they want it to have a meaning that would make this verse fit our time. But the word generation comes from the Greek word "genea." As to trying to force this word to mean "race," Charles Meek points out in his book "Christian Hope through Fulfilled Prophecy:"

> Excuse our bluntness, but this is eisegesis, not exegesis – and borders on the dishonest. The Greek word for "race" is **genos.** The word genea is used 43 times in the New Testament and not once in any standard Bible is it translated "race." [13]

But there is so much futurist bias in some of these translations, that although they will not actually translate the word genea as race, they will attempt to convince the reader that this is its meaning by adding it in the footnote. And in his book "Unraveling the End," John Noe makes this important point concerning the use of this word:

> Please notice that after Jesus' "this generation" time statement in Matt 24:34 some Bibles place a footnote clarifying its meaning or possible meaning as being "race." However, no footnote is added to the identical usage of this phrase in Matthew 23:36. If, however, Jesus' "this generation" meant "race," then Jesus did not answer his disciples time question in Matthew 24:3, which preceded this entire discourse: "Tell us," they said, "when will this happen, and what will be the sign of your coming and the end of the age? [14]

Yes, my friend John Noe has hit the nail on the head on this one. Jesus excoriated the scribes and Pharisees in Matthew 23:34-36 when he told them:

> Mat 23:34 Therefore I send you prophets and wise men and scribes, some of whom you will kill and crucify, and some you will flog in your synagogues and persecute from town to town,
> Mat 23:35 so that **on you may come all the righteous blood shed on earth**, from the blood of righteous Abel to the blood of Zechariah the son of Barachiah, whom you murdered between the sanctuary and the altar.
> Mat 23:36 Truly, I say to you, all these things will come upon this generation.

And this passage further confirms the judgment that Jesus was pronouncing upon this group. Nowhere is there any attempt to say that in this verse the word "genea" means race. And Charles Meek is right...the attempt to say genea means "race" in Matt. 24:34 is not exegesis, but eisegesis. This term is defined as an interpretation, especially of Scripture, that expresses the interpreter's own ideas, bias, or the like, rather than the actual meaning of the text.

Next, Jesus tells these four disciples how much they can depend upon what he said with these words in Matt. 24:35:

> Mat 24:35 "Heaven and earth will pass away, but My words will not pass away.

As Matthew Henry words it in his commentary, "The word of Christ is more sure and lasting than heaven and earth." Albert Barnes says: "You may sooner expect to see the heaven and earth pass away and return to nothing, than my words to fail." Commentator John Lightfoot adds that Jesus' words had a deeper meaning when he noted concerning this verse. After surveying how this language is used throughout the Bible and in Jewish literature, he believes the "passing away of heaven and earth" refers to the "destruction of Jerusalem and the whole Jewish state...as if the whole frame of this world were to be dissolved." I believe his notion is absolutely correct. But whether or not Jesus' meaning was this deep, one thing is certain: _We can depend on Jesus' words_. They did come to pass, and we can depend on **all of his precious promises.**

As for the remainder of the _Olivet Discourse,_ there is also much controversy as to its fulfillment. This will be discussed in detail in the following chapter.

NOTES

1. Strong, James (2011-05-07). Strong's Greek Dictionary of the Bible (with beautiful Greek, transliteration, and superior navigation) (Strong's Dictionary) (Kindle Locations 5855-5857). Miklal Software Solutions, Inc.. Kindle Edition.

2. Ibid, (Kindle Locations 4842-4844). Miklal Software Solutions, Inc.. Kindle Edition.

3. http://www.newadvent.org/fathers/250103.htm (Eccl. Hist. 3:5:3)

4. The Works of Josephus, Translated by William Whiston, AM, Hendrickson Publishers, Peabody, Mass. 1987, The Wars of the Jews, Book 6, Chapter 9, verse 3, page 749

5. History of the Christian Church, Volume 1, Chapter 6, under "The Jewish Rebellion," http://www.ccel.org/s/schaff/history/1_ch06.htm

6. The Works of Josephus, Translated by William Whiston, AM, Hendrickson Publishers, Peabody, Mass. 1987, The Wars of the Jews, Book 2, Chapter 13, Section 5, page 614

7. Taken from Foxes Book of Martyrs, Chapter 1, http://www.ccel.org/f/foxe/martyrs/fox101.htm

8. The Works of Josephus, Translated by William Whiston, AM, Hendrickson Publishers, Peabody, Mass. 1987, Wars of the Jews Book 6. Chapter 5. Section 3, page 742

9. Ibid.

10. Ibid.

11. http://www.centuryone.com/josephus.html Magen Broshi of The Israel Museum

12. The Worlds Last Night and other Essays - Harvest Book 2002 Pages 97,98

13. Christian Hope through Fulfilled Prophecy, 2013, Faith Facts Publishing, Spicewood, TX Charles Meek, page 98

14. Unraveling the End, 2014, East2West Press, Indianapolis, IN, John Noe, page 288

15. Albert Barnes Notes on the Bible, taken from e-Sword, Version 10.2.1, 2013, Rick Meyers (Free download at www.e-sword.net)

16. Adam Clarke's Commentary on the Bible, taken from e-Sword, Version 10.2.1, 2013, Rick Meyers (Free download at www.e-sword.net)
17. John Gill's Exposition of the Entire Bible, taken from e-Sword, Version 10.2.1, 2013, Rick Meyers (Free download at www.e-sword.net)

Chapter 6

Matthew 24 & 25: The Olivet Discourse - Part 2

As we continue to the remainder of the Olivet Discourse from Matthew chapters 24 and 25, we notice that there are differences of opinion as to the timing of when these things would occur. There are many who would tell us that this was but a shadow of what is coming in our future...that the events of the Olivet Discourse given here in Matthew 24 are going to play out all over again as we are staring down the Last Days in our time. But to those who would say this, I issue a challenge. _Where is there even the slightest hint in Jesus words that this was going to happen twice?_ You can search all three accounts of this, and you will find that there is **not a single word** conveying anything that would **hint** of a dual fulfillment. If there is no indication of this, then what is the reasoning behind there being a dual fulfillment?

In verse 34 and 35 Jesus tells his disciples that everything prior to that would happen in the generation in which they were living. But there are those who would argue that from this point on, we do not have the words bracketing "this generation." Thus, from this argument, it is said that we can be open to futuristic possibilities for the following verses. Those making this argument state that whereas in verses 1-35, Jesus gives predictable signs, which we showed actually happened, there appears to be less certainty about the timing of the things which he states from this point forward. But if this is true, we should see some indication from our Lord's words that this is the case, some words indicating a delay. This is a must; otherwise the disciples would be left confused, and misled. As we examine these verses, let's look for such an indication.

> Mat 24:36 "But of **that day** and hour no one knows, not even the angels of heaven, nor the Son, but the Father alone.
> Mat 24:37 "For the coming of the Son of Man will be just like the days of Noah.
> Mat 24:38 "For as in those days before the flood they were eating and drinking, marrying and giving in marriage, until the day that Noah entered the ark,
> Mat 24:39 and they did not understand until the flood came and took them all away; so will the coming of the Son of Man be.
> Mat 24:40 "Then there will be two men in the field; one will be taken and one will be left.
> Mat 24:41 "Two women *will be* grinding at the mill; one will be taken and one will be left.

Notice in verse 36 we have a reference to what was **already spoken** in the earlier verses when it says, "But of that day...." Does not this language and what follows show the imminence of the situation? Adam Clarke points out that this would be an unexpected attack. However, if the early Christians had heeded the words of Jesus, they _would have already_ fled to the mountains when Roman General Titus returned to finish the job. Notice Adam Clarke's words:

> **But of that day and hour -** Ωρα, here, is translated season by many eminent critics, and is used in this sense by both sacred and profane authors. As the day was not known, in which Jerusalem should be invested by the Romans, therefore our Lord advised his disciples to pray that it might not be on a Sabbath; and as the season was not known, therefore they were to pray that it might not be in the winter; Mat_24:20. See on Mar_13:32

Also Albert Barnes notes:

But of that day and hour - Of the precise time of the fulfillment. The "general signs" of its approach have been given, as the budding of the fig-tree is a certain indication that summer is near; but "the precise time" is not indicated by these things. One part of their inquiry was Mat_24:3 when those things should be. He now replies to them by saying that the precise time would not be foretold.

And as regards the women grinding, Adam Clarke's notes:

Then shall two men - two women - one shall be taken, and the other left - The meaning seems to be, that so general should these calamities be, that no two persons, wheresoever found, or about whatsoever employed, should be both able to affect their escape; and that captivity and the sword should have a complete triumph over this unhappy people.

Two women shall be grinding - Women alone are still employed in grinding the corn in the east; and it is only when dispatch is required, or the uppermost millstone is heavy, that a second woman is added. See Wakefield, and Harmer, Obs. vol. i. 253. That they were formerly thus employed, see Exo_11:5, and the note there. See also Isa_47:2.

Watch - Be looking for his coming. Be expecting it as near; as a great event; as coming in an unexpected manner. Watch the signs of his coming, and be ready.

As Clarke notes here, this calamity would be inescapable, and would come on all of those to whom it was predicted to come. Of course, if the Christians obeyed, they would be spared, as we previously noted. The Lord said that no one knows the day or hour, but even if he had that information, would it be prudent to give it to them? To have been very specific and given them an exact time would have taken from them one of the most powerful motives for being watchful, and on guard. They needed to be watchful about all of the events taking place. They needed to draw close to God in prayer, for what was about to happen was the most magnificent and horrific event in the history of the Jews.

Now we see that verses 42-44 read as follows:

Mat 24:42 Watch, then, for **you** do not know **in what hour** your Lord comes.

Mat 24:43 But know this, that if the housemaster had known in what watch the thief comes, he would have watched and not have allowed his house to be dug through.

Mat 24:44 Because of this, you also be ready, for **in that hour you** think not, the Son of Man comes. **(LITV)**

I have quoted this verse from Green's literal translation to note that he is regulating this time in terms of **hours** and not in terms of **decades or centuries**! Jesus is speaking of a more precise time than this. The "general signs" of its approach have been given, as the budding of the fig-tree is a certain indication that summer is near; but although the precise time is not indicated by these things, we do notice that *he says nothing about the notion that this was something that was to happen in some future generation*. Also notice that our Lord is still using the term **YOU** in these verses, and not **THEY.** This was definitely something these disciples would see happen, if even from a distance, having fled the city.

And finally, as we complete chapter 24, we have the ending passage:

Mat 24:45 Who then is the faithful and wise servant whom his Lord has set over His household, to give to them the food in season?

Mat 24:46 Blessed *is* that servant whom his Lord shall find so doing when He comes.

Mat 24:47 Truly I say to you, He will set him over all His substance.

Mat 24:48 But if that wicked slave says in his heart, My Lord delays to come,

Mat 24:49 and begins to beat *his* fellow servants, and to eat and to drink with the *ones* drinking,

Mat 24:50 the Lord of that slave will come in a day in which he does not expect and in an hour which he does not know,

Mat 24:51 and will cut him in two, and will appoint his portion with the hypocrites. There will be weeping and gnashing of the teeth.

Although not expressly stated as such, this passage is a parable. It is designed to show his disciples that they should act as if he could return at any minute. So with this in mind, it begs the question: Why would he have them act in such a way if his "Parousia" was not to happen for centuries, even thousands of years? Do we see anything in here which in anyway indicates a break in time, so that these events should be spoken of as far off into the future? Is he playing a cruel joke on them? **No.** He is telling them to be obedient because as he stated earlier, this judgment would happen *__in this same generation!__*

Verse 51 tells of that horrendous judgment: "and will cut him in pieces and put him with the hypocrites. In that place there will be weeping and gnashing of teeth." What does he mean by those words? Is it really as horrendous as the words indicate?

Notice what Adam Clarke says in this comment of this verse:

> **Cut him asunder -** This refers to an ancient mode of punishment used in several countries. Isaiah is reported to have been sawed asunder. . . . . It may also have reference to that mode of punishment in which the different members were chopped off *seriatim*, first the feet, then the hands, next the legs, then the arms, and lastly the head. This mode of punishment is still in use among the Chinese. But we find an exact parallel among the Turk. . . . . "If a Turk should happen to kill another Turk, his punishment is thus: After he is adjudged to death, he is brought forth to the market place; and a blocke being brought hither of four foot high, the malifactor is stript naked, and then laid thereon with his belly downward; they draw in his middle together so small with running cords that they strike his body a-two with one blow: his hinder parts they cast to be eaten by hungry dogs kept for the same purpose; and the forequarters and head they throw into a grievous fire, made there for the same end. And this is the punishment for manslaughter."

What a horrendous form of capital punishment this is. It is literally *__killing a person a little at a time!!__* It is done by cutting off first hands, then feet, then limbs, and finally the head of the victim.

Adam Clarke continues:

> This is the very same punishment, and for the same offense, as that mentioned by our Lord, the killing of a fellow servant - one of the same nation, and of the same religion.
>
> The reader has no doubt observed, in the preceding chapter, a series of the most striking and solemn predictions, fulfilled in the most literal, awful, and dreadful manner. *Christ has foretold* **the ruin of the Jewish people, and the destruction of their polity;** *and in such a circumstantial manner as none else could do,* but He, under whose eye are all events, and in whose hands are the government and direction of all things. *Indeed he rather declared* **what he would do,** *than predicted what should come to pass.* And the fulfillment has been as circumstantial as the prediction. Does it not appear that the predicted point was so literally referred to by the occurring fact, by which it was to have its accomplishment, *as* **to leave no room to doubt** *the truth of the prediction, or the certainty of the event by which it was fulfilled?* Thus the wisdom of God, as also his justice and providence, have had a plenary manifestation. (emphasis mine)

Even in the early 1800's theologian Adam Clarke was confident that this dreadful, hideous event was a judgment assigned to the Jewish people to whom Jesus spoke at the end of Matthew chapter 23. The writings of Josephus in the Wars of the Jews make this manifestation apparent. The awfulness of the situation at the end was indescribably bad. As Clarke concludes his thought here, we become convicted of the absolute sovereignty of God. With it comes the necessity of being obedient and faithful unto death.

Notice how powerfully he makes his point:

> But this wisdom appears, farther, in preserving such a record of the prediction, and such evidence of its accomplishment, as cannot possibly be doubted. The New Testament, given by the inspiration of God, and handed down uncorrupted from father to son, by both friends and enemies, **perfect in its credibility and truth,** inexpugnable in its evidences, and astonishingly circumstantial in details of future occurrences, which the wisdom of God alone could foreknow – that New Testament is the record of these predictions. The history of the Romans, written by so many hands;

the history of the Jews, written by one of themselves; triumphal arches, coins, medals, and public monuments of different kinds, are the evidence by which the fulfillment of the record is demonstrated. Add to this the preservation of the Jewish people; a people scattered through all nations, yet subsisting as a distinct body, without temple, sacrifices, or political government; and who, while they attempt to suppress the truth, yet reluctantly stand forth as an unimpeachable collateral evidence, that the solemn record, already alluded to, is strictly and literally true! Who that has ever consulted the Roman historians of the reigns of Vespasian and Titus, the history of Josephus, and the 24th chapter of St. Matthew's Gospel, and who knows anything of the present state of the Jews over the face of the earth, or even of those who sojourn in England, can doubt for a moment the truth of this Gospel, or the infinite and all-comprehensive knowledge of Him who is its author! Here then is one portion of Divine Revelation that is incontrovertibly *and absolutely proved to be the truth of God.* Reader! If he, who, while he predicted the ruin of this disobedient and refractory people, wept over their city and its inhabitants, has so, minutely fulfilled the threatenings of his justice on the unbelieving and disobedient, will he not as circumstantially fulfill the promises of his grace to all them that believe? The existence of his revelation, the continuance of a Christian Church upon earth, the certainty that there is one individual saved from his sins by the grace of the Gospel, and walking worthy of his vocation are continued proofs and evidences that he is still the same; *that he will fulfill every jot and tittle of that word* on which he has caused thee to trust; and save to the uttermost all that come unto the Father by him. *The word of the Lord endureth for ever;* and they who trust in him shall never be confounded. (emphasis mine)

We must keep in mind that Adam Clarke wrote this commentary **almost 200 years ago.** At that time, the re-establishment of the nation of Israel was still over **100 years in the future.** He was correct - they stood in judgment, the judgment that _was fulfilled_ in AD 70.

The Parable of the Virgins – Matthew 25:1-13

As these verses are examined, once again we must **look closely** to see if there is any indication whatsoever that our Lord has changed the subject and is now referring to a time period hundreds, perhaps even thousands of years in the future. If it was to entail a different era, wouldn't it make sense for there to be some kind of indication of this in his transitional phrase at the start of the parable? But, in fact, the opposite is true. We see in these verses to follow absolutely no indication of such a thing. In fact the transitional word which starts out the verse is "Then", indicating a continuation along the same lines. Reading verses 1-13, notice the words as chapter 25 begins:

Mat 25:1 "Then the kingdom of heaven will be comparable to ten virgins, who took their lamps and went out to meet the bridegroom.

Mat 25:2 "Five of them were foolish, and five were prudent.

Mat 25:3 "For when the foolish took their lamps, they took no oil with them,

Mat 25:4 but the prudent took oil in flasks along with their lamps.

Mat 25:5 "Now while the bridegroom was delaying, they all got drowsy and *began* to sleep.

Mat 25:6 "But at midnight there was a shout, 'Behold, the bridegroom! Come out to meet *him*.'

Mat 25:7 "Then all those virgins rose and trimmed their lamps.

Mat 25:8 "The foolish said to the prudent, 'Give us some of your oil, for our lamps are going out.'

Mat 25:9 "But the prudent answered, 'No, there will not be enough for us and you *too*; go instead to the dealers and buy *some* for yourselves.'

Mat 25:10 "And while they were going away to make the purchase, the bridegroom came, and those who were ready went in with him to the wedding feast; and the door was shut.

Mat 25:11 "Later the other virgins also came, saying, 'Lord, lord, open up for us.'

Mat 25:12 "But he answered, 'Truly I say to you, I do not know you.'

Mat 25:13 "Be on the alert then, for you do not know the day nor the hour.

Once again we see a transitional word, this time it is "Then," a reference to the previous time frame. Regarding these last two parables, much has been made of the delays in them. Yes, there are delays mentioned in these two parables, but does it make any sense that such delays would be for periods of hundreds and thousands of years? Gary DeMar makes a good point in this respect:

> The parables of Matthew 24–25 are clear on the duration of the delays—the two masters who go on a journey return to the same people they left. There is no need to allegorize these parables to force them to depict a distant coming of Christ. In addition, the delay of the bridegroom in the parable of the ten virgins is not very long, **unless the virgins are related to Rip Van Winkle.** The virgins get drowsy at dusk, and the bridegroom returns at midnight (Matt. 25:6). How can this "delay" be turned into a span of time nearly two thousand years in length?[1] (emphasis mine)

So the question here is, what is the point our Lord was making to the disciples? It is clear from this passage that he was teaching his disciples the importance of always being in a watchful mode – they should always be ready, because they will not know when these things will occur.

The Parable of the Talents – Matthew 25:14-30

Now we consider the parable of the talents. This parable denotes the importance of being responsible stewards. It is an excellent example for all of us in this respect. We have been given much by God. It is our responsibility to be good stewards, and if we are, we will be rewarded. But once again, the question here is: "What was the meaning of this passage for the disciples who were given this message directly?" As we examine these verses, let's look for any time related indication that there is a delay.

Let's begin by considering this passage:

Mat 25:14 "For *it is* just like a man *about* to go on a journey, who called his own slaves and entrusted his possessions to them.

Mat 25:15 "To one he gave five talents, to another, two, and to another, one, each according to his own ability; and he went on his journey.

Mat 25:16 "Immediately the one who had received the five talents went and traded with them, and gained five more talents.

Mat 25:17 "In the same manner the one who *had received* the two *talents* gained two more.

Mat 25:18 "But he who received the one *talent* went away, and dug *a hole* in the ground and hid his master's money.

Mat 25:19 "Now after a long time the master of those slaves *came and *settled accounts with them.

Mat 25:20 "The one who had received the five talents came up and brought five more talents, saying, 'Master, you entrusted five talents to me. See, I have gained five more talents.'

Mat 25:21 "His master said to him, 'Well done, good and faithful slave. You were faithful with a few things, I will put you in charge of many things; enter into the joy of your master.'

Mat 25:22 "Also the one who *had received* the two talents came up and said, 'Master, you entrusted two talents to me. See, I have gained two more talents.'

Mat 25:23 "His master said to him, 'Well done, good and faithful slave. You were faithful with a few things, I will put you in charge of many things; enter into the joy of your master.'

Mat 25:24 "And the one also who had received the one talent came up and said, 'Master, I knew you to be a hard man, reaping where you did not sow and gathering where you scattered no *seed.*

Mat 25:25 'And I was afraid, and went away and hid your talent in the ground. See, you have what is yours.'

Mat 25:26 "But his master answered and said to him, 'You wicked, lazy slave, you knew that I reap where I did not sow and gather where I scattered no *seed.*

Mat 25:27 'Then you ought to have put my money in the bank, and on my arrival I would have received my *money* back with interest.

Mat 25:28 'Therefore take away the talent from him, and give it to the one who has the ten talents.'

Mat 25:29 "For to everyone who has, *more* shall be given, and he will have an abundance; but from the one who does not have, even what he does have shall be taken away.
Mat 25:30 "Throw out the worthless slave into the outer darkness; in that place there will be weeping and gnashing of teeth.

James Stuart Russell writes,

> "The connecting particle 'for' in verse 14 distinctly marks the continuation of the discourse. The theme is the same, the time is the same, the catastrophe is the same. Up to this point, therefore, *we find no break, no change*, no introduction of a different topic; all is continuous, homogeneous, one. Never for a moment has the discourse swerved from the great, all-absorbing theme, -- the approaching doom of the guilty city and nation, the solemn events attendant thereon, all to take place within the period of that generation, and which the disciples, or some of them, would live to witness."[2]

Russell's point is well taken. There is absolutely nothing which indicates a change of theme or timing. However, in this parable we find the message of the stewardship of the treasure which all of God's servants have been given. The nation of Israel stood before God as one *who hated the message of the Kingdom.* Now, it was the responsibility of those disciples to be diligent in their stewardship of the gift of the Kingdom they have been given. As for the wicked servant who disregarded the Kingdom of Heaven as nothing and put to death the Son of God, he will come under a very severe judgment.

The Son of Man will Judge the Nations - Matthew 25:31-46

The fulfilled viewpoint is that from the beginning of the Olivet Discourse until now our Lord has given his disciples one connected and continuous prophecy, which was all to take place, according to our Lord's prediction, before the existing generation should pass away (Matt 24:34).

If we look at our English Version of the verses which follow, it **may appear** that Jesus is now starting a new subject, not connected with the previous context. In fact, we find by a survey that most commentators believe that this passage cannot be understood as referring to Jerusalem or Israel in general, but to all of mankind in the final judgment. *However, James Stuart Russell makes a very valid point* that is overlooked by almost all commentators:

> This parable, though in our English version standing apart and unconnected with the context, is really connected by a very sufficient link with what goes before. This is a parent in the Greek, where we find the particle, the force of which is to indicate transition and connection, -- transition to a new illustration, and connection with the foregoing Context. Alford, in his revised New Testament, preserves the continuative particle-- '**But when** the Son of man shall have come in his glory,' etc. It might with equal propriety be rendered -- **And when**,' etc.[3] (emphasis mine)

This Greek word, δε; which means "And or But" is **crucial** to the understanding of this text.

Upon examination of the Greek text as delivered by Novum Testamentum Graece, [9] we note the following in the Greek:

"Οταν δε ελθη ο νιος τον ανθρωπον," when translated into English it reads "**And (or But)** when comes the Son of Man...."

Since this transitional word **is in** the original Greek language, I am completely puzzled why so many translators do not include this word in the translation. It **is included** in the following translations:

American Standard Version (ASV), New American Standard Bible (NASB):

> Mat 25:31 **But** when the Son of man shall come in his glory, and all the angels with him, then shall he sit on the throne of his glory:

Also the LITV "Literal Translation of the Holy Bible"

> Mat 25:31 **But** when the Son of Man comes in His glory, and all the holy angels with Him, then He will sit on the throne of His glory.

The Modern King James Version MKJV:

> Mat 25:31 **But** when the Son of Man comes in His glory, and all the holy angels with Him, then He shall sit on the throne of His glory.

Young's Literal Translation reads:

> Mat 25:31 `**And** whenever the Son of Man may come in his glory, and all the holy messengers with him, then he shall sit upon a throne of his glory; (YLT)

This word is *missing* in the **KJV, NKJV, NIV, ESV** to name a few of the most popular.

Nonetheless, Russell is correct. The connecting word **de** is there in the Greek, and it **does** without question play an important role in that it ties this to the other parables, all of which refer to "This generation" (Matt 24:31).

Now we shall examine this passage, Matthew 25:31-46. I will be quoting from the New American Standard Version since it includes the particle present in the Greek. Beginning with verses 31-33:

> Mat 25:31 "But when the Son of Man comes in His glory, and all the angels with Him, then He will sit on His glorious throne.
> Mat 25:32 "All the nations will be gathered before Him; and He will separate them from one another, as the shepherd separates the sheep from the goats;
> Mat 25:33 and He will put the sheep on His right, and the goats on the left.

These verses sound very much like something Jesus already stated in Matt. 16: 27,28:

> Mat 16:27 For the Son of Man is going to come with his angels in the glory of his Father, and then he will repay each person according to what he has done.
> Mat 16:28 Truly, I say to you, there are some standing here who will not taste death until they see the Son of Man coming in his kingdom." (ESV)

As James Stuart Russell points out in his book, "The Parousia," we should notice several things about these passages at this point:

(a) That in both passages the subject referred to is the same, viz. the coming of the Son of man- the Parousia.
(b) In both passages He is described as coming in glory.
(c) In both He is attended by the holy angels.
(d) In both He comes as a King. ' Coming in his kingdom; ' He shall sit upon his throne; Then shall the King,' etc.
(e) 'In both He comes to judgment.
(f) In both the judgment is represented as in some sense universal. 'He shall reward every man 'Before him shall be gathered all the nations.'
(g) In Matt. xvi. 28 it is expressly stated that this coming in glory, etc., was to take place in the lifetime of some then present. This fixes the occurrence of the Parousia within the limit of a human life, thus being in perfect accord with the period defined by our Lord in His prophetic discourse. 'This generation shall not pass,' etc. We are fully warranted, therefore, in regarding the coming of the Son of man in Matt. xxv. as identical with that referred to in Matt. xvi., which some of the disciples were to live to witness. Thus, notwithstanding the words 'all the nations' in Matt. xxv. 32, we are brought to the conclusion that it is not the 'final consummation of all things ' which is there spoken of, but the judgment of Israel at the close of the [Jewish] ,aeon or age.[4]

With these seven statements, Russell has made a very strong case for the idea that this coming judgment **was not** sometime in the distant future, but within the generation to whom Jesus spoke. There seems to be just one hitch in this theory. But what about the phrase "and before him shall be gathered all the nations," doesn't this indicate that there is a much broader reference than just those local nations at this time?

The word translated in our Bibles as "nations" stems from the Greek word in this verse which is εθνη, or the nominative form of the noun εθνος pronounced in English as **ethnos**. This word refers to ethnic groups, which allows for it to be translated as follows according to Strong's Greek dictionary:

> 1484. ἔθνος éthnos eth'-nos probably from 1486; a race (as of the same habit), i.e. a tribe; specially, a foreign (non-Jewish) one (usually, by implication, pagan):--Gentile, heathen, nation, people.[5]

With this we see that Jesus most likely was referring to the ethnic groups around Judea. Russell makes this point as he continues:

> There is no impropriety in designating the tribes as nations. The promise of God to Abraham was that he should be the father of many nations (Gen. xvii. 5; Rom. iv. 17, 18). In our Lord's time it was usual to speak of the inhabitants of Palestine as consisting of several nations. Josephus speaks of ' the nation of the Samaritans,' 'the nation of the Batanaeans,' ' the nation of the Galileans,'-- using the very word (etnoj) which we find in the passage before us. Judea, was a distinct nation, often with a king of its own; so also was Samaria; and so with Idumea, Galilee , Paraea, Batanea, Trachonitis, Ituraea, Abilene,-- all of which had at different times princes with the title of Ethnarch, a name which signifies the ruler of a nation. It is doing no violence, then, to the language to understand as referring, to 'all the nations' of Palestine, or ' all the tribes of the land.' (3) This view receives strong confirmation from the fact that the same phrase in the apostolic commission (Matt. xxviii. 19), 'Go and teach all the nations,' does not seem to have been understood by the disciples as referring to the whole population of the globe, or to any nations beyond Palestine . It is commonly supposed that the apostles knew that they had received a charge to evangelise the world. ....[6]

In Russell's statement above, some may challenge it by saying, "Surely, they understood 'Go and teach the nations' as a reference to going outside of the area of Palestine." But if this is true, then why did the first century church challenge Peter for going in to uncircumcised men such as he did with Cornelius?

Adding to this, notice this passage:

Mat 10:23 When they persecute you in one town, flee to the next, for truly, I say to you, you **will not have gone through all the towns of Israel before the Son of Man comes.**

With these words, spoken by Jesus himself, *can there be any doubt* from this that he was speaking of his coming judgment upon the Jewish nation including the destruction of Jerusalem within "this generation" in AD 70?

Continuing on with this parable we read beginning again in Matthew 25:34-40:

Mat 25:34 "Then the King will say to those on His right, 'Come, you who are blessed of My Father, inherit the kingdom prepared for you from the foundation of the world.

Mat 25:35 'For I was hungry, and you gave Me *something* to eat; I was thirsty, and you gave Me *something* to drink; I was a stranger, and you invited Me in;

Mat 25:36 naked, and you clothed Me; I was sick, and you visited Me; I was in prison, and you came to Me.'

Mat 25:37 "Then the righteous will answer Him, 'Lord, when did we see You hungry, and feed You, or thirsty, and give You *something* to drink?

Mat 25:38 'And when did we see You a stranger, and invite You in, or naked, and clothe You?

Mat 25:39 'When did we see You sick, or in prison, and come to You?'

Mat 25:40 "The King will answer and say to them, 'Truly I say to you, to the extent that you did it to one of these brothers of Mine, *even* the least *of them,* you did it to Me.'

Now let's put this in the time frame of the subject of which Jesus is speaking here. He is speaking of the time that he was alive on the earth. Those who existed before Jesus was born *could not be judged* according to his words here *for the very fact that he was not yet present.* Therefore those alive before he was born *could not have* forsaken him in such a manner! Yes, he was speaking to the sheep on his right, *who were alive* during his lifetime and did the deeds spoken of here. Continuing on in Matthew 25:41-46:

Mat 25:41 "Then He will also say to those on His left, 'Depart from Me, accursed ones, into the eternal fire which has been prepared for the devil and his angels;

Mat 25:42 for I was hungry, and you gave Me *nothing* to eat; I was thirsty, and you gave Me nothing to drink;

Mat 25:43 I was a stranger, and you did not invite Me in; naked, and you did not clothe Me; sick, and in prison, and you did not visit Me.'

Mat 25:44 "Then they themselves also will answer, 'Lord, when did we see You hungry, or thirsty, or a stranger, or naked, or sick, or in prison, and did not take care of You?'

Mat 25:45 "Then He will answer them, 'Truly I say to you, to the extent that you did not do it to one of the least of these, you did not do it to Me.'

Mat 25:46 "These will go away into eternal punishment, but the righteous into eternal life."

Now we clearly see the judgment of those who were called the "goats" on his left. From the accounts of the Acts of the Apostles all the way through the epistles of John, we see that the persecution of the Church was not only undertaken by the religious leaders of the Jewish nation, it was started and led by them! This parable shows how the rejected King of the Jews was now judging the nation and was about to bring an end to the Jewish Age. Notice the words of Russell as he makes this very valid point:

Their treatment of His disciples, especially of His apostles, might most fitly and justly be made the criterion of character in ' discerning between the righteous and the wicked.' Such a test would be most appropriate in an age when Christianity was a persecuted faith, and this is evidently supposed by the very terms of the King's address: -- 'I was hungry, thirsty, a stranger, was naked, sick, and in prison.' The persons designated as 'these my brethren ,' and who are taken as the representatives of Christ Himself, are evidently the apostles of our Lord, in whom He hungered, and thirsted, was naked, sick, and in prison. All this is in perfect harmony with the words of Christ to His disciples, when He sent them forth to preach-- 'He that receiveth you receiveth me, and he that receiveth me receiveth him that sent me. He that receiveth. a prophet in the name of a prophet shall receive a prophet's reward; and he that receiveth a righteous man in the name of a righteous man, shall receive a righteous man's reward. And whosoever shall give to drink unto one of these little ones a cup of cold water only in the name of a disciple, verily I say unto you, he shall in no wise lose his reward' (Matt. x. 40-42). *We are thus brought to the conclusion,* **the only one which in all respects suits the tenor of the entire discourse,** *that we have here, not the final judgment of the whole human race,* **but that of the guilty nation or nations of Palestine,** *who rejected their King, despitefully treated and slew His messengers* (Matt. xxii. 1-14), *and whose day of doom was now near at hand.* [7] (emphasis mine)

With these words, the Lord Jesus concluded what is commonly referred to as the Olivet Discourse. There is no reason to believe that the disciples did not **understand every word** of his parables. What reason would Jesus have to confuse them by jumping from a discussion of "this generation" to events of some future generation without some indication that he was changing the time reference? From what we have seen here, it is clear. It is not a judgment upon the world in general, **but a judgment of "guilty" upon the entire religious system of the Jewish Age.**

There are many who would say that this prophecy, and these parables may have been fulfilled at the end of the Jewish Age in AD 70, but there is a second fulfillment yet to come. To those who would say this, we reiterate: **Where does it say anything in Scripture to indicate this?** To proclaim such a thing would be outside of the scope of **exegesis** (drawing facts **out of** the text), and would put this view clearly in the realm of **eisegesis** (reading things **into** the text). It simply is not in there!

But there is another point which must be considered. The destruction of Jerusalem and the temple had significance like no other event in human history. If you will recall, the Lord said:

> Mat 24:21 "For then there will be a great tribulation, such as has not occurred since the beginning of the world until now, nor ever will.

When we look closely at it, there is no history that parallels it from many perspectives. The calamities included famine of such a terrible nature that cannibalism occurred, murder, rape, pestilence, and a destruction by fire and sword that reduced a thriving city and religion to ruin and destruction. As we read the writings of Josephus, we had to be appalled at the horror he presented. Luke presented it properly when he said:

> Luk 21:22 because these are days of vengeance, so that all things which are written will be fulfilled.

All of the predictions of the prophets and the Savior came together here to be fulfilled in the most horrible manner possible on that generation. It is also remarkable that this magnificent temple was burned and reduced to rubble on exactly the same day and the same month as the original temple was burned by the Babylonians.

> However, one cannot but wonder at the accuracy of this period thereto relating; for the **same month and day** were now observed, as I said before, wherein the holy house was burnt formerly by the Babylonians. [8]

This destruction is remarkable since it marked the end of the Jewish system of worship as set forth in Leviticus. The entire Mosaic economy, over which God presided for over fifteen centuries was now completely abolished.

As we look at this prophecy from the viewpoint of the promises of God, it gives us faith that we **can trust** God's prophetic promises. They are true; they are just; and they do get fulfilled exactly as prophesied! This builds our faith in God's promise of redemption. It also is true, and we can depend on it.

Now that we have examined the Olivet Discourse, what does the rest of the New Testament have to say about the "Last Days?" In the next chapter, we will begin this consideration.

NOTES

1. Last Days Madness, Gary Demar, American Vision,1999, p201
2. Russell, James Stuart (2013-12-13). Parousia: The New Testament Doctrine of Our Lord's Second Coming (Kindle Locations 1537-1540). . Kindle Edition.
3. Russell, James Stuart (2013-12-13). Parousia: The New Testament Doctrine of Our Lord's Second Coming (Kindle Locations 1564-1568). . Kindle Edition.
4. Ibid, (Kindle Locations 1576-1584). . Kindle Edition.
5. Strong, James (2011-05-07). Strong's Greek Dictionary of the Bible (with beautiful Greek, transliteration, and superior navigation) (Strong's Dictionary) (Kindle Locations 2484-2486). Miklal Software Solutions, Inc.. Kindle Edition.
6. Russell, James Stuart (2013-12-13). Parousia: The New Testament Doctrine of Our Lord's Second Coming (Kindle Locations 1592-1600). . Kindle Edition.
7. Ibid, (Kindle Locations 1623-1630). . Kindle Edition.
8. The Works of Josephus, Translated by William Whiston, AM, Hendrickson Publishers, Peabody, Mass. 1987, Wars of the Jews, Book 6, Chapter 4, Section 8. (The date was reported elsewhere as August 10)
9. Note: Novum Testamentum Graece is the Greek version of the New Testament published by Kurt Aland and Matthew Black. The copy from which this material was taken is the 1995 version ISBN 3-438-05100-1 Kunststoff, 3-438-0501-7 Leder
10. Albert Barnes Notes on the Bible, taken from e-Sword, Version 10.2.1, 2013, Rick Meyers (Free download at www.e-sword.net)
11. Adam Clarke's Commentary on the Bible, taken from e-Sword, Version 10.2.1, 2013, Rick Meyers (Free download at www.e-sword.net)

Chapter 7

The Last Days – Part 1

Many have said that the early Christians were wrong in their view of what constituted the Last Days. But stop and think about this for a minute. Who was it that led them to believe Jesus was coming back in a short time? Wasn't it the Lord Jesus himself? Let's look at a passage we read in the last chapter again:

> Mat 10:23 But whenever they persecute you in one city, flee to the next; for truly I say to **YOU, YOU** will not finish *going through* the cities of Israel **until the Son of Man comes.** (emphasis mine)

Now if you were alive at that time, and heard Jesus say this, what would you have thought that he meant? Look at this passage closely. How could he be more specific? He was speaking to the twelve apostles. How long would it take the disciples to go through all of the cities of Israel and tell them the good news about Christ? Well actually, we do not have to guess about this, because we know when Paul and Barnabas left Judea on the first missionary journey. If you look at your map section in the back of your Bible, you will find that many of them state the time of leaving for this at about AD 46. Prior to this we find the following in the book of Acts:

> Acts 10:36   The word which He sent to the sons of Israel, preaching peace through Jesus Christ (He is Lord of all)--

Acts 10:37 you yourselves know the thing which took place throughout all Judea, starting from Galilee, after the baptism which John proclaimed.

Additionally we are told:

Acts 12:24 But the word of the Lord continued to grow and to be multiplied.

Acts 12:25 And Barnabas and Saul returned from Jerusalem **when they had fulfilled their mission,** taking along with *them* John, who was also called Mark. (emphasis mine)

Yes, the first 12 chapters of the book of Acts make it clear that getting the message of Christ to all the cities of Israel had, for the most part, been accomplished. In Acts chapter 13, and verse 4, they began the first missionary journey where they set sail for Cyprus. Therefore, we know that this was just 16 years at the very most, from when Jesus died on the cross. So easily within the time frame Jesus told them of this generation, they got through most of the cities of Israel. Jesus said that *he would* come again, *not thousands of years later*, but within *the specific time frame* of their completion of spreading the Gospel in Israel. Of course we know that after AD 46, they continued moving around the cities of Israel due to the tremendous persecution that was put on them by the hard line Jews. As far as Jerusalem is concerned, they left when they were told and fled to the mountains of Pella. Looking at this passage, once again, we see a simple statement by our Lord. So I ask you in all sincerity, how could it mean anything else, except that our Lord would return within the generation that saw his death?

In fact, we know that the entire Roman world had heard the message of Christ only 11 years later. By the year AD 57, Paul had completed his third missionary journey. Listen to what is recorded in Acts 19:10:

Acts 19:10 This took place for two years, so that **all who lived in Asia** heard the word of the Lord, both Jews and Greeks. (emphasis mine)

In fact, by the time Paul reached Rome, at the end of his missionary journeys, he declared:

Rom 1:8 First, I thank my God through Jesus Christ for you all, because your faith is being proclaimed **throughout the whole world.** (emphasis mine)

Did you hear what Paul said here? This message of Christ had already reached the entire Roman world. This fulfills what Jesus told them in Matthew 24:14, where it says:

Mat 24:14 This gospel of the kingdom shall be preached in the whole world as a testimony to all the nations, and then the end will come.

If we look up the Greek word here for "world" in Strong's Greek dictionary, we find that it is **οικουμενε** (pronounced oi-kou-mene) which is narrowly defined as "land" and more specifically defined in this case as the "The Roman Empire." In contrast to this, only 12 verses later Jesus makes reference to the world, but used a different Greek word. That word is **κοσμος** (pronounced kos-mos), which is a much more broadly defined word meaning the entire orderly arrangement, and sometimes even refers to the entire human race, and even the universe. Let's read that verse:

Mat 16:26 For what will it profit a man if he gains the whole world (kosmos) and forfeits his soul? Or what shall a man give in return for his soul? (ESV)

The Apostle Paul confirms that this had already happened again later in the book of Romans when he said:

Rom 10:18 But I ask, have they not heard? Indeed they have, for "Their voice has gone out to all the earth (**γη** – **pronounced gae - land**), and their words to the ends of the world (**οικουμενε - oikoumene – in effect, the Roman World**)."(ESV)

The Greek word **γη** here commonly also means "land." So in summary, we now know from looking at this evidence that Jesus' words in Matt 10:23 were fulfilled. He was speaking of a **short period of time**. It only took 16 years at best for most of the land of

Judea to hear the message. But by the time Paul wrote the letter to the Romans in about AD 57, the entire Roman world had been reached. Of course, the work continued even after this. Thus Jesus' words, "**YOU** will not finish *going through* the cities of Israel until the Son of Man comes." This indicates that **THEY** would keep working **until he returned**. It also fell within the generation to whom Jesus spoke.

Commentator Albert Barnes acknowledges this fact when he stated of Matt 10:23:

> By "the coming of the Son of Man," that is, of "Christ," is probably meant the destruction of Jerusalem, which happened about thirty years after this was spoken.

Now let's look at another passage that is recorded by Matthew. From what we know, his Gospel was probably the last one written of what is called the "Synoptic Gospels." The term "synoptic" is a reference to the three Gospel accounts including Mark and Luke which are a synopsis of Jesus' life. Matthew records Jesus saying **this** in the following verses:

> Mat 16:27 For the Son of Man is **about to come** with His angels in the glory of His Father. And then "He will give reward to each according to his practice." *Pro. 24:12; MT-Psa. 62:12*
> Mat 16:28 Truly I say to you, There are some standing here who will **not taste of death, never,** until they see the Son of Man coming in His kingdom.(LITV) (emphasis mine)

Was this just a teaser? Did Jesus mean something different than what he led the disciples to believe? Is there any question that he was referring to the fact that he was to return in "this generation?" Commentator Adam Clarke correctly says of this verse:

> This verse seems to confirm the above explanation, as our Lord evidently speaks of the establishment of the Christian Church after the day of pentecost, and its final triumph after the destruction of the Jewish polity; **as if he had said, "Some of you, my disciples, shall continue to live until these things take place."** The destruction of Jerusalem, and the Jewish economy, which our Lord here predicts, took place about forty-three years

after this: and some of the persons now with him doubtless survived that period, and witnessed the extension of the Messiah's kingdom; and our Lord told them these things before, that when they came to pass they might be confirmed in the faith, and expect an exact fulfillment of all the other promises and prophecies which concerned the extension and support of the kingdom of Christ. (emphasis mine)

Now there are some who would say that these passages should be separated, because verse 27 speaks of a time of judgment, and verse 28 speaks of a different event. Why do they say this? Because they want you to believe that Jesus changed the subject between these two verses. Most of them want you to believe that verse 28 speaks of the transfiguration which occurred just 6 days later as shown in the very next verse.

But if this is true, why would he say that "**some** standing here would not taste of death" until this occurred? What is implied here? Isn't he, in effect saying, "Although **most** of you will die, **some** of you will not taste of death until they see the Son of Man coming in his Kingdom." Did Jesus expect that **most of them would die** in the next 6 days? **Of course not!** Additionally, he did not say, "some of you will see a vision of the Son of man." He told them they would **actually** see the Son of Man coming in his Kingdom, which ties directly with what he said all along....that it would happen within this generation, but it would be far enough away, that **most of them** would have tasted death before this happened!

Some have said that this is a reference to his return at Pentecost, but this cannot be for at least two reasons. First, Jesus told them that he would not return then, but that he would send the Holy Spirit to them at that time and the Holy Spirit would act as a comforter to them.

Second, it is very unlikely that **any** of them died between the time Jesus said this and Pentecost. Jesus' statement in Matthew 16:28 made it clear that when he returned, although some would still be alive, most of them would be dead!

But there is one more reason why these verses cannot be separated. If we look in the Interlinear Bible, we see that the Greek phrase that is used to start the verse is αμην λεγω υμιν, which means "Truly I say to you."

Now just looking at this first Greek word, αμην, which translates into English as amen, we find that it means exactly the same thing as in our English. Strong's Greek dictionary has this to say about that word:

> ἀμήν amến am-ane' of Hebrew origin (0543); properly, firm, i.e. (figuratively) trustworthy; adverbially, surely (often as interjection, so be it):--amen, verily.[1]

When do we use this word? Yes, even today we use this word when we want to completely affirm something! We say **AMEN!** And this is what Jesus was doing here in verse 28.

I did a search of this phrase in my ESV Bible, and here is what I found. This phrase, αμην λεγω υμιν (ahmain lego humeen) was **only used by Jesus**. No one else in the Bible ever used this phrase. And in all 72 cases in which it is found in the English Standard version, it _is always used to confirm, emphasize, or give additional information_ about what is said just previous to this.

Let me repeat this, because it is crucial to understanding this passage in Matthew 16:27, 28. This phrase was **only used by Jesus**. No one else in the Bible ever uses this phrase. _And in all 72 cases_ in which it is found in the English Standard version, it is _always used to confirm, emphasize, or give additional information_ about what is said just previous to this. Therefore, because of these reasons, verse 27 is NOT speaking of one thing, and verse 28 of something else.

So now as we read this passage again, please realize that Jesus conveyed what he said in verse 27, and then added emphasis to it in verse 28.

This time from the Contemporary English Version:

> Mat 16:27 The Son of Man will **soon come** in the glory of his Father and with his angels to reward all people for what they have done.
> Mat 16:28 **I promise you** that some of those standing here **will not die** before they see the Son of Man coming with his kingdom. (emphasis mine)

Do you see how he put emphasis on verse 27, and then added to it in verse 28. Yes, he told them he was coming _within a generation_ to judge their contemporaries, and some of them would live to see it! And he _**fulfilled this**_ when the entire Jewish system of worship was brought to an end _**at his coming**_ in **AD 70!**

This is why the writer of Hebrews made the statement:

> Heb 8:13 In speaking of a new covenant, he makes the first one obsolete. And what is _**becoming**_ obsolete and growing old _**is ready**_ to vanish away. (ESV)(emphasis mine)

Yes, even up to the year AD 66 or 67, when Hebrews was written, the old covenant was still in effect, but would soon pass away with the destruction of the Jewish Levitical sacrificial system of government. And then, after Jesus completed his judgment of the Jewish nation here, the sacrifice of himself as the Lamb of God that he presented in heaven was completely and fully in effect. This is when the old covenant vanished completely. We will have much more to say on this subject in a later chapter.

Now we will focus on the Apostles Peter's sermon in Acts the second chapter when he said:

Acts 2:17 "'And in the last days it shall be, God declares, that I will pour out my Spirit on all flesh, and your sons and your daughters shall prophesy, and your young men shall see visions, and your old men shall dream dreams; (ESV)

Now up to this point, we have mostly focused on what the Bible writers have said concerning the Last Days from the viewpoint of the Synoptic Gospels. Now let's expand our coverage outside of these to the other writings in the New Testament. First let's go to the book of Acts. Jesus told them just before he ascended into heaven:

Act 1:4 And while staying with them he ordered them not to depart from Jerusalem, but to wait for the promise of the Father, which, he said, "you heard from me;
Act 1:5 for John baptized with water, but you will be baptized with the Holy Spirit not many days from now." (ESV)

As we know, in the next chapter we see that Jesus was right, for just 10 days later, the Holy Spirit did come to them and the impact was profound. Once again, the Jews got a sign. The various language groups were able to hear what was being preached in their own language.

It was during this time that Peter made this statement:

Act 2:16 But this is what was uttered through the prophet Joel:
Act 2:17 "'And in the last days it shall be, God declares, that I will pour out my Spirit on all flesh, and your sons and your daughters shall prophesy, and your young men shall see visions, and your old men shall dream dreams; (ESV)

Note that Peter said in this passage that God would pour his spirit out on "all flesh"(from Joel 2:28). This meant that there was no longer an exclusive community of Jews who were considered God's people. The Holy Spirit could be received by all who accepted Christ regardless of ethnicity. Continuing with this thought he said:

Act 2:18 even on my male servants and female servants in those days I will pour out my Spirit, and they shall prophesy. (ESV)

Then Peter says to them something which looks like he is changing the subject, but he is not. Notice these words: He is still stating that the prophecy of Joel is being fulfilled here when he says:

Act 2:19 And I will show wonders in the heavens above and signs on the earth below, blood, and fire, and vapor of smoke;

Act 2:20 the sun shall be turned to darkness and the moon to blood, before the day of the Lord comes, the great and magnificent day. (ESV)

Do these words sound familiar to us? Yes, for in the last chapter, in the exposition of Matthew 24, we read Jesus telling them:

Mat 24:29 "But immediately after the tribulation of those days THE SUN WILL BE DARKENED, AND THE MOON WILL NOT GIVE ITS LIGHT, AND THE STARS WILL FALL from the sky, and the powers of the heavens will be shaken.

Mat 24:30 "And then the sign of the Son of Man will appear in the sky, and then all the tribes of the earth will mourn, and they will see the SON OF MAN COMING ON THE CLOUDS OF THE SKY with power and great glory.

When Peter was speaking here, he **remembered** these words that Jesus told him and his three companions on that occasion at the Mount of Olives. He remembered that Jesus told him these things would occur in that generation! And now Peter was passing this information along, showing that these words were first prophesied by the prophet Joel, and that because of them murdering Jesus as they had done, they were about to see what Jesus told them they would see….his power and glory!! Yes, these ones to whom Peter was preaching were part of the group that Jesus said would see these terrible things that were about to befall them. Why? He tells them in verse 36:

Act 2:36 Let all the house of Israel therefore know for certain that God has made him both Lord and Christ, this Jesus whom you crucified." (ESV)

But looking back at verse 21, Peter showed them the way out of this mess they were in when he said:

Act 2:21 . . . everyone who calls upon the name of the Lord shall be saved.'(**ESV**)

How did they respond to Peter's words? The next verse tells us:

Act 2:37 Now when they heard this they were cut to the heart, and said to Peter and the rest of the apostles, "Brothers, what shall we do?" (ESV)

Yes, because of the **power of the Holy Spirit,** and the convincing words of Peter relating this time as the fulfillment of Joel's prophecy, they could see that they were in desperate trouble and appealed to Peter fervently. There _was_ a genuine spirit of repentance in the heart of those gathered. And Peter told them their next step – repentance and baptism for the remission of their sins, especially the sin of the cold blooded murder of the Son of God! He said:

Act 2:38 "Repent and be baptized every one of you in the name of Jesus Christ for the forgiveness of your sins, and you will receive the gift of the Holy Spirit.
Act 2:39 For the promise is for you and for your children and for all who are far off, everyone whom the Lord our God calls to himself."
Act 2:40 And with many other words he bore witness and continued to exhort them, saying, "Save yourselves **from THIS crooked generation.**" (ESV) (emphasis mine)

And once again with these words, Peter makes plain the meaning of the Greek word, γενεα. It was this wicked generation to whom Jesus made reference in Matt. 24:34. It was **THIS generation** that rejected him, and said:

Mat 27:25 "His blood be on us and on our children!" (ESV)

And not only did they reject him, but murdered him in the process! When Jesus was speaking to the scribes and Pharisees in Matthew 12, he told them how vile this generation would become. Notice his words:

Mat 12:43 "When the unclean spirit has gone out of a person, it passes through waterless places seeking rest, but finds none.
Mat 12:44 Then it says, 'I will return to my house from which I came.' And when it comes, it finds the house empty, swept, and put in order.
Mat 12:45 Then it goes and brings with it seven other spirits more evil than itself, and they enter and dwell there, and the last state of that person is worse than the first. **So also will it be with this evil generation."** (ESV) (emphasis mine)

Speaking of the evil which developed in that generation in verse 45, commentator Adam Clarke reiterates:

And so it was: for they grew worse and worse, as if totally abandoned to diabolic influence; till at last the besom of destruction swept them and their privileges, national and religious, utterly away. What a terrible description of a state of apostasy is contained in these verses! May he who readeth understand!

Yes, for just under 40 years later, their entire system of worship was destroyed. But now as we have seen in this second chapter of the book of Acts, there was true repentance that came when those present at Pentecost put their trust in him!

Later on in the book of Acts, we find the Apostle Paul, after his conversion, in the city of Athens, speaking in the Aereopagus. He said that he noticed that they had a monument to the unknown God. Using this as his backdrop he tells them that this is the God to whom they must render their worship, because God created men to worship him, and him alone. Why? Because in him we have been born as his offspring. Then after this notice what he says (from Young's literal translation):

Act 17:29 `Being, therefore, offspring of God, we ought not to think the Godhead to be like to gold, or silver, or stone, graving of art and device of man;
Act 17:30 the times, indeed, therefore, of the ignorance God having overlooked, doth now command all men everywhere to reform,

Act 17:31 because He did set a day in which He is **about to judge the world** in righteousness, by a man whom He did ordain, having given assurance to all, having raised him out of the dead.' (YLT) (emphasis mine)

If you look verse 31 up in your Interlinear Bible, you will find that the Greek word μελλει, which is a form of the Greek word μελλω which means "about to." Then as we read the phrase "εν η μελλει κρινειν την οικουμενην"in the Greek, we see that it is properly translated in Young's Literal translation as "in which he is **about to** judge the world." So looking at the Greek here in verse 31 shows that this judgment was to happen in the **NEAR** future, **NOT** in the distant future!

And later on when speaking to Roman official, Felix, Paul reiterates the closeness of the judgment where he says:

Act 24:24 And after certain days, Felix having come with Drusilla his wife, being a Jewess, he sent for Paul, and heard him concerning the faith toward Christ,
Act 24:25 and he reasoning concerning righteousness, and temperance, and the judgment that is **ABOUT TO BE**, Felix, having become afraid, answered, `For the present be going, and having got time, I will call for thee;' (YLT) (emphasis mine)

Yes, as recorded here, God was **ABOUT TO bring judgment.** Young's Literal Translation shows that it was imminent. Looking closely at this passage, we see that Felix got Paul's message that it **was going to be soon.** Why do we know this? It is because the verse said that **he became afraid!** Yes, judgment was indeed to happen soon.

How does this information impact our lives today? What can we take away from this?

Once again as we will continue to see in the coming chapters, the words of Jesus **have been fulfilled**. It is vitally important to realize this to help us know that since Jesus DID keep his promises to judge the nation of Israel, and that his promise of redemption for us is an absolute certainty!

But there is much more ahead. In the next chapter, we will look at what Peter had to say about this coming judgment.

NOTES

1. Strong, James (2011-05-07). Strong's Greek Dictionary of the Bible (Kindle Locations 497-498). Miklal Software Solutions, Inc.. Kindle Edition.
2. Adam Clarke's Commentary on the Bible, taken from e-Sword, Version 10.2.1, 2013, Rick Meyers (Free download at www.e-sword.net)
3. Albert Barnes Notes on the Bible, taken from e-Sword, Version 10.2.1, 2013, Rick Meyers (Free download at www.e-sword.net)

Chapter 8

The Last Days – Part 2

In our last chapter, one of the things highlighted was how corrupt the generation of the first century had become. And this was after God gave them a second chance by allowing them to build a second temple. This second temple was a far cry from the first one in many ways, but it did allow them to continue the Levitical sacrificial form of worship.

Now Ezra was a very dedicated priest, who was sent to Jerusalem to teach the people the law. The book of Nehemiah shows Ezra reading the law to the people every day in the city of Jerusalem after the completion of the rebuilding of the walls of the city.

In the ninth and tenth chapters of the book of Nehemiah, we find the people gathered together dressed in sackcloth, with dust on their heads recounting all of the sins of the past, and then strongly vowing in great detail to be faithful to follow the law of Moses. But even after the vows of faithfulness made in Nehemiah chapter 10, it was not long before there was widespread corruption and disobedience to every facet of the law once again.

But as regards the priesthood, we have still not heard the half of it. Before we continue what Peter had to say concerning the Last

Days in the book of Acts, I would like you to look at one more thing that reiterates how wicked this priesthood had become during the last 300 years before Jesus came on the scene.

Concerning the second temple Jewish Rabbi Ken Spiro said:

> The intense spiritually of the First Temple cannot be compared to the Second. The constant open miracles are gone. Prophecy will also disappear during the early years of the second Temple. The Ark of the Covenant is gone — and although there is a Holy of Holies, it stands empty.....
>
> According to the Talmud, during the First Temple period of about 410 years, there were only 18 High Priests. During the Second Temple period of 420 years, there were more than 300 High Priests! We know (from the Talmud, Yoma 9a) that Yochanan was High Priest for 80 years, Shimon was High Priest for 40 years, and Yishmael ben Pabi was High Priest for 10 years. That means in the remaining 290 years there were AT LEAST 300 PRIESTS — one every year or so. What accounts for that? [1]

Spiro goes on to point out that the office of high priest **went to the highest bidder!** This is a total violation of the law, and certainly shows how corrupt the priesthood had become.

All of this went on for a period of almost 300 years, until our loving and patient God had enough of their disgusting behavior. Finally, in chapter 4, the prophet Malachi warns them of the coming desolation for those who do not fear him. He follows this by telling them God would send Elijah the Prophet before "the great and awesome day of the Lord."

> Mal 4:5 Behold, I *am* sending you Elijah the prophet before the coming of the great and dreadful day of Jehovah.
> Mal 4:6 And he shall turn the heart of the fathers to the sons, and the heart of the sons to their fathers, that I not come and strike the earth *with* utter destruction. (LITV)

And we know that Jesus told the disciples that this "Elijah" was actually John the Baptist when he said:

Mat 11:12 From the time of John the Baptist until now, violent people have been trying to take over the kingdom of heaven by force.
Mat 11:13 All the Books of the Prophets and the law of Moses told what was going to happen up to the time of John.
Mat 11:14 And if you believe them, John is Elijah, the prophet you are waiting for. (CEV)

Because they continued shamelessly to disobey, even to the point of crucifying the Son of God, this prophecy would eventually result in the most severe of judgments. But now, let's go back to Peter's discourse at Pentecost. I want you to notice what Peter said once again:

Act 2:14 Peter stood with the eleven apostles and spoke in a loud and clear voice to the crowd: Friends and everyone else living in Jerusalem, listen carefully to what I have to say!
Act 2:15 You are wrong to think that these people are drunk. After all, it is only nine o'clock in the morning.
Act 2:16 But this is what God had the prophet Joel say,
Act 2:17 "When the last days come, I will give my Spirit to everyone. Your sons and daughters will prophesy. Your young men will see visions, and your old men will have dreams. (CEV)

Yes, we discussed this passage at length in the last chapter, but the point I want you to notice here is that what Peter said happened **right there and then** at Pentecost was what the prophet Joel said would happen in the **LAST DAYS**. He carried this theme over in the epistles which he wrote as general letters to the persecuted Christians.

But before we begin an examination of Peter's general epistles, let's look at a little background information which will actually come to bear on his motive for writing his epistles. Now we know it is generally agreed upon that Peter wrote this epistle to the persecuted Christians during the timeframe just before, during, or after the city of Rome burned. We also know that this was most likely just prior to Peter's martyrdom, thus dating his writings in the mid 60's (AD), just a few years before the destruction of Jerusalem.

Yes, Peter was speaking to those who were undergoing a very powerful wave of persecution at the hands of Nero. In order to deflect suspicion from him as having set the fire that burned Rome, Nero blamed the early Christians, whom Nero considered to be nothing more than a despicable sect of the Jews. He hated these Jews anyway, and the fact that they worshiped this man Jesus instead of him, made him all the more furious. Foxes book of Martyrs reports that Nero was so diabolic that he would skin animals and sew the skins onto the Christians, who were thereafter, and I quote "worried by dogs until they expired."

This madman would also soak the shirts of the Christians in stiff wax and then make them wear them as he set them on fire in his gardens, all for his enjoyment. Did it work? Did it cause the Christians to give up their faith? Quoting from Foxes book of Martyrs it says:

> This persecution was general throughout the whole Roman Empire; but it rather **increased** than diminished the spirit of Christianity. In the course of it, St. Paul and St. Peter were martyred.[2] (emphasis mine)

So how did Peter's writings reflect all of this? What was **he** anticipating the near future to bring? And how would he encourage those struggling persecuted Christians to whom he wrote those epistles? Reading from J.P. Green's Literal Translation, we see that he immediately calls attention to the time in which they were living, early in the first chapter of his first epistle:

1Pet 1:3 Blessed *be* the God and Father of our Lord Jesus Christ, He according to His great mercy having regenerated us to a living hope through *the* resurrection of Jesus Christ from *the* dead,
1Pet 1:4   to an inheritance incorruptible and undefiled and unfading, having been kept in Heaven for you
1Pet 1:5 *the ones* in *the* power of God being guarded through faith to a salvation ready to be revealed in the last time; (LITV)

This last phrase we read in 1 Pet. 1:5 in the Greek is **καιρω εσχατος (kairo eschatos).** The word "eschatos" in the Greek is where we get the word Eschatology, which is a study of the Last Days. The word "kairo" translates as "occasion, opportunity, or time." Clearly from these words, Peter expected that they were on the verge **of the end of something important,** and was encouraging them that they had a wonderful future beyond it. **This is what strengthened them during this intense persecution by Nero!**

Then later in the same chapter we read even more encouragement:

1Pet 1:19 but with precious blood of Christ, as a lamb without blemish and without spot,
1Pet 1:20 indeed having been foreknown before *the* foundation of *the* world, **but revealed in** *the* **last times (εσχατου των χρονων)** because of **you,** (LITV)

Again we see a form of the word "eschatos", this time with the Greek word "crahnown." The Greek word χρονων "crahnown" is where we get our word chronology. So two times in this first chapter we see an indication that Peter believed they were living in the Last Days, a time which would bring about the "end of chronology."

Do you get the drift here? Peter was writing about **the end of the Jewish chronology!!**

Already in chapter one of his epistle, he wrote of this. And notice who his audience was. As I have already stated, it was those

Christians who were being heavily persecuted at that time. It was **not** a message addressed to people thousands of years later. To reiterate this point, he says in the fourth chapter of his first epistle:

> 1Pet 4:7 But **the end of all things has drawn near.** Be of sound mind, then, and be sensible to prayers; (LITV)

In the Greek, this phrase reads, παντων δε το τελος ηγγικε (Pahntone de tah tellahs aingeekay, (all things of the end drawn near). The Greek word "pahntone" here is important because we see that it is a declension of the Greek word "pahs" which means "the whole" or all of it. Thus by Peter telling them the end of all things has drawn near, he was telling them that the entire old covenant system of things or the "whole part of it" was about to end, and they were covered by their continued faith which they should display by their sound minds and prayers.

Then later in the same chapter.....

> 1Pet 4:17 Because the time *has come* to begin **the judgment from the house of God;** and if firstly from us, what *will be* the end of the ones disobeying the gospel of God? (LITV)

Notice that he says that judgment is "to begin from the house of God." This is the Greek phrase

του οικου του Θεου (tone oikou tone Theyoo) "The house of God" **What was the house of God?**

Albert Barnes states of this in his commentary,

> Benson, Bloomfield, and many others, suppose that this refers to the Jews, and to the calamities that were to come around the temple and the holy city about to be destroyed. But the more obvious reference is to Christians, spoken of as the house or family of God. There is probably in the language here an allusion to Eze 9:6; "Slay utterly old and young, both maids, and little children, and women; and begin at my sanctuary."[3]

Yes, this judgment would begin very soon. And not only would the temple of God be destroyed, but those early Christians would experience this wrath as a byproduct, in the form of persecution. Thus, he encouraged them to remain strong. And the record shows that the early church did just that and grew amidst this intense persecution.

All of this is reminiscent of what Jesus said in Luke 21:

> Luk 21:22 For these are days of vengeance *when* **all things** that have been written are to be fulfilled. (LITV)(emphasis mine)

That judgment completely consumed "The house of God" or the temple, and it was completely reduced to rubble, and ended the Levitical system of sacrificial worship. But despite severe persecution, the church continued to grow, watered by the precious blood of the saints!

So now, we have looked at how the Apostle Peter addressed the Christians who were being heavily persecuted by a self-centered, sociopathic emperor by the name of Nero Caesar, and some of the awful things they had to endure. I cannot emphasize enough how important it is to look at the _context_ of Peter's message, and also his audience. Yes, as we look at the context of his second epistle, we see that Peter's mission in writing _both of these_ epistles _was to encourage his suffering brothers and sisters,_ and to let them know _they could unequivocally depend on the promises of their Lord Jesus._ And although we can draw some application for us today as we live in this world, we are **not** Peter's audience.

So now, as we move forward to look at the verses leading up to the statement about the heavens and earth being burned up, I would ask you to once again keep in mind _Peter's purpose in writing this epistle._ As I just said, it was to encourage those Christians being martyred for the cause of Christ!

Remember that he himself *had actually seen the glory of Jesus* in the transfiguration along with two other Apostles. Can you imagine how forcefully Peter could witness to these suffering Christians with such a testimony as this? He did *just this* when he told them:

> 2Pet 1:16 When we told you about the power and the return of our Lord Jesus Christ, we were not telling clever stories that someone had made up. But **with our own eyes** we saw his true greatness.
>
> 2Pet 1:17 God, our great and wonderful Father, truly honored him by saying, "This is my own dear Son, and I am pleased with him."
>
> 2Pet 1:18 **We were there with Jesus on the holy mountain and heard this voice speak from heaven.** (CEV)(emphasis mine)

Can you imagine yourself being in that position, hearing what Peter said back then? I am sure that it would be so powerful as to give you chills running up and down your spine. He said in effect: "Look, I have seen this with my own eyes. I saw our Lord Jesus transformed in his glory, and **he has promised** us that we will **without question** escape this corruption, one way or another!" Yes notice what he had already told them as we step back to verse 3 and 4:

> 2Pet 1:3 We have everything we need to live a life that pleases God. It was all given to us by God's own power, when we learned that he had invited us to share in his wonderful goodness.
>
> 2Pet 1:4 God made great and marvelous promises, so that his nature would become part of us. Then we could escape our evil desires and the corrupt influences of this world. (CEV)

Do you see what he told them? He said in effect: "You have **Christ living within you!!** And **he** is going to **give you the strength to endure** all of these horrible things you are suffering at the hands of these corrupt people!" This is why Foxes book of Martyrs made it clear that this persecution at the hands of Nero did not discourage these Christians. Peter's divinely inspired words **absolutely propelled them to remain faithful,** showing them **beyond a shadow of doubt that they were safe** in the hands of their loving Savior!

Then as we look at chapter 2, we see a dire warning of the things Peter remembered Jesus telling him concerning the Last Days. These words were riveted in Peter's mind and this whole chapter is in effect a reiteration of what Jesus said:

Mat 24:10 At that time many will fall away and will betray one another and hate one another.
Mat 24:11 Many false prophets will arise and mislead many.
Mat 24:12 Because lawlessness is increased, most people's love will grow cold.
Mat 24:13 But the one who endures to the end, he will be saved.

In this chapter he told them the testimonies of the Old Testament, and several examples of God's judgment, including judgments on angels, those in Sodom and Gomorrah, and false prophets such as Balaam, warning them to beware of such influences. He warned them that some would fall away and concluded the chapter by telling them:

2Pet 2:22 It has happened to them according to the true proverb, "A dog returns to its own vomit," and a sow, after washing, returns to wallowing in the mire." (NASB)

Continuing in chapter 3, he reiterated that this information he was delivering to them was from the prophets of old, and from the mouth of Jesus:

2Pet 3:1 My dear friends, this is the second letter I have written to encourage you to do some honest thinking. I don't want you to forget
2Pet 3:2 what God's prophets said would happen. You must never forget what the holy prophets taught in the past. And you must remember what the apostles told you our Lord and Savior has commanded us to do. (CEV)

Yes, he continued to encourage them, and to admonish them to remember the promises they had been given, that they were reliable and dependable. He even told them that there would be those who will laugh at them and call them fools for believing these things:

> 2Pet 3:3 But first you must realize that in the last days some people won't think about anything except their own selfish desires. They will make fun of you
> 2Pet 3:4 and say, "Didn't your Lord promise to come back? Yet the first leaders have already died, and the world hasn't changed a bit." (CEV)

Do you see what Peter did here? He clarified that the Lord Jesus promised that he would return **in that same generation** and that people would make fun of them for believing this.

Remember that we said in the last chapter, that Peter wrote these words in the mid to late 60's just a few years before the destruction of Jerusalem. Yes, in just a few more years, these scoffers would no longer be laughing at the Lord Jesus! They would directly see his awesome power in the complete annihilation of the temple and the holy city.

As we continue in this chapter we see that Peter reminded them that God has judged the land in the past, and he was about to do so again, very soon.

> 2Pe 3:5 For this is hidden from them *by their* willing *it so*, that heavens were of old, and earth by water, and through water, having subsisted by the Word of God,
> 2Pe 3:6 through which the world which then was, being flooded by water, perished.
> 2Pe 3:7 But the heavens and the earth now, having been stored up by the same Word, are being kept for fire to a day of judgment and destruction of ungodly men. (LITV)

But wait, did Peter tell them that the literal heavens and the literal earth were **about to be burned up?** Or did he change subjects and tell them about something that would not happen for **thousands of years?**

Do you remember what he just said in verse 3? He told them that people made fun of them because the Lord Jesus had not yet fulfilled his promise to return. No, he did not change subjects here, and he did not wander off and start talking about something that would happen thousands of years later. Had he done this, it would have been of no encouragement to them, and they would have actually lost courage.

Yes Peter was still informing them of something that was **about to** happen. We'll get to this explanation in a minute but let's continue reading.

> 2Pe 3:8 But let not this one thing be hidden *from* you, beloved, that one day with *the* Lord *is* "as a thousand years, and a thousand years as one day." *Psa. 90:4*
> 2Pe 3:9 The Lord of the promise is not slow, as some deem slowness, but is long-suffering toward us, not having purposed any to perish, but all to come to repentance. (LITV)

Do you see what he did here? Since people were laughing at these Christians for putting their complete confidence in Jesus' words about returning in this generation, he told them why the Lord had still not returned after over 30 years as he promised. He quoted Psalm 90 verse 4, in order to tell them that the Lord was still giving all who would listen a chance. But make no mistake about it. **Jesus would keep his promise.** This generation Jesus spoke of was not over yet. And he wanted them not to lose heart. Then he went on to explain why the Lord has waited over thirty years to return in judgment.

> 2Pet 3:9 The Lord of the promise is not slow, as some deem slowness, but is long-suffering toward us, not having purposed any to perish, but all to come to repentance.
> 2Pet 3:10 But the day of the Lord **will come** as a thief in *the* night, in which the heavens will pass away with rushing sound, and having burned *the* elements will be dissolved, and earth and the works in it will be burned up.

2Pet 3:11 Then all these **being** *about* **to be** dissolved, *of* what sort ought **you to be** in holy behavior and godliness,

2Pet 3:12 looking for and **hastening** the coming of the Day of God, through which *the* heavens having been set afire will be dissolved; and burning, *the* elements will melt?

2Pet 3:13 But according to His promise, we look for "new heavens and a new earth," in which righteousness dwells. *Isa. 65:17* (LITV)

As you look at this passage, you are probably now confused by all of this, thinking that there is no question that this verse absolutely applies to something which is yet to occur in our future. After all, doesn't it say that the heavens and the earth will be burned up? Doesn't it say that the elements will be dissolved? Doesn't it say that there will be a new heavens and a new earth? Yes, admittedly, this does sound like what it is saying, **but as you take a closer look at this passage, things start to change.**

First of all, this passage cannot mean a literal destruction of the earth. Eccl 1:4 tells us:

Ecc. 1:4 tells us: "A generation passes away, and *another* generation comes; but the earth stands forever." (LITV)

Also in support of this are Psalm 37:29, and Psalm 78:69.

Psa 37:29 The righteous will inherit the land And dwell in it forever.

Psa 78:69 And He built His sanctuary like the heights, Like the earth which He has founded forever.

Yes, I know that most Christians believe that Peter told those to whom he was writing that the literal heavens and the literal earth would be burned up. They say this because they interpret verse 9 to mean that God is speaking to them in what is commonly referred to as "God's time," but I would like to ask you just from a logical perspective the following questions:

If we interpret verse 8 to mean Peter was speaking to them in "God's time," how can we believe that any prophecy would be fulfilled in "man's time?" What if those people to whom Jeremiah spoke when he told them about the destruction of the first temple would have said: "but remember, David wrote in the Psalms that 'a thousand years is as one day in the eyes of the Lord,' so we don't have to worry?" Yes, if we take this view, all prophecy **has no time value** at all. Additionally, looking at Peter's previous words, and after all that we have just revealed about the horrible persecutions that those Christians were enduring, why would he tell them that the end of all things has drawn near, and then tell them the that someday in the distant future, the whole world is going to be dissolved?

Does that sound logical? And then further to follow up, why would he tell them that these things **are about to be** dissolved, meaning **soon?** These words would be confusing and contradictory. And they certainly would not be encouraging to the early church. In order to get a better perspective of what Peter said, let's go back to verse 11, and look at this verse again:

> 2Pe 3:11 Then all these **being** *about* **to be** dissolved, *of* what sort ought **you to be** in holy behavior and godliness, (LITV)

If we look at this phrase in the Interlinear Bible in the Greek we find the words: τουτων ουν παντων λυομενων (tootone oon pahntone loomenone) which means "these things then (or now) all being **about to be** dissolved" what sort ought you to be in holy behavior and godliness? Do you see the urgency here? Peter was asking them that since these things were about to be dissolved, how should they be conducting themselves? Now this would not make sense if he were speaking about an event that would not take place for thousands of years, would it? Well then what does he mean by these words?

Was he expecting a sort of cosmic renewal to happen soon? And if he did not believe that this sort of thing would happen soon, but thousands of years later, how would this in anyway be comforting or encouraging to them? So then, how can we see this making sense? How does it all fit together?

As we begin to look closely at this, the point I want to emphasize above all else with regard to Peter's epistles is this: Peter wrote it **to strongly encourage those early Christians**, and let them know that they could **absolutely trust the Lord Jesus** to do what he said he would do, even though they were undergoing the most severe persecution imaginable! Everything he wrote in these epistles was for that purpose. So with this in mind, let's closely examine this passage:

> 2Pet 3:10 But the day of the Lord will come like a thief, in which the heavens will pass away with a roar, and the elements will be destroyed with intense heat, and the earth and its works will be burned up.
> 2Pet 3:11 Since all these things are to be destroyed in this way, what sort of people ought you to be in holy conduct and godliness,

Now when Peter wrote these words, it is obvious that Peter told them something would happen soon because he told them there would be **implications for THEM**. After all, did he not already tell them, "The end of all things is at hand?" As we go back again to our basic interpretive principle, the question we must ask is: What did Peter want these words to mean for those to whom it was first written?

The fact is, as you will see, those early Christians understood what he meant. When he said that the elements would be burned up, they weren't thinking of the elements in the scientific periodic table. It is doubtful that they even knew anything of this. No! They were familiar with the elements as meaning something entirely different. We find that the word for the elements is the Greek word (στοιχεια) [stoichayah].

This word only appears 5 other times in the New Testament, and in all 5 of these cases which we are about to read, it is used in its relationship to the basic principles, or rudimentary things of the old covenant. The Apostle Paul wrote four of these. Notice what he says:

> Gal 4:3 So we also, when we were children, we were held in bondage under the elemental things,(στοιχεια) (stoichayah) of the world,
>
> Gal 4:9 But now that you have come to know God, how is it that you turn again to the weak and worthless elemental things, (στοιχεια) (stoichayah) to which you desire to be enslaved all over again?
>
> Col 2:8 See to it that no one takes you captive through philosophy and empty deception, according to the tradition of men, according to the elementary principles ,(στοιχεια) of the world, rather than according to Christ.
>
> Col 2:20 If you have died with Christ to the elementary principles, (στοιχεια) of the world, why, as if you were living in the world, do you submit yourself to decrees

Yes, here in these verses, Paul admonished them not to return to the legalistic ways of the old law covenant, but to embrace the freedom that comes from the new covenant and the grace of the Lord Jesus. The writer of Hebrews mentions the last instance of this word in Chapter 5.

> Heb 5:12 For though by this time you ought to be teachers, you have need again for someone to teach you the elementary principles,(στοιχεια) (stoichayah) of the oracles of God, and you come to need milk, and not of solid food;

The Greek phrase used here in the Greek is στοιχεια της αρχης των λογιων του Θεου (stoikayah tays arkays tone logeeown tahn thayoo) which translates as "the rudiments of the beginning of the Words of God." So now you have seen every incidence in which this word is used by the writers of the New Testament.

Yes, they all spoke of the very basics of the old covenant law! So then from this, we can surmise that Peter spoke about the destruction of the old covenant under which Paul said these early Christians were at one time in bondage.

Next, as we continue with 2 Pet. 3:10, let's look at the translation of the Greek word κατακαησεται, (katakaisetai) for "burned up," which we find in our King James and New King James translations, and ευρεθησεται (yourethaysetai) for 'discovered, exposed to judgment, or laid bare' which we find in the ESV, NLT, and NIV translations." Without getting too technical on these Greek terms, suffice it to say that these translations all convey the message that there was about to be a severe judgment upon earth which would lay bare its works, which leads us to our next point.

As regard the terms heaven and earth, let's look at a little background information. If we go all the way back to the book of Exodus, in chapter 20, we find that Moses was called by God up to Mount Sinai and given the 10 commandments, which were the very basics of the old covenant. This was followed by God giving him a whole host of detailed laws that they were to practice. In chapter 24 of the book of Exodus, God called Moses up again to Mount Sinai, and he was there for 40 days and forty nights. During this time God gave him a very detailed description of the tabernacle. This tabernacle **WAS** built, and it **WAS** a representation of heaven and earth, with the Most Holy compartment representing the heavens, where only the high priest was allowed to go once a year, and the holy compartment where the rest of the priesthood was allowed on occasion, was a representation of earth.

And now with this background information let's read how Moses began his accusation of the corruption of the Israelite people in the book of Deuteronomy just prior to the song of Moses.

> Deut 31:28 Assemble to me all the elders of your tribes and your officers, that I may speak these words in their hearing and call the heavens and the earth to witness against them.

And then as he begins the song of Moses, which is Moses' last address to the people, he said:

> Deut 32:1 "Give ear, O heavens, and let me speak, And let the earth hear the words of my mouth.
> Deut 32:6 Do you thus repay the LORD, O foolish and unwise people? Is not He your Father who has bought you?

Yes, from this we see why Moses called the tabernacle of God as a witness against them. He knows the evil which existed in this people, and he addressed them with a final warning just before his death.

Continuing this line of evidence, in Isaiah 51:15,16 we read:

> Isa 51:15 "For I am the LORD your God, who stirs up the sea and its waves roar (the LORD of hosts is His name).
> Isa 51:16 "I have put my words in your mouth, and have covered you with the shadow of my hand, **to establish the heavens,** to found the earth, and to say to Zion, 'you are my people.'"

Now just looking at the words of this passage from a logical perspective, do you think that God put words in the mouths of the Israelites in order to establish the literal heavens and literal earth? **Of course not!** But when he brought this nation out of Egypt, God **did establish** the heavens and earth when he had them build the tabernacle which **REPRESENTED** heaven and earth, thus forming a theocratic government, ruled from heaven with Almighty God himself as their leader. And from this founding, he established this nation as the only theocratic government ever to be in existence on the face of the earth.

The fact that this was all represented in the tabernacle, and later in the temple was common knowledge among the Israelite people. Even Jewish historian Josephus wrote about this.

Note what Josephus recorded:

> Now the room within those pillars was the most holy place; but the rest of the room was the tabernacle, which was open for the priests. However, this proportion of the measures of the tabernacle proved to be an imitation of the <u>system of the world;</u> for that third part thereof which was within the four pillars, to which the priests were not admitted, is, as it were, <u>a heaven peculiar to God.</u> But the space of the twenty cubits, is, as it were, <u>sea and land</u>, on which men live, and so this part is peculiar to the priests only. [4]

Jesus confirmed all of this when he said in the Sermon on the Mount:

> Mat 5:17 "Do not think that I came to abolish the Law or the Prophets; I did not come to abolish but to fulfill.
> Mat 5:18 For truly I say to you, **until heaven and earth pass away**, not the smallest letter or stroke shall pass from the Law until all is accomplished."

Yes! When Jesus said heaven and earth, he **meant the temple**, and here's why. Now if we look at what Jesus said here, we know that we absolutely **cannot** take it in the literal sense. Let's read verse 18 again:

> "For truly I say to you, **until heaven and earth pass away**, not the smallest letter or stroke shall pass from the Law until **ALL** is accomplished."

Now just think about this for a minute. If this **IS** literal, it means that until the **literal** heaven and the **literal** earth pass away, **that we are still, and will always be under the law of Moses!**

But **NO**, as the verse says, **Jesus fulfilled the law.** He knew that heaven and earth would pass away in this generation as he prophesied, all of this allowing us to be under **HIS** loving grace and not under the law of Moses! That's why the writer of Hebrews said:

> Heb 8:8 For finding fault with them He says: "Behold, days are coming, says the Lord, when I will effect a new covenant with the house of Israel and with the house of Judah,
> Heb 8:13 When he said "a new covenant", he makes the first one obsolete. But whatever **is becoming obsolete and growing old is ready to disappear.**

Yes, the present form of government **WAS** passing away! The old covenant **WAS** becoming obsolete. It **WAS** about to disappear, but had not yet done so completely.

Of course we know that the early Christians were not under the obligation to keep the law, but it **DID** exist simultaneously until the destruction of the temple in AD 70. The passages we have already read concerning the στοιχεια (elements) clarify the point that the early Christians were no longer under the law, just as Paul reiterated:

> Eph 2:8 For by grace you have been saved through faith, and not of yourselves; *it is* the gift of God;

These words were written because until "heaven and earth" (which was the temple and the Jewish system of government and worship) passed away, the new covenant established by Christ existed side by side with the old law covenant. Yes, this new covenant did finally and completely replace that old covenant when Jerusalem **and** the temple, including the entire Jewish system of government and worship were completely destroyed and reduced to rubble! And this is the essence of Peter's words in 2 Peter 3:9-13, as we have covered in these two segments of this series.

Yes, "heaven and earth" **would be** destroyed, in which "the elements" or the "old law covenant" would be dissolved, and in so doing its lawless works would be exposed. But these early Christians would soon see a "new heavens, and a new earth" in the form of a new covenant which took effect **finally and completely** at the destruction of Jerusalem, the temple, and with it the total annihilation of the Jewish system of worship. In this new covenant they would be dwelling in righteousness and only so by the grace of our Lord Jesus.

Yes, it is only by this amazing grace established with the new covenant, and the precious blood of Jesus that they could be declared righteous and dwell with one another in peace and harmony, and we also, as we walk in the love of Christ. Left on our own, they, and we, could never earn salvation. **God's promise of redemption is** in this new covenant!

When we return in the next chapter, we will examine what the writer of the book of Hebrews had to say about the Last Days.

NOTES

1. http://www.aish.com/jl/h/cc/48938582.html
2. Foxes Book of Martyrs, Chapter 2, taken from e-Sword, Version 10.2.1, 2013, Rick Meyers (Free download at www.e-sword.net)
3. Albert Barnes Notes on the Bible, taken from e-Sword, Version 10.2.1, 2013, Rick Meyers (Free download at www.e-sword.net)
4. The Works of Josephus, Translated by William Whiston, AM, Hendrickson Publishers, Peabody, Mass. 1987, Antiquities of the Jews, Book 3,chapter 6, section 4

Chapter 9

The Last Days – Part 3

The book of Hebrews is one of the most important and useful of all the apostolic writings. All the doctrines of the Gospel are in it. It is full of illustrations and references which are striking, and arguments which are cognitive and convincing. However, the author is unknown. The title simply states, "The Letter to the Hebrews." No author's name was given. And although I would say that the majority of commentators believe it was the Apostle Paul, the writing style of this book does not particularly match Paul's style. Additionally there is some internal evidence against it. For it says in Hebrews 2:3:".... After it was at the first spoken through the Lord, it was confirmed to us by those who heard." In so many words here the writer stated that he had received the message from others who had heard directly from the Lord Jesus. Paul stated in Gal 1:11-12:

> Gal 1:11 For I would have you know, brethren, that the gospel which was preached by me is not according to man.
> Gal 1:12 For I neither received it from man, nor was I taught it, but *I received it* through a revelation of Jesus Christ.

Martin Luther, the great reformer, was convinced that Apollos wrote it. Others have said it was Barnabas. Regardless, we know that whoever wrote this book knew the Scriptures; he was eloquent; and he thought and argued in the way that a person knowledgeable of the Hebrew culture would. However, the fact is, we have no way of positively knowing who the author was. And so, with these thoughts in mind, when referring to the author, I will merely state him as the author, or writer of Hebrews.

The book of Hebrews is all about showing the Jewish community to whom he was writing, the **supremacy of Christ, and the new covenant.** A brief outline of the book might look something like this:

1. Christ is superior to the angels. He created them, is above them, and they worship him. (Chapters 1-2)
2. Christ is superior to Moses, Aaron, and all other high priests who ever existed.(Chapters 3-7)
3. The superiority of the Priesthood of Christ and the new covenant. (Chapters 8-9)
4. The blessings bestowed on the believers is superior to old covenant blessings. (Chapters 10-12)
5. The believers are called to a superior behavior in every relationship, even the direct relationship they now have with God. (Chapter 13)

But why was so much written here in this book to show them the supremacy of Christ? After all, the Hebrew Christians were those to whom it was primarily written was it not? Yes, that is true. But just as in several of the other epistles, the writer of Hebrews wrote this book primarily to encourage those who were believers in the supremacy of Christ, since they were undergoing tremendous rejection and persecution at the hands of their fellow countrymen, the Jews. They were under overwhelming pressure to return to following the law of Moses. Yes, this book (Hebrews) was written to boost their confidence that the Lord Jesus **WAS** superior to the angels, to Moses, and to any high priest who had ever lived, and **they could absolutely TRUST HIM** to keep his promises.

At this point, I would like to point out that **we know** this epistle was written before the destruction of Jerusalem because the book is replete with present tense references to the Levitical Priesthood which ended in AD 70. For example:

> Heb 5:1   For every high priest taken from among men **IS** appointed on behalf of men in things pertaining to God, in order to offer both gifts and sacrifices for sins;
> Heb 7:26   For it was fitting for us to have such a high priest, ...
> Heb 7:27   who **does not** need daily, like those high priests, to offer up sacrifices,

And also there are references in the 8th, 9th, 10th and 13th chapters.

Now, since we are concerned in this series with what the writers of the New Testament taught concerning the Last Days, let's begin an examination of what is contained about this in the epistle to the Hebrews. The writer of Hebrews opened his epistle as follows:

> Heb 1:1   In many ways and in various ways of old, God spoke to the fathers in the prophets;
> Heb 1:2   in these last days *He* spoke to us in *the* Son, whom He appointed heir of all; through whom He indeed made the ages; (LITV)

The last word in this passage is the Greek word αιωνας which translates as "ages." Although many translations use the word "world" here, the best translation is "ages" because it conveys an important fact. The Jews during that period of time were accustomed to a division of time in which there were two great periods known as ages. The first one was the time period before the Messiah, and the age to come was the age of the Messiah, or the age of "The Kingdom of God." The book of Hebrews was written at the end of the Jewish age, just a few years prior to the destruction of the temple.

Yes, it was now over thirty years, since Jesus told them that he would return in "this generation," and there was considerable anticipation of this event being soon to take place. In chapter 3 of this epistle, the writer again emphasized the important point that they keep their confidence in their Savior **firm until the end.** This was one of the most important points the author made in the third chapter and he reiterates it for us twice and once again in Chapter six.

> Heb 3:6 but Christ *was faithful* as a Son over His house--whose house we are, if we hold fast our confidence and the boast of our hope firm **until the end.**
> Heb 3:14 For we have become partakers of Christ, if we hold fast the beginning of our assurance firm **until the end,**
> Heb 6:11 And we desire that each one of you show the same diligence so as to realize the full assurance of hope **until the end,**

In Hebrews 9:24-26, the writer of Hebrews makes it clear that the end was soon when he said:

> Heb 9:24 For Christ did not enter a holy place made with hands, a *mere* copy of the true one, but into heaven itself, now to appear in the presence of God for us;
> Heb 9:25 nor was it that He would offer Himself often, as the high priest enters the holy place year by year with blood that is not his own.
> Heb 9:26 Otherwise, He would have needed to suffer often since the foundation of the world; **but now once** at the consummation of the ages He has been manifested to put away sin by the sacrifice of Himself.

Yes, as it is written here, Christ would enter into the Most Holy in Heaven **ONE TIME**, and one time only, and this would be enough to compensate for the sin of man forever. As Adam Clarke mentions concerning verse 26 in his commentary, the consummation of the ages that was spoken of here was a reference to the end of the Jewish age, and the beginning of the age of Christianity which would continue forever, and was possible because Christ performed this loving act on behalf of man. But finally, of all of the verses in the New Testament which point out that these early Christians knew they were living in the Last Days, **none is more forceful** than what the author wrote in Hebrews 10:37 where he said:

> Heb 10:37 For yet "a very, very little *while, and* the one who is coming will come and will not delay." (LEB)

Now I have quoted this passage from the Lexham English Bible for a very good reason. If you look at the Greek phrase spoken here, you see that it is:

ετι γαρ μιχρον οσον οσον ο ερχομενος ηξει και ου χρο
νισει
For yet little   very very the coming(one) will come and
will not delay
(Zondervan Parallel Greek English)

What I want you to notice is that the Greek word **οσον** "hoson" which is translated "very" is put in here **twice!** Most of our commonly used translations only put this word in there once, such as the NASB, ESV, and NIV. But in the Greek it is there twice to emphasize the fact that the writer of Hebrews was confident that the Lord Jesus was coming very, very soon and would not delay.

Now I want to ask you, if you were living in the time of this writing, and you heard that our Lord was coming very, very, soon, **is there any possibility** that you would think he was not going to be coming **until thousands of years later?**

Thus we see further proof that the book of Hebrews is in line with the other books we have examined, and that the one who wrote it was sure that the Lord Jesus would be coming very very soon, and would not under any circumstances delay that coming. And once again we know that the facts of history confirm that he fulfilled his promise, putting an end to the old covenant.

Heb 8:13 When He said, "A new *covenant*," He has made the first obsolete. But whatever is becoming obsolete and growing old is ready to disappear.

Yes, that old covenant disappeared finally and forever when the Roman armies **completely** destroyed the temple and the Levitical Sacrificial Form of Worship.

References from the book of James

The book of James has, perhaps the most interesting history of any of the epistles. It had an extremely difficult battle just to be recognized as a part of the Bible canon. And although the history of this is long and varied, I would like to relate some of it. For example, the great reformer Martin Luther, wanted the book banished from the New Testament altogether. In his preface to the New Testament, he stated it, which I will quote in part:

> I think highly of the epistle of James, and regard it as valuable although it was rejected in early days. It does not expound human doctrines, but lays much emphasis on God's law. Yet to give my own opinion, without prejudice to that of anyone else, I do not hold it to be of apostolic authorship. …. I therefore refuse him a place among the writers of the true canon of my Bible; but I would not prevent anyone else placing him or raising him where he likes, for the epistle contains many excellent passages. [1]

The Syrian church, which produced the **very first** New Testament (2nd century), sometimes called the "Syriac Peshitta" excluded it, along with 2 Peter, 2 John, 3 John, Jude, and Revelation, and those books were not added back until the 6th century.

Additionally some of the same issues caused a delay in including James into the Bible by the Latin church. But when church fathers Jerome and Augustine accepted it, it finally gained acceptance in the Bible canon.

Then, there is the question of authorship. Which one of the 5 individuals mentioned in the Bible, by the name of James, actually wrote this epistle? Without going into great detail, by process of elimination, we come down to either James the apostle, or James, the brother of the Lord and the overseer of the church in Jerusalem. In this case, we must eliminate James the apostle, because he was the first apostle to be martyred, having been beheaded upon the orders of Herod Agrippa in the year AD 44. Thus, we finally arrive at the conclusion that it had to be James, the brother of our Lord Jesus, who was referred to as "James the Just."

James, the overseer of the Christian church in Jerusalem was a Jew through and through. He was used to living under the law of Moses; therefore we see much of what Luther objected to in his epistle. If you will notice in its pages, there is almost nothing in there that would be unacceptable to a law abiding orthodox Jew, except those references to Jesus as Christ, which only occur in the opening of chapters one and two.

This very fact of how closely the book of James looks at the principles of the Mosaic law proves to us, that the law was still in existence side by side with Christianity in the first century. It existed, and was still revered by the first century Christian church, even though in actuality it was a dead law because our Lord died on the cross and became the last sacrifice needed. Thus, it was only after the destruction of the temple, that it would completely pass away since there was no longer any possible way to practice the law. This is in harmony with what the writer of Hebrews pointed out in Heb. 8:13:

Heb 8:13 When He said, "A new *covenant*," He has made the first obsolete. But whatever is becoming obsolete and growing old is ready to disappear.

Next, we come to the question of the time of the writing of the epistle. This question cannot be answered positively, but the preponderance of evidence seems to tip slightly in favor of a late date. The best evidence is that James was martyred in about AD 62, although some have said it could be as late as AD 69. James the Just was respected for his proper oversight of the Jewish Christian Church. But eventually the leaders of the Jewish Sanhedrin decided that this beloved saint had to die. They cast him down and began stoning him, but he prayed that they be forgiven for their lack of knowledge. Apparently the stoning was not working, so one of the Fullers took a club down into the pit and brought it down on the head of James, killing him in a vicious, brutal attack.

There are 3 points which seem to indicate a late date for the book of James. First, as Luther pointed out, the book of James hardly mentions Jesus at all, but focuses on the inequities of those members of the Jerusalem church. This would favor a late date because in the early years after Pentecost, the church was focused on the glory of the risen Lord and the grace bestowed on the believers. Second, there is evidence of the idea that the church was becoming corrupt, meaning that it was well founded and had time to develop.

Also there were apparently rich members of this church who were spoken to in Chapter 5. In the early days of the church, there were very likely no rich ones. But the nation was becoming more and more corrupt, and these values were affecting the church, particularly the rich ones as spoken of in Chapter 5:1-3. Notice these words as we read:

> Jas 5:1 Come now, you rich, weep and howl for your miseries which are coming upon you.
> Jas 5:2 Your riches have rotted and your garments have become moth-eaten.
> Jas 5:3 Your gold and your silver have rusted; and their rust will be a witness against you and will consume your flesh like fire. **It is in the last days** that you have stored up your treasure!

Adam Clarke notes concerning this verse:

> St. James seems to refer here, in the spirit of prophecy, to the destruction that was coming upon the Jews, not only in Judea, but in all the provinces where they sojourned. He seems here to assume the very air and character of a prophet; and in the most dignified language and peculiarly expressive and energetic images, foretells the desolations that were coming upon this bad people.[2]

In Henry Alford's commentary he notes concerning this verse, and verse 3:

> These miseries are not to be thought of as the natural and determined end of all worldly riches, but are the judgments connected with the coming of the Lord: cf. James 5:8, It may be that this prospect was as yet intimately bound up with **the approaching destruction of the Jewish city and polity**: for it must be remembered that they are Jews who are here addressed.
>
> Vs 3: i. e. in these, the last days **before the coming of the Lord**, ye, instead of repenting and saving your souls, laid up treasure to no profit; employed yourselves in the vain accumulation of this world's wealth.[3] (emphasis mine)

Clearly, James proclaimed that they were living in the Last Days, just before the coming of the Lord as mentioned by Alford. Also, Alford makes mention of James 5:8. I would like to back up to chapter 5 and verse 7 and begin reading:

> Jas 5:7 Therefore be patient, brethren, **until the coming of the Lord**. The farmer waits for the precious produce of the soil, being patient about it, until it gets the early and late rains.
> Jas 5:8 You too be patient; strengthen your hearts, **for the coming of the Lord is near.**

Jas 5:9 Do not complain, brethren, against one another, so that you yourselves may not be judged; behold, **the Judge is standing right at the door.**

Albert Barnes notes of this passage:

> The most natural interpretation of the passage, and one which will accord well with the time when the Epistle was written, is, that the predicted time of the destruction of Jerusalem Matt. 24 was at hand; that there were already indications that that would soon occur; and that there was a prevalent expectation among Christians that that event would be a release from many trials of persecution, ... **The destruction of Jerusalem and of the temple would contribute to that by bringing to an end the whole system of Jewish types and sacrifices; by convincing Christians that there was not to be one central rallying-point, thus destroying their lingering prejudices in favor of the Jewish mode of worship; and by scattering them abroad through the world to propagate the new religion.**[4] (emphasis mine)

So once again, we see it confirmed. The leader of the church in Jerusalem knew what was coming. He knew the destruction of the temple was near. He knew the beloved saints needed patience, for their cry was "How long O Lord?"

He was in agreement with Paul when he said: "The God of peace will soon crush Satan under your feet." (Rom 16:20) He was in agreement with Peter when he said: "The end of all things is near."(1 Pet 4:7) He was in agreement with the writer of Hebrews when he said: "For yet a very, very little *while, and* the one who is coming will come and will not delay." (Heb 10: 37)(LEB)

Once again, I must ask the question. If you were living at that time in the city of Jerusalem, and undergoing tremendous persecution as were these Christians, and heard such a message, is there any possibility that you would think the Lord was not coming for thousands of years? Of course not! They trusted the Lord Jesus to do what he said he would do, and he did come back in that very same generation and put an end to the Jewish system of worship and the persecution that was severely hampering the work of proclaiming the Gospel of Jesus Christ. And the Lord did return. He did provide them with a way of escape for this judgment, and they were spared. So I ask you today: Why can't we just trust the Lord Jesus, and believe **that he did exactly what he said he would do**?

The remaining epistles

After the book of 2 Peter, and prior to the book of Revelation, there remains only the epistles of John and Jude. Although some of the commentators believe that these books were written after the destruction of Jerusalem, most plainly state that they are unsure of when these were written.

But at this point we must ask an important question. And that question is this: Is there any possibility that the destruction of Jerusalem and the destruction of the temple would not be mentioned in the final writings of the New Testament? After all, this is the most profound event in the history of both the Jewish political and religious system, and that of the early Christians?

And because there is the expectation in both of these epistles that the end was near, we cannot see that it is possible that they could have been written after this profound event.

Now we will examine the evidence found in these epistles that they were waiting for a very powerful event to occur, and that event was the Parousia or the coming of our Lord. Looking first at 1 John 2:17,18 we see:

> 1Jn 2:17 The world is passing away, and *also* its lusts; but the one who does the will of God lives forever.

1Jn 2:18 Children, it is the last hour; and just as you heard that antichrist is coming, even now many antichrists have appeared; from this we know that **it is the last hour.**

You can feel the urgency in the words of the apostle as he wrote this verse. A crisis is at hand. How much more emphasis could he put on it than to state "it is the last hour."

The sense of urgency is the same as it was with James when he wrote:

Jas 5:9 ... behold, **the *Judge is standing right at the door.* (NASB)**

Of this passage Matthew Henry notes:

Little children, it is the last time; our Jewish polity in church and state is hastening to an end; the Mosaic institution and discipline are just upon vanishing away; Daniel's weeks are now expiring; the destruction of the Hebrew city and sanctuary is approaching, *the end whereof must be with a flood, and to the end of the war desolations are determined,* Dan 9:26. It is meet that the disciples should be warned of the haste and end of time, and apprised as much as may be of the prophetic periods of time.[5]

Then later of verse 18 he notes:

They were foretold also as the sign of this last time. *For there shall arise false Christs and false prophets, and shall show great signs and wonders, insomuch that, if it were possible, they shall deceive the very elect,* Mat 24:24. And these were the forerunners of the dissolution of the Jewish state, nation, and religion: *Whereby we know it is the last time,* 1Jo 2:18.[6]

Yes, and as John ends the second chapter of his first epistle, he reaffirms this point by telling those to whom he wrote:

1Jn 2:28 Now, little children, abide in Him, **so that when He appears, we may have confidence** and not shrink away from Him in shame at His coming.

Yes, John is showing in this verse the full confidence of his coming soon. There is no question that he expects "an appearing" soon because he tells them that when this happens, if they are abiding in him, they will have full confidence.

And then in Chapter 2 he states something very interesting in the following verse:

1Jn 3:2 Beloved, now we are children of God, and **it has not appeared as yet what we will be.** We know that when He appears, we will be like Him, because **we will see Him just as He is.**

From this we see two things: First of all, it tells us that John did not expect to see the same type of body as he had seen after the resurrection. This has strong implications for the type of body they would get at their resurrection from the dead. And secondly, it shows that they unequivocally expected to see him themselves.

And finally concerning John's epistle in 1 John 4:17, we read:

1Jn 4:17 By this, love is perfected with us, so **that we may have confidence in the day of judgment;** because as He is, so also are we in this world.

Again we see him reaffirming that there was an expectation of the judgment that was at hand.

And finally in the book of Jude, which is only one chapter long, we see more affirmation of what our Lord said in Mark 13 concerning apostates within the church. Note what he wrote in Jude 17-19:

Jud 1:17 But you, beloved, ought to remember the words that were spoken beforehand by the apostles of our Lord Jesus Christ,

Jud 1:18 that they were saying to you, "**In the last time** there will be mockers, following after their own ungodly lusts."
Jud 1:19 These are the ones who cause divisions, worldly-minded, devoid of the Spirit.

These words are almost identical to what Peter wrote in his first epistle. These people were apostates from the faith. They denied the truth that Jesus was the Messiah, and thus they were to be lumped in with those who would see the wrath of the Lord. Yes, the Jewish nation was about to receive its judgment, when the Lord would use the Roman armies as his instrument of wrath in the great and dreadful day of the Lord. That judgment was described in the Revelation given to John by our Lord. This will be discussed in the next chapter.

Once again we see that there is consistency among the writers of the New Testament. They believed Jesus' words when he said: "this generation will not pass away until all these things take place" (Matt 24:34). All of this builds trust in the promises of our Lord, that they are trustworthy and true. This includes that most precious of all promises, the promise of redemption.

NOTES

1. http://www.cogwriter.com/news/church-history/martin-luther-changed-andor-discounted-18-books-of-the-bible/
2. Adam Clarke's Commentary on the Bible, taken from e-Sword, Version 10.2.1, 2013, Rick Meyers (Free download at www.e-sword.net)
3. Henry Alford's The Greek Testament, taken from e-Sword, Version 10.2.1, 2013, Rick Meyers (Free download at www.e-sword.net)
4. Albert Barnes Notes on the Bible, taken from e-Sword, Version 10.2.1, 2013, Rick Meyers (Free download at www.e-sword.net)
5. Matthew Henry's Commentary on the Whole Bible, taken from e-Sword, Version 10.2.1, 2013, Rick Meyers (Free download at www.e-sword.net)
6. Ibid.

Chapter 10

The Revelation of Jesus Christ

When we hear anything about the Bible book of Revelation, we often think of horrific things stored up for the future. Why is this so? It is because of how **obsessed** the prophecy pundits are with their interpretation of this book, and how they say that it lies directly in our future.

From the standpoint of the topic of this book, which concerns the *promise of redemption and the fulfillment of this promise,* it is important because **we also need to know** if this promise is **yet to be** fulfilled in our future, or if it **has already been fulfilled** in our past. If it is yet to be fulfilled in our future, then much of what has been said in the previous chapters of this book is questionable. However, if the promise of redemption **has been** fulfilled, then we should see evidence of this in the final book of the New Testament. This is the question we must tackle, and find a definitive answer relative to the topic of this book.

Let's begin with first things first. So, as we begin a discussion of "The Revelation of Jesus Christ," we must first look at **the name of the book**. The word revelation in the Greek language is the word αποκαλυψις. The correct pronunciation of this word is apocaloopsis. This is a noun, with the English meaning of "the revealing" or the "unveiling." This book was inspired to the mind of the Apostle John by the Lord Jesus Christ to reveal something relevant to him. The problem that has existed with those trying to understand this throughout the centuries is just exactly **what** was being revealed to the Apostle John.

Among those attempting such an interpretation there are a vast diversity of opinions. We will look at the ones that seem to be the most prevalent. These views are categorized around the words of Revelation 20 which speaks of a 1000 year period of time called the millennium. Some believe this to be a figurative period of time, others a literal period of time. Here are the most prevalent views:

1. By far the most prevalent is that after the first three chapters, the remainder of the book is **entirely in our future.** This view is called **the dispensational view,** and through its various descriptions, all interpretations under this heading point to a "soon coming" event which will be a millennial reign of Jesus Christ on the earth followed at some point by a complete recreation of heaven and earth. Those who interpret this book in this form spend a huge amount of time developing "the Antichrist." But a close examination of the book shows that there is not even a whisper of this enigmatic individual in the pages of this book.

2. Then there is the **partial fulfillment view.** Under this view, some believe the events of Revelation are partially fulfilled. The millennium is said to be a figurative period of time that began in the first century and has continued through the centuries up to and including now. This view is called **Amillenialism** and was also described in an earlier chapter.

3. As explained in the next view, the Revelation contains a prophetical description of a past event. This is the most important event in the history of Israel, the destruction

of Jerusalem. This includes the Jewish war, and the related civil wars of the Romans. There are two camps of thought here. One is that the book is entirely in our past **(Preterist – meaning past)**. The other one is that although **most** of it is in our distant past, **some** of it is yet in our distant future **(Preterist-Postmillenial)**.

4. Though these are the primary views, there is another one that is somewhat popular. This view is called the **idealistic** view, although it may have literal components. This view states that the book is predominately apocalyptic in nature, but it is also an epistle as is indicated by the opening and closing of the book. As such the book may have no actual connection with any particular events. Yet, it may have various fulfillments throughout the ages without exhausting its meaning.

The Date of Writing the Book

The next most important thing to discuss, before any discussion of the contents of the book, **has to be the time of the writing of the book**. Why is this so? The reason is because **if** the book is about **the destruction of Jerusalem** and the events surrounding it, then it **must have** been written prior to this event. If it was written after the year AD 70, when Jerusalem was destroyed, then it has nothing to do with this book whatsoever. This would totally eliminate two of the aforementioned views as detailed in item 3 above.

So now, let's consider the evidence that the book was written prior to AD 70. This will not be by any means an exhaustive look at this evidence, but an overview of the evidence. For a detailed description of these events, I will be referring to a book written by Kenneth L. Gentry Jr. entitled "Before Jerusalem Fell." Dr. Gentry has solidly documented this in fine detail, and I would like to show why I agree with his conclusions.[1]

The External Evidence

Those who say the book of Revelation was written after the destruction of Jerusalem, primarily rest their evidence on comments made by Irenaeus, the Bishop of Lyons who was born in the first half of the second century, or somewhere around 100 years after Christ walked the earth. His life spans from perhaps AD 130 through AD 202. As one of the early church fathers, his writings are considered by many to be foundational to the early development of Christian theology. He also was acquainted with Polycarp who was a disciple of the Apostle John.

Some of the comments of Irenaeus seem to be directly applicable to the dating of the book of Revelation. Irenaeus wrote his most famous work entitled _Against Heresies_ to dispute the teachings of the Gnostics, and it is in Book 5 that the question of the time of writing of The Revelation is taken up. Although originally composed in the Greek language, most of the copies did not survive in its original form, although the statement in question upon which the late date advocates rest their conclusion is preserved in Greek for us in Eusebius' _Ecclesiastical History_.

For those who profess belief in the later dating of the book of Revelation, the writings of Irenaeus seem to provide them with their most potent information to prove the late date, or a writing which is post-AD 70.

The words translated in English below are what we find when we search for this statement now. It says:

> We will not, however, incur the risk of pronouncing positively as to the name of Antichrist; for if it were necessary that his name should be distinctly revealed in this present time, it would have been **announced by him who beheld the apocalyptic vision.** For

that was seen no very long time since, but **almost in our day**, towards the end of Domitian's reign.[2]

To say the least, this statement, even when translated in English as done so above is very vague in its contents. Those who advocate a late date for the writing of the Apocalypse (Revelation) state that it means that John wrote the Apocalypse toward the end of Domitian's reign. Domitian is said to have reigned from AD 81 to AD 96. But Albert Barnes, in his introduction to the book of Revelation mentions (from Dr. Nathaniel Lardner) that this last statement by Irenaeus was a reference *to a copy of the book*, "The Revelation of John."[13] He indicates that *this book* was seen toward the end of Domitian's reign. Wouldn't this emphasize the notion that *the book was written much earlier?* Thus, when Irenaeus said "For that was seen no very long time since," it finally makes sense in that he was referring to a book which had already been written, and *NOT* to John himself.

When looking at the statement above of Irenaeus, we must realize that this statement is a translation of a translation. It was written in Greek, then translated to Latin. From that Latin translation, it was translated into English. This multiplies the chance of error. Second of all, as we said before, the statement is vague. Due to the wording, there is some lack of clarity to what is actually meant here. But from what we have noted above, *it would make sense* in reference to *the book of Revelation*. It should be noted that Irenaeus is also known to have made errant statements throughout his volumes. For example he is specifically stated as saying that Jesus' ministry embraced a period of 10 and even up to 20 years as noted below in Book two of *Against Heresies*:

> He preached only one year reckoning from His baptism. On completing His thirtieth year He suffered, being in fact still a young man, and who had by no means attained to advanced age. Now, that the first stage of early life embraces thirty years,(1) and that this extends onwards to the fortieth year, every one will admit; *but from the fortieth and fiftieth year a* man begins to decline

towards old age, which our Lord possessed while He still fulfilled the office of a Teacher, even as the Gospel and all the elders testify; those who were conversant in Asia with John, the disciple of the Lord, [affirming] that John conveyed to them that information.(2) And he remained among them up to the times of Trajan. (3) Some of them, moreover, saw not only John, but the other apostles also, and heard the very same account from them, and bear testimony as to the [validity of] the statement[3] (emphasis mine)

Yes, even this passage from _Against Heresies_ is plagued with vague statements, making just exactly what Irenaeus is saying about Jesus, John, and the other apostles difficult to understand. But he certainly appears to be saying that Jesus lived to the age of forty or fifty.

Additional evidence concerning the Apostle John shows that he was **banished to Patmos by the emperor Nero** during his reign. This is from the Syriac Writings: _The History of John, the son of Zebedee,_ and also the _Syriac Peshitta_ version from the sixth and seventh century which contains _The Apocalypse of St. John._ The title of this latter volume states: "**written in Patmos, whither John was sent by Nero Caesar.**" Nero ruled from AD 64-68, prior to the destruction of Jerusalem. Having said that, there are also statements which show John was exiled to Patmos during the reign of Domitian (AD 81-96). Of course John could have been exiled twice, which would solve this problem. (See _Before Jerusalem Fell,_ pp45-67 Kenneth Gentry,. 1998 Victorious Hope Publishing, pp 105, 106.)

There is much more that could be considered. If this documentation is of interest to you, please explore Dr. Gentry's book as listed above.

The Internal Evidence

When we say that we need to look at the internal evidence of why the book of Revelation was written before AD 70, we mean that we need to show why we know that the city of Jerusalem and the temple were still in existence. And in this category, there appears to be **overwhelming evidence** that it was written prior to the demise of the holy city. To begin with, the churches to which the book was written were warned of an impending crisis. What other crisis was there at hand during that entire time period that would affect the churches mentioned? As you read the passages below, the urgency of the warnings almost scream at you. The Apostle John wrote this letter specifically to those seven churches, and he wanted them to understand the words he was writing. Notice these instances:

To the loveless church at Ephesus he warns:

Rev 2:5 'Therefore remember from where you have fallen, and repent and do the deeds you did at first; or else I am coming to you and will remove your lampstand out of its place--unless you repent.

To the persecuted church at Smyrna he writes:

Rev 2:10 'Do not fear what **you are about to suffer**. Behold, the devil is about to cast some of you into prison, so that you will be tested, and you will have tribulation for ten days. Be faithful until death, and I will give you the crown of life

To the compromising church at Pergamum he writes:
Rev 2:16 'Therefore repent; or else **I am coming to you quickly**, and I will make war against them with the sword of My mouth.
To the corrupt church at Thyatira, to those tolerating the woman Jezebel and acts of immorality and Idol worship, he writes:

Rev 2:21 'I gave her time to repent, and she does not want to repent of her immorality.
Rev 2:22 'Behold, I will throw her on a bed *of sickness,* and those who commit adultery with her into great tribulation, unless they repent of her deeds.

Rev 2:23 'And **I will kill her children with pestilence**, and all the churches will know that I am He who searches the minds and hearts; and I will give to each one of you according to your deeds. Rev 2:24 'But I say to you, the rest who are in Thyatira, who do not hold this teaching, who have not known the deep things of Satan, as they call them--I place no other burden on you.

To the dead church of Sardis he writes:

Rev 3:3 'So remember what you have received and heard; and keep *it,* and repent. **Therefore if you do not wake up**, I will come **like a thief,** and you will not know at what hour I will come to you.

To the faithful church at Philadelphia he writes:

Rev 3:10 'Because you have kept the word of My perseverance, **I also will keep you from the hour of testing,** that *hour* which is about to come upon the whole world, to test those who dwell on the earth.
Rev 3:11 **'I am coming quickly;** hold fast what you have, so that no one will take your crown.

To the lukewarm church at Laodicea he writes:

Rev 3:16 'So because you are lukewarm, and neither hot nor cold, **I will spit you out of My mouth.**

And then in general he writes to all of these churches:

Rev 3:20 'Behold, **I stand at the door and knock**; if anyone hears My voice and opens the door, I will come in to him and will dine with him, and he with Me.
Rev 3:21 'He who overcomes, I will grant to him to sit down with Me on My throne, as I also overcame and sat down with My Father on His throne.
Rev 3:22 'He who has an ear, let him hear what the Spirit says **to the churches.'"**

Now as we look at these warnings, we have to realize that **the only cataclysmic event** of that time period which involved those churches was the **destruction of Jerusalem and the temple,** which occurred in the year AD 70. Of course we know that these churches were not in Jerusalem, but the impact of this coming destruction was felt strongly by these churches. The persecution of that era was brought on primarily by the Jews, and also severely at the hands of the emperor Nero. Thus, the second and third chapters without question were addressing these churches, **which were all real churches** present within the Roman Empire. And they would feel the effects of this judgment that was **soon to come**, spoken by the Lord Jesus through the pen of the Apostle John.

As we look at more of the internal evidence, we see in looking at Rev 1:7 the words:

Rev 1:7 Lo, he doth come with the clouds, and see him shall every eye, even those who did pierce him, and wail because of him shall all the tribes of the land. Yes! Amen! (Young's Literal Translation)

This unquestionably refers to the prophecy Jesus himself made to the members of the Jewish Sanhedrin, upon the occasion of his trial before his crucifixion. Although not literally driving the nails in his hands and feet, **they are the ones who pierced him!** It is impossible that the time reference could be any other than this same generation! Notice how specific Jesus is on this occasion:

Mat 26:63 But Jesus remained silent. And the high priest said to him, "I adjure you by the living God, tell us if you are the Christ, the Son of God."
Mat 26:64 Jesus said to him, "You have said so. But I tell you, from now on **YOU** will see the Son of Man seated at the right hand of Power and coming on the clouds of heaven."

Jesus was not speaking to some future group of people, but was speaking **directly** to this group of scribes and Pharisees, and directly to the high priest. And in Josephus' account of the destruction of Jerusalem, we have presented the evidence that this prophetic event **did** happen, and **was** fulfilled.

Next, we see that the book of Revelation speaks of the temple as still in existence, followed by the trampling of the city for 42 months.

> Rev 11:1 Then I was given a measuring rod like a staff, and I was told, "Rise **and measure the temple of God** and the altar and those who worship there,
> Rev 11:2 but do not measure the court outside the temple; leave that out, for it is given over to the nations, and they will **trample the holy city for forty-two months**.
> Rev 11:3 And I will grant authority to my two witnesses, and they will prophesy for 1,260 days, clothed in sackcloth."

First of all, from verse 1, we know that measuring the temple would be impossible if the temple was not present at the time of the writing. Some have said that this was not a literal measurement, but if this is so, why was he given a measuring rod? Unmistakably, the sources for this time statement are Luke 21:24: "and Jerusalem will be trampled underfoot by the Gentiles, until the times of the Gentiles are fulfilled," and Daniel's referent to "the time, times, and half time" in (Daniel 7:25).

Don Preston notes concerning verse two and three:

> This is confirmed when we remember, as noted above, that the sealed book that John has seen, that only the Lamb is worthy to open, is the sealed book of Daniel's prophecy of the time of the end (Daniel 8: 25-26; 12: 4). Space forbids an exhaustive analysis of each of the texts in which these synonymous terms, i.e. forty -two months, time, times and half times, 1260 days, etc. are used. However, note that there is a common thread in them that ties them all together: 1.) The persecution of the saints (Daniel 7: 25). 2.) The time of the Great Tribulation and the time of the end (Daniel 12: 7). 3.) The treading down of the holy city (Revelation 11: 2). 4.) The ministry of the two witnesses (Revelation 11: 3). 5.) The protection of the woman during the persecution (Revelation

12: 6). 6.) The blasphemy and persecution by the beast (13: 5). What emerges from these references is that there would be a period of intense persecution of God's people, during which time Jehovah would providentially–and even miraculously (Revelation 11: 5f)– prevent the church from being overwhelmed and defeated, although for all appearances sake, the outlook was bleak. Nonetheless, at the end of the foreordained time, the persecutor would be judged and God's saints would be identified, vindicated, avenged, and glorified.[4]

Eighteenth century commentator Adam Clarke states concerning chapter eleven and verse one:

This **must** refer to the temple of Jerusalem; and this is **another presumptive evidence** that it was yet standing.[5] (emphasis mine)

The Beast of Revelation

When we consider the internal evidence for the dating of the book of Revelation, it is imperative that we consider the seven headed, ten horned beast. This beast is first identified in Rev. 13:1:

Rev 13:1 And the dragon stood on the sand of the seashore. Then I saw a beast coming up out of the sea, having ten horns and seven heads, and on his horns *were* ten diadems, and on his heads *were* blasphemous names.

There have been a great number of commentators who have identified this beast by proclaiming that it is a history lesson which spans several centuries. However, I reiterate that **we must keep in mind** that the Revelation given to John was given to him **for the purpose outlined** in the opening verse of the book:

Rev 1:1 The Revelation of Jesus Christ, which God gave Him to show to His bond-servants, the things which **must soon take place**; and He sent and communicated *it* by His angel to His bond-servant John,
Rev 1:2 who testified to the word of God and to the testimony of Jesus Christ, *even* to all that he saw.

Rev 1:3 Blessed is he who reads and those who hear the words of the prophecy, and heed the things which are written in it; for the time is near.

Rev 1:4 John to the seven churches that are in Asia: Grace to you and peace, from Him who is and who was and who is to come, and from the seven Spirits who are before His throne,

Rev 1:5 and from Jesus Christ, the faithful witness, the firstborn of the dead, and the ruler of the kings of the earth. To Him who loves us and released us from our sins by His blood--

Rev 1:6 and He has made us to be a kingdom, priests to His God and Father--to Him be the glory and the dominion forever and ever. Amen.

In a way, this sort of reminds us of a last will and testament. Of course it is not, because it speaks of events which are about to take place. But it is the same in that it very specifically outlined to whom it is written and for what purpose. It is not to give the churches a history lesson, nor is it to outline thousands of years of events to take place in the future.

I mentioned earlier that there have been a great number of commentators who have identified this beast by proclaiming that it is a history lesson which spans several centuries. But if we stop and think about this for a minute, this makes no sense to the literary theme of the epistle. Specific to the beast outlined in Rev 13:1 above, there are commentators who would say that this is a reference to seven world monarchies; Egypt, Assyria, Babylon, Persia, Greece, Rome, and then to future dynasties hundreds of years into the future. But this cannot be when we consider the purpose as outlined in the very opening of the book!

The apostle to whom this Revelation was given clearly expects this prophecy to be fulfilled during his lifetime. Why would he imply to these persecuted Christians that they needed to think about the history of the world powers and then speculate on future powers? This would be of absolutely no interest to them. Consequently, we must conclude that this beast outlined in verse one of chapter thirteen is a first century figure.

When John writes this book, the emperor Nero is ruling. In addition to the passage in chapter 13, we see a clue to the identity in chapter seventeen. In Revelation 17:1-6 John gives a vision of a seven headed beast. And then in verses 9-11 the interpreting angel gives the meaning of the seven headed beast.

> Rev 17:9 "Here is the mind which has wisdom. The seven heads are seven mountains on which the woman sits,
> Rev 17:10 and they are seven kings; five have fallen, one is, the other has not yet come; and when he comes, he must remain a little while.
> Rev 17:11 "The beast which was and is not, is himself also an eighth and is *one* of the seven, and he goes to destruction.

This passage is properly explained by Jonathan Welton in his book, "*The Art of Revelation*:"

> This passage, which speaks of the line of rulers in Rome, tells us exactly how many rulers had already come, which one was currently in power, and that the next one would only last a short while. Take a look at how perfectly it fits with Nero and the Roman Empire of the first century. The rule of the first seven Roman Emperors is as follows: "Five have fallen... " Julius Caesar (49–44 BC) Augustus (27 BC–AD 14) Tiberius (AD 14–37) Caligula (AD 37–41) Claudius (AD 41–54) "One is... Nero (AD 54-68) "the other has not yet come; but when he does come, he must remain for only a little while." Galba (June AD 68–January AD 69, a six-month rulership) Of the first seven kings, five had come (Julius Caesar, Augustus, Tiberius, Gaius, and Claudius), one was currently in power (Nero), and one had not yet come (Galba), but would only remain a little time (six months). The current Caesar at the time of John's writing was the sixth Caesar, Nero.[6]

Let me reiterate the incredible specificity of this! The angel is telling John that these kings represent the emperors in succession of the Roman Empire. If we look up these emperors according to secular history, we find that they are:

1. Julius Caesar (49 - 44 BC), (followed by civil war)
2. Augustus Caesar (27BC – AD 14),
3. Tiberius Caesar (14 - AD 37),
4. Gaius Caesar (37 - AD 41),
5. Claudius (41 - AD 54),
6. Nero (54 - AD 68),
7. Galba (June AD 68 – January AD 69)

The five that have fallen:
Julius, Augustus, Tiberius, Gaius, and Claudius.
One is: Nero
One is yet to come:
Galba (only a little while)

Notice **how precisely** the succession of emperors is described in the book! There is no way this could be a coincidence! All of them reigned over a period of years with the exception of Galba who only reigned for about 6+ months. The reason Galba reigned such a short period of time is because it was the beginning of a civil war in Rome, and amazingly, this exact scenario was described **precisely** in verse 10 of chapter 17.

With this established it appears very evident that the book of Revelation **had to be written prior to June 8, AD 68**, the day that Nero committed suicide.

Then finally we must consider the information found in the final chapter of the Revelation. It says:
Rev 22:10 And he said to me, "**Do not seal up** the words of the prophecy of this book, **for the time is near."**

Is it reasonable to think that we could have gone nearly 2000 years since these words were written, and yet this "time that is near" has not yet happened? The notion of this is preposterous! Especially is this true when we compare it to the words written by the prophet Daniel:

Dan 12:4 "But as for you, Daniel, conceal these words and **seal up the book** until the end of time;

From the time of Daniel's prophecy to the time of the destruction of Jerusalem, it is only a period of 530 years or so. Wow! Do you see the impossibility of this? Daniel was only 490 years away from the fulfillment of his prophecy, and he was told to **seal up the book**. It is **just not possible** that John told the seven churches that the time **was near**, and **not to seal up the book**, yet we are still waiting for the fulfillment **almost 2000 years later!**

The Contextual Evidence

All of the evidence we have considered here leads us to believe that the book of Revelation was written **for** the seven churches to which it was addressed. But considering all of the hype that has been attached to this book, we must ask some important questions. Was it written to be understood? Or was it meant to be an enigma, and completely unintelligible to the readers? The prophecy pundits have told us that it speaks of our future. Some have proposed that it has reference to tanks, helicopters, and modern nations, not even in existence during the time of its writing. Some have said that it has reference to the Catholic church and medieval popes, as well as historical figures throughout the centuries, sometimes labeled as "the antichrist."

But if this were true, **of what possible value** would this information have been to those seven churches addressed in the first three chapters of the Revelation? These Christians, as citizens of the nations of the Roman Empire, were undergoing persecution from two sources, Jerusalem, and Rome. They were suffering greatly. The Apostle John was inspired to send them a message with a warning, **an urgent warning!** So then, how is it possible that John would send them all of this irrelevant information, especially considering that the message was urgently inspired by the Lord Jesus? Would this not be a form of mockery? Of course it would!

Therefore, we must conclude that the Apocalypse was without question meant to be understood by the **original** readers. It must be speaking of events relative to the time of those early Christians, and that period of time **had to be relatively short** in its span. This is not a matter of speculation. For in the very beginning of the book we read:

> Rev 1:1 The Revelation of Jesus Christ, which God gave Him to show to His bond-servants, the things which **must soon take place**...
>
> Rev 1:3 Blessed is he who reads and those who hear the words of the prophecy, and heed the things which are written in it; **for the time is near.**

In his book "Christian Hope through Fulfilled Prophecy," Charles Meek points out the following fact:

> Some two dozen passages in the book of Revelation tie the date of the events of Revelation to first-century Israel, either (a) by specific time -reference , (b) by correlating to other texts that are limited by a time-reference (some of which we have studied in previous chapters), (c) by pointing specifically to Jerusalem or the nation of Israel, or (d) by being confirmed by actual historical accounts of first-century Jerusalem as the place and time of the apocalypse. Here is a list of such passages:
>
> Revelation **1: 1; 1: 3;** 1: 7; 1: 9-10; 1: 19; 2: 10; **2: 16;** 2: 25; 3: 10; **3: 11;** 4: 1; 6: 12-17; 8: 13; **10: 6-7;** 11: 2; 11: 8; 11: 15-19; 12: 5; 14: 7; 14: 14-20; 15: 5-8; 16: 6; 16: 19; 17: 8; 18: 19, 24; 20: 7-10; 20: 11-15; **22: 6; 22: 7; 22: 10; 22: 12; 22: 20.**
>
> If the reader takes the time to look up each of these passages he will note familiar language that we have already discussed. The passages in bold specifically say that the events in view, including the Second Coming, were to happen soon or were near or were going to take place without delay ("must shortly take place.").[7]

We have already looked at some of these passages, specifically in the opening of the book, and in the warnings to the seven churches. Now in chapter ten we read:

> Rev 10:6 and swore by him who lives forever and ever, who created heaven and what is in it, the earth and what is in it, and the sea and what is in it, **that there would be no more** delay, (ESV)

And from the final chapter of the book, we read:

> Rev 22:6 And he said to me, "These words are trustworthy and true. And the Lord, the God of the spirits of the prophets, has sent his angel to show his servants what must soon take place."
> Rev 22:7 "And behold, I am coming soon. Blessed is the one who keeps the words of the prophecy of this book."
> Rev 22:10 And he said to me, "Do not seal up the words of the prophecy of this book, for the time is near.
> Rev 22:12 "Behold, I am coming soon, bringing my recompense with me, to repay each one for what he has done.
> Rev 22:20 He who testifies to these things says, "Surely I am coming soon." Amen. Come, Lord Jesus!

So from these passages in both the front and back of the book, it should be obvious to the reader that these events would happen soon. The book of the Apocalypse was without question meant to be understood by the readers. But what is the meaning? When we consider who the author is, namely the Apostle John, an interesting question pops up. Where is John's version of the Olivet Discourse? As we examine his Gospel account, we find no trace of it. Is it possible that the Revelation of Jesus Christ as given to John **was a form of the Olivet Discourse** that he gave to his Apostles?

In his book, _Who is this Babylon_, Don Preston notes the following comparison:

> Very few deny that Matthew 24 predicts the fall of Jerusalem. However, many have failed to realize that **Revelation recreates the Olivet Discourse** in form and outline. R.H. Charles was one of the first to recognize that the seals of Revelation 6 follow exactly the pattern predicted by Jesus in Matthew 24:7. The pattern of judgment in Matthew— as well as Mark 13 and Luke 21 is:
>
> 1.) War (Matthew 24: 6; compare Revelation 6: 1-2).
> 2.) International strife (Mat. 24: 7a; Rev. 6: 3-4).

3.) Famine (Mat. 24: 7b; Rev. 6: 5-6).
4.) Earthquakes (Mat. 24: 7c; Rev. 6: 12;16: 18).
5.) Persecutions (Mat. 24: 9-13; Rev. 6: 9-11).
6.) De-creation (Mat. 24: 15-31; Rev. 6: 12-17) (de-creation). [8]

Preston continues the analogy as follows:

In addition to the above, there are other parallels between Revelation and the Olivet Discourse.

1.) Both speak of the judgment of a sinful city following the completion of the world mission (Mat. 24: 14; Rev. 14: 6f).
2.) Both speak of the Great Tribulation (Mat. 24: 21; Rev. 14).
3.) Both speak of the Abomination of Desolation (Mat. 24: 15; Rev. 13).
4.) Both urge the faithful to flee from the city (Mat. 24: 15f; Rev. 18: 4).
5.) Both speak of false prophets and the workers of false miracles (Mat. 24: 24; Rev. 13: 12-15).
6.) Both speak of the coming of the Son of Man on the clouds (Mat. 24: 30; Rev. 14: 14f). 7.) Both speak of the sounding of the Trumpet at the time of the end (Mat. 24: 31; Rev. 11: 15f).
8.) Both speak of the salvation of the elect (Mat. 24: 31; Rev. 14: 15-16).
9.) Both speak of the gathering of the birds of the air to feast on the carcass of the dead (Mat. 24: 28; Rev. 19: 17f).

Compare this with Deuteronomy 28: 25-26; Psalms 79; Jeremiah 34, etc.. This is a common theme associated with punishment on Israel. 10.) Both predictions were to be fulfilled soon (Mat. 24: 34; Rev. 1: 1-3; 22: 6, 10, 12, 20). These, and other similarities, show that the Olivet Discourse and Revelation are parallel. The significant thing about these parallels, for the amillennialist and postmillennialist, is that every one of them is taken from the section of Matthew 24 that is almost universally agreed to be speaking about the fall of Jerusalem. If Revelation is parallel to Matthew 24, and Matthew 24 speaks of the impending judgment on Jerusalem, then Revelation must speak of the fall of Jerusalem. In Revelation, judgment is against Babylon. The judgments on Babylon are the judgments Jesus proclaimed against Jerusalem.

> Unless one can show that Revelation and the Olivet Discourse speak of two identical judgments, to come on two different cities, then Babylon must be Jerusalem.[9]

We have to be wowed by this analogy! As Preston concludes after showing 15 likenesses, the book of Revelation is a parallel passage to Matthew 24. **Both speak of the impending judgment on Jerusalem**. It is obvious that the Revelation given to John is a parallel passage, speaking of the fall of Jerusalem. He further surmises that In Revelation, judgment is against Babylon. The judgments on Babylon are the judgments Jesus proclaimed against Jerusalem. Unless one can show that Revelation and the Olivet Discourse speak of two identical judgments, to come on two different cities, then Babylon must be Jerusalem. Preston's logic here is impeccable!

This brings us to an outline!

Thus from the information above, we can form an outline for the first nineteen chapters. It is **not** an outline that is unfamiliar to the first readers of the words penned by the Apostle John, because **it is similar** to other sections of the Bible. The first of such sections is from the Torah, specifically, Leviticus 26 and Deuteronomy 28. God's relationship with Israel was always defined **in terms of the covenant.** That covenant in Leviticus 26 was a simple one. If Israel would **obey God,** she would be **blessed.** If Israel **disobeyed God,** she would be subject to the **horrible curses** outlined in these two chapters (Leviticus 26:14-39; Deut. 28:15-68). Just listen to what is said in Leviticus 26. It is so exact in the precision with which God acted upon the nation of Israel, and it is **such a close match** for what happened during the destruction of Jerusalem, that it **literally will raise the hair up** on the back of your neck! Notice the words:

> Lev 26:29 You shall **eat the flesh of your sons**, and you shall eat the flesh of your daughters.

Lev 26:30 And I will destroy your high places and cut down your incense altars and cast your dead bodies upon the dead bodies of your idols, and my soul will abhor you.

Lev 26:31 And I will **lay your cities waste** and will **make your sanctuaries desolate**, and I will not smell your pleasing aromas.

Lev 26:32 And I myself will **devastate the land**, so that your enemies who settle in it shall be appalled at it.

Lev 26:33 And I will **scatter you among the nations**, and I will unsheathe the sword after you, and your land shall be a desolation, and your cities shall be a waste.

And from Deuteronomy 28 we also read the shockingly accurate words:

Deu 28:25 "The LORD will cause you to be defeated before your enemies. You shall go out one way against them and flee seven ways before them. And you shall be a horror to all the kingdoms of the earth.

Deu 28:26 And **your dead body shall be food for all birds of the air** and for the beasts of the earth, and there shall be no one to frighten them away.

Deu 28:49 The LORD will bring **a nation against you from far away, from the end of the earth, swooping down like the eagle**, a nation whose language you do not understand,

Deu 28:50 a hard-faced nation who shall not respect the old or show mercy to the young.

Deu 28:51 It shall eat the offspring of your cattle and the fruit of your ground, until you are destroyed; it also shall not leave you grain, wine, or oil, the increase of your herds or the young of your flock, until they have caused you to perish.

Deu 28:56 **The most tender and refined woman among you**, who would not venture to set the sole of her foot on the ground because she is so delicate and tender, will begrudge to the husband she embraces, to her son and to her daughter,

Deu 28:57 **her afterbirth that comes out** from between her feet and her children whom she bears, because lacking everything **she will eat them secretly**, in the siege and in the distress with which your enemy shall distress you in your towns.

Deu 28:64 "And the LORD will **scatter you among all peoples**, from one end of the earth to the other, and there you shall serve other gods of wood and stone, which neither you nor your fathers have known.

Deu 28:65 And among these nations you shall find no respite, and there shall be no resting place for the sole of your foot, but the LORD will give you there a trembling heart and failing eyes and a languishing soul.

Now as shockingly accurate as this is, I want you to notice something else. Notice what it says in Leviticus 26:18, 21, 24, and 28:

Lev 26:18 And if in spite of this you will not listen to me, then I will discipline you again **sevenfold for your sins,**

Lev 26:21 "Then if you walk contrary to me and will not listen to me, I will continue striking you, **sevenfold for your sins.**

Lev 26:24 then I also will walk contrary to you, and I myself will strike you **sevenfold for your sins.**

Lev 26:28 then I will walk contrary to you in fury, and I myself will discipline you **sevenfold for your sins.**

Not just once does he say this in the chapter, but **four times**! And yes, there is significance even in this. It is **not** just happenstance that he would mention this four times in Leviticus. Notice the words of the prophets in other judgments that would happen in Israel's future:

Jer 15:3 I will appoint over them four kinds of destroyers, declares the LORD: the sword to kill, the dogs to tear, and the birds of the air and the beasts of the earth to devour and destroy.

Eze 14:21 "For thus says the Lord GOD: How much more when I send upon Jerusalem my four disastrous acts of judgment, sword, famine, wild beasts, and pestilence, to cut off from it man and beast!

So as we can see from this, the numbers **four** and **seven** have **profound significance** when looking through the Bible's prophetic history, and it is no different in looking at the last book of the Bible. In fact, we find this scenario fully developed in the book of Revelation, for there are **four sets of seven** present in its pages. These are:

1. The letters to the **Seven** churches;
2. The book containing the opening of the **Seven** Seals;
3. The sounding of the **Seven** Trumpets;
4. The judgment of the **Seven** Bowls of Wrath.

Thus we see that the structure is the same. The use of the numbers four and seven are once again used in the final prophecy of the Bible. These match the prophecy given to the Apostle John.

Thus, we can make an outline for the book of Revelation as follows:

1. Introduction
   a. An opening statement of the Revelation of Jesus Christ (1:1-3)
      i. A definitive time statement that this would happen **soon.**
      ii. A blessing for those who read and hear, for the time is **near.**
   b. Introduction to the message John was to send to the **seven** churches (1:4-7)
      i. Jesus now in a position of power and glory.
      ii. Soon to be coming in the clouds of Glory.
      iii. He is the Alpha and the Omega, Lord and God of all!
   c. The Island of Patmos Vision
      i. A command to write that which he is about to see, including the fact that this **is written for** the seven churches.
      ii. An astounding vision of the glorified Jesus, profoundly testifying that he is now the glorious King of Kings and Lord of Lords.

iii. He is no longer a man. He has now returned to his glory as God the Son.

2. The Letters to the churches (2:1-3:22)
   a. Ephesus (2:1-7)
   b. Smyrna (2:8-11)
   c. Pergamum (2:12-17)
   d. Thyatira (2:18-29)
   e. Sardis (3:1-6)
   f. Philadelphia (3:7-13)
   g. Laodicea (3:14-22)
3. The Throne Room in Heaven (4:1-5:14)
   a. The scene in heaven
   b. A vision of the throne
   c. The book of the seven seals
   d. The appearance of the Lion who was also the Lamb who is worthy
   e. The worship of the Lamb of God
4. Judgment (6:1-14:19)
   a. The seven seals (6:1-8:5)
   b. The seven trumpet judgments (8:6-11:19)
   c. The ouster of Satan (12:1-17
   d. The beasts (13:1-18)
   e. The Lamb and the 144,000 (14:1-5)
   f. The Gospel and the wine of wrath (14:6-13)
   g. The harvest for wrath (14:14-19)
5. Victory in Heaven (15:1-19:21)
   a. The bowls
   b. Babylon's doom
   c. The Lambs victory
   d. The marriage of the Lamb
   e. The doom of the false prophets
6. Satan bound, freed, and judged (20:1-15)
7. New heaven and new earth (21:1-27)
8. The river of the water of life, The tree of life (22:1-9)
9. The final message (22:10-21)
   a. Do not seal up – **The time is near**

b. Plagues given for adding to or taking away from
   the book
c. **Jesus coming quickly – repeated twice**

Considering that the subject of this book concerns proof that we can depend on God's promise of redemption, it is beyond the scope of this book to do an exegesis of the book of Revelation. However, there are a few things that must be said. The Revelation given to John by Jesus contains the Lord's greatest prophecy, which though the use of much figurative and symbolical dress, he has expanded, and as others have said, dramatized. As Preston noted earlier, the same facts and events which are predicted in the Gospels are shown in the Revelation, only clothed in symbology. In the words of James Stuart Russell:

> They pass before us like scenes exhibited by the magic lantern, magnified and illuminated, but not on that account the less real and truthful. In this view the Apocalypse becomes the supplement to the gospel, and gives completeness to the record of the evangelist.[10]

But the Revelation does contain its own set of bookends which restrict the time period. It opens and closes with words telling those to whom it was written that the events were about to happen. This fits closely with the events given by the Lord Jesus in his greatest prophecy in the Olivet Discourse. Indeed, the outline presented earlier by Don Preston makes it clear that this is indeed the expanded, dramatized version of it dressed in symbolic language not at all foreign to the recipients of the message. **Precisely as expounded** in the warning in Leviticus 26, the judgment upon Israel contains **four sets of seven judgments**. This shows the power and harmony of God's words throughout all of his written word.

The Dispensationalists say that the Revelation depicts events entirely in our future after chapter three. The Amillenialists say the dividing line is in chapter 20. However, we see that the "bookends" restrict the time period to the first century. There is no question that by the way the book starts and ends, it is meant to have occurred soon in its entirety to those to whom it was written, thus it is a fulfilled prophecy, and stands as a single unit. It was given to the seven churches. This was the audience. They were undergoing severe persecution and needed the encouraging words given to the Apostle by the Lord Jesus.

When speaking of timelines, however, we must not overlook the fact that John was told in Revelation chapter ten something very unique:

> Rev 10:8 Then the voice which I heard from heaven, *I heard* again speaking with me, and saying, "Go, take the book which is open in the hand of the angel who stands on the sea and on the land."
> Rev 10:9 So I went to the angel, telling him to give me the little book. And he said to me, "Take it and eat it; it will make your stomach bitter, but in your mouth it will be sweet as honey."
> Rev 10:10 I took the little book out of the angel's hand and ate it, and in my mouth it was sweet as honey; and when I had eaten it, my stomach was made bitter.
> Rev 10:11 And they said to me, "**You must prophesy again** concerning many peoples and nations and tongues and kings."

Concerning this passage, commentator Henry Alford (1810-1871) stated:

> It remains that we say something on the circumstances accompanying the Apostle's reception of the mysterious book. Its *sweetness*, when he tasted it, allusive as it is to the same circumstance in Ezekiel's eating the roll which was all lamentation, mourning, and woe, doubtless represents present satisfaction at being informed of, and admitted to know, a portion of God's holy will: of those words of which the Psalmist said, Psa_119:103, "How sweet are thy words unto my taste, yea sweeter than honey unto my mouth!" But when the roll came to be not only tasted, but digested,—the nature of its contents felt within the man,—bitterness took the place of sweetness: the persecutions, the apostasies, the judgments, of the church and people of the Lord, saddened the spirit of the Seer, and dashed his

joy at the first reception of the mystery of God.[11]

But just exactly what is the meaning of verse eleven as stated here? Could it mean that John would write again? Or does it mean that the book is timeless in its application? Could it be that the Revelation given to John was the beginning of his writing? Could it be that Divine providence saw to it that John felt the bitterness of the apostasies that were occurring in the church, thus, inspiring him to continue his writing which included prophesying?

We have no way of knowing for certain. However, I would like to propose the following solution to this dilemma. Since we **do not** know the order in which John wrote his books, could it be that John **was given the Revelation first?** Could it be that this is what compelled him to write his Gospel account and the other epistles which contained prophecies?

Note this quotation from Eusebius:

> 5. Again, in the same books, Clement gives the tradition of the earliest presbyters, as to the order of the Gospels, in the following manner:

> 6. The Gospels containing the genealogies, he says, were written first. The Gospel according to Mark had this occasion. As Peter had preached the Word publicly at Rome, and declared the Gospel by the Spirit, many who were present requested that Mark, who had followed him for a long time and remembered his sayings, should write them out. And having composed the Gospel he gave it to those who had requested it.

> 7. When Peter learned of this, he neither directly forbade nor encouraged it. **But, last of all, John,** perceiving that the external facts had been made plain in the Gospel, being urged by his friends, and inspired by the Spirit, composed a spiritual Gospel. This is the account of Clement.[12]

Since there is no way of dating any of these writings, it could be that John was given the Revelation first, then in view of what he saw in the Christian community prior to fleeing to the mountains, he wrote the three general epistles, and finally, long after the

Synoptic Gospels were written, he was given inspiration to write an entirely different Gospel, which is the Gospel of John.

So now we have examined in these last few chapters the truth that every one of those who wrote in the New Testament were soundly convinced that the Last Days, as Jesus laid out in the Olivet Discourse was indeed the generation that lived after the time when Jesus walked the earth and went to the cross.

The prophecy pundits have continued to pour out new theories of how the Last Days are still in our future for over a hundred years now, and every one of them has proven false. Jesus did in fact return in that first century generation. He returned in the same manner as he has always returned. And as we have seen in numerous passages in the Old Testament, **this did not mean** that he was **literally and physically** returning to the earth in a human body. He did exactly as he told them. It is similar to the warning of Jeremiah in chapter 4 when Nebuchadnezzar was soon his instrument of destruction:

> Jer 4:13 Behold, he shall come up like clouds, and his chariots like a tempest. His horses are swifter than eagles. Woe to us, for we are plundered!
> Jer 4:14 O Jerusalem, cleanse your heart from evil so that you may be saved. Until when will your vain thoughts lodge within you? (LITV)

He returned again **in the clouds**, using as his instrument of destruction another physical kingdom that was present at the time. This time he used the Roman legions to bring an end to the sacrificial, Levitical system of government and worship.

In the past, it was a temporary end. This time it was permanent. Following the destruction of Jerusalem by the Romans in AD 70, there was now **no place on the face of the earth** where anyone could carry out the rituals of the old covenant. And that circumstance has prevailed for the past two thousand years. Yes, after centuries of disobedience, this end was permanent. The prophet Jeremiah was given a similar description of the harlotry with which Jerusalem is charged in this Revelation to John. Note the words:

> Jer 3:6 Then the LORD said to me in the days of Josiah the king, "Have you seen what faithless Israel did? She went up on every high hill and under every green tree, and she was a harlot there.
> Jer 3:7 "I thought, 'After she has done all these things she will return to Me'; but she did not return, and her treacherous sister Judah saw it.
> Jer 3:8 "And I saw that for all the adulteries of faithless Israel, I had sent her away and given her a writ of divorce, yet her treacherous sister Judah did not fear; but she went and was a harlot also.

The Revelation to John confirmed the nature of Jerusalem's harlotry, and likewise pronounced judgment, a **permanent judgment**. Thus, we are now living in the new covenant, a covenant of Grace in which we are promised eternal life for those who believe. Jesus himself made this promise when he said in John 5:24:

> Truly, truly, I say to you, he who hears my word, and **believes** Him who sent me, has eternal life, and does not come into judgment, but has passed out of death into life.

This is not easy believeism, as some would have you think. As James pointed out in his epistle, the fact is that our faith is made evident by our works. We cannot under any circumstances con the God of the universe. He reads our hearts. But we can humble ourselves and put our complete confidence in him because our Lord Jesus has **always done WHAT** he said he would do, **WHEN** he said he would do it!

The promise of redemption **was REAL!** The fulfillment **was REAL!** The Revelation given to the Apostle John by our Lord reiterates the fact that our Lord was intent on keeping this promise of redemption which has proven to be the theme of the

Bible. The details of the redemption are elaborated on in the ninth chapter of the book of Hebrews. In the next chapter, we will take the time to look at this fulfillment.

NOTES

1. Before Jerusalem Fell, Dating the book of Revelation, Third Edition, copyright by Gentry Family Trust, udt April 2, 1999, Victorious Hope publishing, Fountain Inn, SC
2. *Against Heresies*, Book 5, Chapter 30, section 3, By Irenaeus of Lyons, http://www.newadvent.org/fathers/0103530.htm
3. Against Heresies, Book 2, chapter 22, section 5, By Irenaeus of Lyons, http://www.newadvent.org/fathers/0103222.htm
4. D. Div., Don K. Preston (2012-06-17). Who Is This Babylon? (Kindle Locations 925-935). JaDon Management Inc.. Kindle Edition.
5. Adam Clarke's Commentary on the Bible, taken from e-Sword, Version 10.2.1, 2013, Rick Meyers (Free download at www.e-sword.net)
6. Welton, Jonathan (2013-11-01). Raptureless: An Optimistic Guide to the End of the World - Revised Edition Including The Art of Revelation (Kindle Locations 4468-4472). BookBaby. Kindle Edition. "
7. Meek, Charles S. (2014-11-24). Christian Hope through Fulfilled Prophecy: An Exposition of Evangelical Preterism (Kindle Locations 2796-2806). BookBaby. Kindle Edition.
8. D. Div., Don K. Preston (2012-06-17). Who Is This Babylon? (Kindle Locations 145-156). JaDon Management Inc.. Kindle Edition.
9. Ibid.
10. Russell, James Stuart (2013-12-13). Parousia: The New Testament Doctrine of Our Lord's Second Coming (Kindle Locations 4681-4685) Kindle Edition.
11. Henry Alford's Greek Testament, taken from e-Sword, Version 10.2.1, 2013, Rick Meyers (Free download at www.e-sword.net)
12. (Ecclesiastical History, Eusebius, 6.14.5,6,7) http://www.newadvent.org/fathers/250106.htm

13. Taken from "Introduction to Revelation" under "The Direct Historical Evidence" (near the end) from Albert Barnes' Commentary on the Bible. Taken from e-Sword, Version 10.2.1, 2013, Rick Meyers (Free download at www.e-sword.net)

Chapter 11

God's Promise of Redemption

From the previous chapters, we have seen that we can trust the promises of our Lord. As we mentioned in the previous chapter, the book of Hebrews is all about the supremacy of Christ, but it also gives us huge insight on the fulfilment of the promise of redemption. In this chapter I would like to focus on _God's promise of redemption_ which is a thread throughout the entire Bible. Chapter nine of Hebrews is a very big key to understanding the amazing grace with which we have been blessed. The writer of Hebrews gives a detailed description of the priestly duties relating to sacrifices required by the old covenant law. The reiteration of these duties helps us to understand what Christ has done for us. First I would like to give a little background for chapter nine.

In chapter 8 verse 1-5, we learned what the writer of Hebrews had to say about the eternal priesthood of Christ. In verses 6-9 we learned of the superiority of the new covenant to the old. In verses 10-12, we looked at the predictions of the prophets with regard to how this new covenant will affect people in the future in a positive way. And finally in verse 13 we heard the writer say that with the establishment of this new covenant, the old covenant is becoming obsolete.

Now as we begin chapter 9 of Hebrews, we will see the writer emphasizing the superiority of Christ's ministry and sacrifice, and how there is no match for the blood of Christ in terms of what it will do for humanity in its sinfulness. As men must die once and be judged, so Christ was **offered once** to bear the sins of many, and shall come again, but this time, _not_ for the purpose of dealing with sin, _but to save those_ who are eagerly awaiting his presence.

> Heb 9:1 Truly, then, the first _covenant_ also had ordinances of service, and the earthly holy place.
>
> Heb 9:2 For the first tabernacle was prepared, in which _was_ both the lampstand and the table, and the setting out of the loaves, which is called holy.
>
> Heb 9:3 But behind the second veil _is_ a tabernacle, being called Holy of Holies,
>
> Heb 9:4 having a golden altar of incense, and the ark of the covenant covered around on all sides with gold, in which _was_ the golden pot having the manna, and Aaron's rod that budded, and the tablets of the covenant;
>
> Heb 9:5 and above it _the_ cherubs of glory overshadowing the mercy-seat (about which now is not _enough time_ to speak piece by piece). (LITV)

The writer of Hebrews noted here that the service that men can offer is only a shadow of the real service which Jesus, the real high priest, alone can offer. But even as he thinks about this, his mind goes back to the tabernacle, which preceded the temple. He is thinking, if earthly service was just a shadow of the reality, then the reality must be incredible.

The tabernacle was divided into two parts. The first part, which was actually two-thirds of the whole--was the holy place. The inner part, the remaining one-third of the whole--a cube, approximately 15 feet on each side, was the Holy of Holies. The curtain which hung in front of the holy place was supported on five brass pillars and made of fine linen wrought in blue, purple and scarlet.

In front of the Holy of Holies there was the veil which was made of fine, twined linen, embroidered in scarlet and purple and blue, and with the cherubim upon it. But no one was ever to go into the Holy of Holies, that is, no one but the high priest. Yes, and then **only once a year** on atonement day, and only after the most elaborate preparations. Within the Holy of Holies stood the ark of the covenant. It contained three things--the golden pot of the manna, Aaron's rod that budded, and the tablets of the law. It was made of acacia wood sheathed outside and lined inside with gold. It was 3 feet 9 inches long, 2 feet 3 inches wide, and 2 feet 3 inches high. Its lid was called the mercy seat. On the mercy seat there were two cherubim of solid gold with overarching wings. It was there that the very presence of God rested, for he had said: "There I will meet with you, and from above the mercy seat, from between the two cherubim that are upon the ark of the testimony" (Exo.25:22).

Now, even after this description, I know you are thinking that it is hard to imagine what we just described. But the point here is this: **It was only a shadow of reality!** Yes with all of its beauty, and lavishly detailed golden coverings, the Holy of Holies was **merely a shadow of the reality in heaven.** But what is even more important to get the grasp of is that **in his great love and mercy,** our loving God sent his only begotten Son **to die** on the cross to take away that barrier and open wide the way to God's presence for those who believe. It is an incredible act of love!

Heb 9:6 And these having been prepared thus, the priests go into the first tabernacle through all, completing the services.
Heb 9:7 But into the second the high priest *goes* alone once *in* the year, not without blood, which he offers for himself and the ignorances of the people;
Heb 9:8 the Holy Spirit signifying *by* this *that* the way of the *Holy of* Holies has not yet been made manifest, the first tabernacle still having *been* standing;

Heb 9:9 which *was* a parable for the present time, according to which both gifts and sacrifices are offered, *but* as regards conscience, not being able to perfect the *one* serving,
Heb 9:10 but only on foods and drinks, and various washings, and fleshly ordinances, until *the* time of setting things right has been imposed. (LITV)

So the writer now is taking us back to the priestly duties. In verse 6 we see the priest regularly going into "the holy" which we just described to perform his ritual duties. Then in verse 7, we see him going into the "Holy of Holies" only on one day a year, and that is strictly for the purpose of making atonement for the people.

Let's take a look at what would happen on atonement day. I think it's important to do this because we need to understand this elaborate ritual. First, I want to warn you that this is going to be a very graphic description of a very bloody ritual. But this is what the Israelite people had to live with as a part of the law. The high priest began by doing the things that were done every day. He burned the morning incense, made the morning sacrifice, and attended to the trimming of the lamps on the seven-branched lampstand. Next he sacrificed a bull, seven lambs and one ram (Num.29:7). Sounds disgusting, doesn't it?

Then he removed his elaborately designed robes, which were to be made exactly as described in Exodus 28, cleansed himself again in water, and dressed himself in the simple purity of white linen. Following this, a bull was brought to him, and it is important to note that the high priest was required to pay for this bull out of his personal funds. At this point, he placed his hands on its head and, standing there in the full sight of the people, confessed his own sin and the sin of his house. Then, for the moment the bull was left before the altar, and he went over to the two goats which were standing by. One lot was marked **for Yahweh**; the other was marked **for Azazel**, which is the scapegoat. The lots were drawn and laid one on the head of each goat. A tongue-shaped piece of scarlet was tied to the horn of the scapegoat. And, once again, for the moment the goats were left.

Then the high priest turned to the bull which was beside the altar and killed it by slitting its throat. The blood of the animal was then caught in a basin. The basin had to be continually stirred so that the blood would not coagulate. This was because it was to be used, but not yet.

I hope, at this point you are still with me!

The next part of the ritual was very important. The high priest took coals from the altar and put them in a censer; he took incense and put it in a special dish; and then he walked into the Holy of Holies to burn incense in the very presence of God. Can you imagine **how scary this must have been**, to literally be in the presence of God inside a 15 foot square area? In fact, it was said that he must not stay too long "lest he put Israel in terror." Yes, it is true that the people literally watched with scary anticipation; and when he came out from the presence of God still alive, they let out a big sigh of relief.

When the high priest came out from the Holy of Holies, he took the basin of the bull's blood, went back into the Holy of Holies and sprinkled it seven times up and seven times down. He came out, killed the goat that was marked for Yahweh, and with its blood re-entered the Holy of Holies and sprinkled again. Then he came out and mingled together the blood of the bullock and the goat and seven times sprinkled the horns of the altar of the incense and the altar itself. What remained of the blood was laid at the foot of the altar of the burnt offering. Thus the Holy of Holies and the altar were cleansed by blood from any defilement that might be on them.

Is this too much detail? ***Sorry, but there is still a lot more to do!***

Next is a most interesting aspect of the ceremony. The scapegoat was brought forward. The high priest laid his hands on it and confessed his own sin and the sin of the people; and the goat was led away into the desert, laden with the sins of the people and there it was killed.

After this, the priest turned to the slain bull and goat and prepared them for sacrifice. Still in his linen garments he read Scripture--Lev.16; Lev.23:27-32, and repeated by heart Num.29:7-11. He then prayed for the priesthood and the people. Then, once again he cleansed himself in water and put on the elaborate robes of the high priest. He sacrificed, first, a kid of the goats for the sins of the people, followed by the normal evening sacrifice; then he sacrificed the already prepared parts of the bull and the goat. Then once again he cleansed himself, took off his robes, and put on the white linen; and for the fourth and last time he entered the Holy of Holies to remove the censer of incense which still burned there. Once again he cleansed himself in water and put on his elaborate priestly robes. Then he burned the evening offering of incense, trimmed the lamps on the golden lampstand, and his work was done. In the evening he held a feast because he had been in the presence of God and had come out alive.

Wow! What a ritual! You can read this elaborate ceremony in **Leviticus chapter 16.** But now as detailed and elaborate as this is, **I do not want you to miss the point!**

The writer of Hebrews was establishing the point that this elaborate ceremony had to be gone through again and again and again, every year. And through all of this ceremony, the sacrifice **was still** that of bulls and goats and animal blood, and would not have atoned for sin **except for one thing.** It pointed to the **ONE AND ONLY true sacrifice--the sacrifice of Christ!** Yes! The **ONLY** priest and the only sacrifice which can open the way to God for all men is the sacrifice of the Lamb of God – the promised Messiah, Jesus Christ!

Let us continue with this chapter:

> Heb 9:11 But when Christ appeared *as* a high priest of the good things to come, *He entered* through the greater and more perfect tabernacle, not made with hands, that is to say, not of this creation;
> Heb 9:12 and not through the blood of goats and calves, but through **His own blood**, He entered the holy place **once for all**, having obtained eternal redemption.
> Heb 9:13 For if the blood of goats and bulls and the ashes of a heifer sprinkling those who have been defiled sanctify for the cleansing of the flesh,
> Heb 9:14 how much more will the blood of Christ, who through the eternal Spirit offered Himself without blemish to God, cleanse your conscience from dead works to serve the living God?

When we try to understand this passage, we must remember some things which are basic to the thought of the writer to the Hebrews. The tabernacle was replaced by the temple during the life of King Solomon. Thus, the temple became the way for the Jews to draw close to God. However, this temple and its worship were only a shadow of the "greater and more perfect tent" as described here in verse 11. Access to God demands absolute purity; and this is something man is incapable of giving, and the animal sacrifices would not suffice. Additionally, as the book of Hebrews is being written, there is on the timeline just ahead a horrific event that is about to take place. The magnificent temple as well as the entire city of Jerusalem are about to be reduced to rubble.

And now in verse 12, the writer of Hebrews goes on to show that Jesus is the only high priest who brings a sacrifice that can open the way to God, and that **that sacrifice is himself.** Therefore, when Christ presents his precious blood in heaven, there will no longer be need of a physical temple.

In addition to the very elaborate ceremony we described earlier, there was another ceremony mentioned in verse 13 here. This was the sacrifice of the red heifer, which we find outlined in detail in Numbers chapter 19. This ritual was performed for the situation where a man touched a dead body. In this case, he was considered by Jewish ceremonial law to be unclean. As such, he was not allowed to worship, and everything and everyone he touched also became unclean. The priest was told to slaughter a red heifer outside the camp, then he sprinkled the blood of the heifer before the tabernacle seven times. After this, the body of the animal was then burned, together with cedar and hyssop and a piece of red cloth. Its ashes were then put in a clean place and were used as purification for sin. Thus, the ashes were kept in a clean place for the cleansing ritual when a man touched the body of a dead person.

But what is being expressed in verse 14 is that the sacrifice that Jesus takes to the altar in heaven is profoundly greater and more effective. As it says in the verse, these sacrifices did not deal with something very important, and that is the guilty consciences of those who sin. No animal blood could cleanse that. So now in verse 14 a new high priest comes—Jesus the Son of God—with **a better sacrifice,** the sacrifice of himself. As the verse says:

> Heb 9:14 how much more will the blood of Christ, who through the eternal Spirit offered Himself without blemish to God, cleanse your conscience from dead works to serve the living God?

Yes, God gave us something called a conscience that becomes guilty when we sin. But isn't it wonderful to know that the sacrifice of our Lord Jesus reaches back to cover all the sins of God's people in the past, and also reaches forward to cover all the sins of God's people in the future! Therefore, when your conscience condemns you, Hebrew 9:14 gives you the answer: _**Turn to the blood of Christ.**_ This is, indeed, the only thing in the universe that can cleanse you and give you relief. Praise God for his awesome goodness in this provision to all of us!

Continuing in verse 15:

> Heb 9:15 For this reason He is the mediator of a new covenant, so that, since a death has taken place **for the redemption** of the transgressions that were *committed* under the first covenant, those who have been called may receive **the promise** of the eternal inheritance.

So now we have mentioned here a _**new covenant!**_ When our Lord died, and became that "Lamb of God that takes away the sin of the world," **HE** became that mediator of the new covenant. And when he entered the Holy of Holies in heaven to present his own blood, _**HE fulfilled the promise of redemption**_ from the transgressions which have separated us from God and have rendered us spiritually dead! This redemption was effective retroactively for those faithful ones under the first covenant. Yes, the blood of bulls and goats, which was only a stop gap measure anyway, was no longer necessary. Praise God for his awesome grace to us!

> Heb 9:16 For where a covenant is, there must of necessity be the death of the one who made it.
> Heb 9:17 For a covenant is valid *only* when men are dead, for it is never in force while the one who made it lives.
> Heb 9:18 Therefore even the first *covenant* was not inaugurated without blood.

If you will recall, this new covenant was the arrangement with his people that God promised in Jeremiah 31:31-34.

> Jer 31:31 "Behold, the days are coming, declares the LORD, when **I will make a new covenant** with the house of Israel and the house of Judah,
> Jer 31:32 not like the covenant that I made with their fathers on the day when I took them by the hand to bring them out of the land of Egypt, my covenant that they broke, though I was their husband, declares the LORD.

Jer 31:33 For this is the covenant that I will make with the house of Israel after those days, declares the LORD: I will put my law within them, and I will write it on their hearts. And I will be their God, and they shall be my people.

Jer 31:34 And no longer shall each one teach his neighbor and each his brother, saying, 'Know the LORD,' for they shall all know me, from the least of them to the greatest, declares the LORD. For I will forgive their iniquity, and I will remember their sin no more." (ESV)

The writer of the book of Hebrews quotes the terms of this covenant in Hebrews 8:10-13. Notice what it says:

Heb 8:10 Because this *is* the covenant which I will covenant with the house of Israel after those days, says *the* Lord, giving My Laws into their mind, and I will write them on their hearts, and I will be their God, and they shall be My people."

Heb 8:11 "And they shall no more teach each one their neighbor, and each one his brother, saying, Know the Lord; because all shall know Me, from the least of them to their great ones.

Heb 8:12 For I will be merciful to their unrighteousnesses, and I will not at all remember their sins and their lawless deeds." *LXX-Jer. 38:31-34; MT-Jer. 31:31-34*

Heb 8:13 In the saying, New, He has made the first old. And the thing being made old and growing aged *is* near disappearing. (LITV)

The message written to these Hebrew Christians also has application to us today. Yes, as this passage implies, the will of God is written on the hearts of people by the movement of the indwelling power of the Holy Spirit. He changes us from the inside out so that **his will becomes a part of our being.** And in verse 12 we see that in the new covenant he is merciful to our transgressions and remembers our sins no more.

Just look at the power of this! In the old covenant there was really _no sacrifice_ that could truly take away the sins of the people. Yes, there were animal sacrifices, and blood was poured out, but Hebrews 10:4 says plainly, "It is impossible for the blood of bulls and goats to take away sin." But now, the new covenant promises that these sins will be completely taken away by the supreme sacrifice of God's own Son. This applies to past, present and future sins.

So when we look closely at the new covenant, we see that it is all about how God deals with sin to make us right with him. But additionally it is how he deals with the guilt and condemnation of sin. As previously stated, God sent his Son to die for sinners and bear our guilt so that there could be forgiveness and cleansing, and good consciences before God. In a nutshell, that's the new covenant. That's Christianity. And the death of Christ, the shedding of Christ's blood, is the basis of it. By God's amazing grace, and the gift of his Son to die for us, John the Baptist called it correctly when he saw Jesus coming to him:

John 1:29 The next day he saw Jesus coming toward him, and said, "Behold, the Lamb of God, who takes away the sin of the world!

And as John prophesied, that sacrifice included the shedding of **HIS** innocent blood. With it our justification was purchased, and it allowed for the process of our sanctification. He took away our guilt and he is in the process of taking away our corruption as we struggle to live the Christian life.

Heb 9:19 For *when* every command had been spoken according to Law by Moses to all the people, having taken the blood of the calves and goats, with water and scarlet wool and hyssop, and he sprinkled both the scroll and all the people,
Heb 9:20 saying, "This *is* the blood of the covenant which God enjoined to you." Ex. 24:8
Heb 9:21 And he likewise sprinkled both the tabernacle and all the service vessels with the blood.
Heb 9:22 And almost all things are purified by blood according to the Law; and apart from shedding of blood no remission occurs. (LITV)

During the time of Moses and the old covenant, it was the custom of the day to purify most everything by blood. Almost everything in the tabernacle and temple service was consecrated or purified by blood. No sins were pardoned except by the shedding of blood. This has been a universal rule as stated in God's word. When we search the Scriptures, we will find **not one case** of sins being forgiven apart from the shedding of blood. Even when Jesus himself forgave sins, it was on the basis of the **future shedding** of his own blood. It is the basis of God's plan of salvation for mankind. It is as Peter said:

> Act 4:11 This Jesus is the stone that was rejected by you, the builders, which has become the cornerstone.
> Act 4:12 And there is salvation in no one else, **for there is no other name under heaven given among men by which we must be saved."**

Now as we continue with chapter nine, we read:

> Heb 9:23 Then *it was* needful for the figures of the things in the heavens to be cleansed *with* these; but the heavenly things themselves by better sacrifices than these.
> Heb 9:24 For Christ did not enter into *the Holy of* Holies made by hands, types of the true things, **but into Heaven itself**, now to appear in the presence of God on our behalf,
> Heb 9:25 not that He should often **offer Himself** even as the high priest enters into the *Holy of* Holies year by year with blood of others;
> Heb 9:26 since He must often have suffered from *the* foundation of the world. But now once for all, at the completion of the ages, He has been manifested **for putting away of sin through the sacrifice of Himself.** (LITV)

So from this passage it is clear that it was in the mind of God that the death of his Son, Jesus Christ, be foreshadowed and anticipated in history among the Jewish people through their animal sacrifices and through the tabernacle and temple worship. The writer says in verse 23 that these earthly things such as the temple, and all of its paraphernalia were all "copies" of an even greater reality in heaven. As copies they could be ceremonially cleansed by blood from the sacrifices of calves and goats. But even though God sanctioned this activity, we are told in verse 23 that these kinds of sacrifices are utterly inadequate to deal with what ultimately matters: not the copies, but the "heavenly things themselves."

So in order to deal with the heavenly things themselves and to cleanse them, there will have to be "better sacrifices." These "better sacrifices" are what Christ offered once when he died on that cross and became as John 1:29 says: "the Lamb of God that takes away the sin of the world." And with this final great offering, verse 24 says, Christ "has entered, not into holy places made with hands, which are copies of the true things, but into heaven itself, now to appear in the presence of God on our behalf."

The words "on our behalf" give us the key to why there has to be cleansing in heaven. **We are going to be there.** Isn't that wonderful! But this cleansing is because we are the ones who will be there, and we will be cleansed. The blood of God's Son was shed for **YOU**. Accept him, put your trust in him, and receive the gift of eternal life.

There was also a very timely lesson here for the Jewish believers. Although the temple was still standing, and although these words were written before the destruction of Jerusalem and the temple, this system of worship was in its last days. As the writer of Hebrews had already stated in chapter 8 and verse 13:

> Heb 8:13 In speaking of a new covenant, he makes _the first one obsolete_. And what is becoming obsolete and growing old _is ready to vanish away._

Yes, they were on the very verge of this event. The old covenant was about to pass away.

As we look at verse 25 and 26 we also see something important. God is holy and pure and perfectly just and righteous. He hates sin and lives in absolute perfection. Yet here we learn how such a great and holy God can and does welcome defiled people like you and me into his presence. How can this be? Answering this question is what history is all about.

Verse 25 tells us that Christ's sacrifice for sin was **NOT** like the sacrifices of the Jewish high priests. They came into the holy place **every year** with animal sacrifices to atone for the sins of the people. If Christ followed the pattern of the priests, then he would have to **die every year**. But no, this was not the case. Verse 26 tells us that Christ only had to appear **once** to atone for the sins of men everywhere.

But I want to call attention to the fact that there are four aspects of this sacrifice that show the glory of Christ in these verses:

1. He says that Christ did this great work "_ONCE_" not repeatedly. It is enough to cover the rest of eternity! It goes on year after year, century after century doing what it was designed to do, save sinners and present them faultless to God.

2. Verse 26 says that "he has appeared once for all at the end of the ages." The death of Jesus is not just one event in a line of similar historical events. **It is the biggest event in the history of man!** It is not just another merely human event. It is the consummation of history.

3. Verse 26 also says Christ **sacrificed himself**, not the blood of another. This underlines the supremacy of Christ again. Not only was his sacrifice once for all. Not only did it mark the consummation of the ages, **it was a sacrifice of the most valuable person in the universe - the Christ, the Son of God**. If you ever doubt that you as a sinner could be made clean before God, just compare your sin to Christ's blood. There is no comparison!! Acts 20:28 states that God

purchased the church **with his own blood**. And as the hymn says: _Christ's blood is greater than all of our sin._

4. Finally, verse 26 says that Christ gave himself once for all at the end of the ages "to put away sin." Yes! **_Christ has completely dealt with this problem of sin!_** The whole sin issue is taken care of. _It is put away._ In one act—the sacrifice of himself, the consummation of history—the Son of God put away sin. All the sins of those who believe are canceled, nullified, and covered.

Let's move on to the last 2 verses of this chapter.

> Heb 9:27 And just as it is appointed for man to die once, and after that comes judgment,
> Heb 9:28 so Christ, having been offered once to bear the sins of many, will appear a second time, not to deal with sin but to save those who are eagerly waiting for him. (ESV)

Notice that there are 2 things mentioned here:

The first one is that we all have an appointment with death. "It is appointed for men to die." Who made this appointment with death? God made it. So death is not an appointment that comes to us only by natural processes. No, our appointment with death comes to us at the divinely appointed moment. God plans our birthday and our death day. Notice what it says in Psalm 139:16

> Psa 139:16 Your eyes have seen my unformed substance; And in Your book were all written The days that were ordained _for me_, When as yet there was not one of them.

Yes, there are a certain number of days ordained for me by God. God sets this appointment, not my health, not my enemies, and not me. But not only that, God sees to it that we keep the appointment. He plans it and he brings it to pass. You recall how Job said, when his children were killed during his time of testing by Satan, "The LORD gave and the LORD has taken away. Blessed be the name of the LORD."(Job 1:21) This reiterates the fact that God is in control – not us.

But did you notice that there is another key word here besides the word "appointed," namely the word "once." This means that there is no such thing as reincarnation. God is not going to bring us back in some other form depending on our karma so that we can die again. We die only one time here on earth. But why do you suppose that the writer of Hebrews put the word "once" in here? I'll tell you why. It's because death is coming to us all and it is coming as sure as the sunrise in the morning! It is a huge event that we all have to face, and it is something to be taken seriously.

Notice the next phrase: "*and after that comes judgment*." Do you see what this means? It means that **_death is not the end of our existence_**. We are not going to just lay down, die, and cease to exist. There is more to come! When it makes the statement: "and after that comes judgment," it means just that. If you stop and think about it for a moment, it really is one of the most terrifying prospects we could possibly imagine! After all, we who are **sinful and defiled** are going to face a **holy God** who is going to hold us accountable for everything we have done. But as mentioned a few verses earlier, **IF** we have put our trust in the Lord Jesus, we have nothing to worry about. He **WILL** stand in the gap for us, and his blood is greater than all of our sin!

And finally, we see from verse 28, that it says Jesus will appear a second time. In fact it tells us that this appearing will be *for an entirely different reason* than the first appearing. Let's look at it again:

> Heb 9:28 so Christ, having been offered once to bear the sins of many, will appear a second time, **not to deal with sin but to save those who are eagerly waiting for him.**

Yes, it was *for those eagerly awaiting his return*! This included those heavily persecuted Christians to whom this letter was written.

There is no question that their Jewish brethren were those doing the persecuting. In his book: "Hebrews: From Flawed to Flawless Fulfilled!" Tony Denton describes it this way:

> The phrase eagerly wait for Him carries with it the idea of "intense yearning." And why would that be, especially in relation to these Hebrews? Because of their suffering of persecution by their Jewish brethren. But there's more. Since the original of the phrase a second time literally means "out of (ek) a/ the second" (no word for "time" being found in the original), this phrase (in this context of Jesus entering the most holy place with His blood, v. 24) obviously means that He was expected to reappear **out of the second place—the most holy place** (cf. 9:3). In other words, just as Aaron entered the most holy place with sin then reappeared without sin resulting in glory (Lev. 9:22-23), so Jesus entered Heaven with our sin and His cleansing blood, then reappeared without sin resulting in glory (salvation); *in fact, the Jonathan Mitchell New Testament (JMNT),* which takes great care in translating the original, *renders the part of this verse about Jesus' reappearance as His coming "forth from out of the midst of the second place." Bingo!* [1] (Emphasis mine)

Denton goes on to point out the significance of this:

> So what coming of Jesus is under consideration here? Well, in context it has reference to Christ's coming in AD 70. Why? Because Jesus' Day of Atonement work was completed within a generation— at the time of the end of the Old Covenant and the fully established New Covenant. (Essentially, one way to view this is that the old wife, Hagar, died at the cross when Deity became engaged to Sarah, Gal. 4: 21-31; then Deity married Sarah ca. AD 70.) When the work of high priest Jesus was accomplished in the true holiest of all and God had accepted His sacrifice on behalf of mankind , *He returned to once and for all time put an end to the Old Testament economy with all its remaining vestiges: Jerusalem, its temple, and its unacceptable sin-offerings which merely spit in the face of God's Son* (cf. Heb. 10:29); this AD 70 coming of Messiah brought to fruition the redemption of mankind in all its totality. [2] (Emphasis mine)

Denton, T. Everett (2011-12-15). Hebrews: From Flawed to Flawless Fulfilled! (pp. 176-177). ASiteForTheLord Publishing. Kindle Edition.

The beauty of this ninth chapter of Hebrews is that it gives the story of how our Lord Jesus _fulfills the promise of redemption_. When he presented HIS blood to God in the Holy of Holies in heaven, it was utterly and completely fulfilled.

Also important to the finality of this is the timing. Let me remind you of what our Lord told the disciples in Luke's version of the Olivet Discourse:

> Luk 21:28 "But when these things begin to take place, straighten up and lift up your heads, because your redemption is drawing near."

This means that the redemption provided by Jesus at the cross was not quite finished. It needed to have one more component, and Jesus himself pointed this out to the disciples on this occasion. That event was the Parousia, which did indeed happen during the generation that saw its beginning.

This agrees with what the Apostle Paul told Titus in his letter:

> Tit 2:13 looking for the blessed hope and the appearing of the glory of our great God and Savior, Christ Jesus,
> Tit 2:14 who gave Himself for us to redeem us from every lawless deed, and to purify for Himself a people for His own possession, zealous for good deeds.

Do you see what Paul is saying here? He is saying that the "appearing of the glory of our great God and Savior, Christ Jesus" completes the blessed hope! Thus, while Christ finished his work on earth by dying on the cross, there was still the promise of a return to complete the process of redemption.

There is also a parallel pointed out by Charles Meek that we do not want to miss:

> The salvation from *worldly* bondage by God in the Old Testament foreshadowed the ultimate salvation from the *spiritual* bondage of *sin*, *death*, and the *Law* brought by the Messiah (Isaiah 25:8-9; Hosea 13:14; Romans 11:25-27; 1 Corinthians 15:26). This salvation was initiated at the cross, but was not quite finished. The Exodus from Egypt and the forty-year period of wandering in the wilderness, foreshadowed the forty-year transition period of the first century, until full deliverance in AD 70.
>
> > This is a remarkable parallel that the reader should not miss. The Hebrew children escaped the *worldly* bondage of slavery in Egypt at the Exodus, but they did not reach their new home for forty years, after much trial and tribulation. In the first century, believers received their promised escape from *spiritual* bondage at the cross, but would enter their *new spiritual dwelling place*—the New Jerusalem/New Heaven and Earth (Revelation 7, 21)—about forty years later, after much trial and tribulation! [3]

It is clear that when Jesus proclaimed "it is finished" (John 19:30) he was finished with his work as the "Son of Man." But when he returned on the clouds as he promised the high priest (Matt. 26:62-64), at the end of the generation to which he spoke, our blessed hope as pointed out by the Apostle Paul was completed (Titus 2:13-14).

Praise God for his awesome goodness to us, and that we can trust his precious promises!

NOTES

1. Denton, T. Everett (2011-12-15). Hebrews: From Flawed to Flawless Fulfilled! (p. 176). ASiteForTheLord Publishing. Kindle Edition.
2. Denton, T. Everett (2011-12-15). Hebrews: From Flawed to Flawless Fulfilled! (pp. 176-177). ASiteForTheLord Publishing. Kindle Edition.
3. Meek, Charles, http://prophecyquestions.com/

Epilogue

God's Promise of Redemption
A story of fulfilled prophecy

God's promise of redemption was a real promise. It was the most important promise in history. The prophetess Anna described in Luke's Gospel account was focused on this promise. Why God saw fit to include the information about this little known prophetess in the book of Luke most likely had to do with her focus. She had a very powerful faith, an unshakeable faith. She was keenly focused on God's promise of redemption.

> Luk 2:38 At that very moment she came up and *began* giving thanks to God, and continued to speak of Him to all those who **were looking for the redemption of Jerusalem.**

From her response here it is obvious that she knew the origin of the promise. She very likely knew the prediction of the prophets. For example:

> Mic 5:2 "But as for you, Bethlehem Ephrathah, *Too* little to be among the clans of Judah, From you One will go forth for Me to be ruler in Israel. His goings forth are from long ago, From the days of eternity."

But as we have discussed in this volume, God had a plan, not a contingency plan. Being omniscient, God knew what would happen in the garden with Adam and Eve. His plan started to unfold in a big way with Abraham. As God made his promise of a great nation come to pass, he put his blessing on Abraham's descendants, the nation of Israel. Using Moses to lead them out of slavery in Egypt, he led them to the land of promise. Moses was not allowed to take them into the Promised Land, but another man was anointed to take over for Moses, a man renamed Joshua by Moses. (Num. 13:16)

By anointing him, Moses obeyed God. Joshua, whose name is the same in Hebrew as Jesus, was **not** named such **by accident.** The name signifies saved, a savior, or the salvation of Jehovah, referring, no doubt, to his being God's instrument in saving the people from the hands of their enemies, and leading them from victory to victory over the different nations inside the land. Eventually they came to be in possession of the land. But soon they started disobeying again. The historical section of the Bible shows constant disobedience. The result of their disobedience was predicted by the prophets. And just as God predicted through the prophets, foreign armies continually invaded their lands.

As we stated in the beginning, the Old Testament shows us that God made a lot of good promises, as well as his terrifying promises. The prophets recorded the future and laid it out before the nation in fine precision. If they refused to obey, their future would be bleak, maybe even devastating to them. Ninety percent of the time they ignored the words of the prophets. The prophets Isaiah and Micah predicted the appearance of the Messiah hundreds of years in advance, but these prophecies also fell on deaf ears.

Their constant disobedience was brought to a climax when they refused to acknowledge God's Son. Not only did they deny him, but they actually tortured and murdered him. But through the pages of this volume, it has been my hope to make it clear that **God kept his promises.** And it is certainly not because of anything that man has done, but because of his great love and undeniable grace. It is as Paul wrote to Titus in his epistle:

Tit 2:11 For the saving grace of God has appeared to all men,

Tit 2:12 instructing us that having denied ungodliness and worldly lusts, we should live discreetly and righteously and godly in the present age,

Tit 2:13 looking for the blessed hope and appearance of the glory of our great God and Savior Jesus Christ,

Tit 2:14 who gave Himself on our behalf, "that He might redeem us from all lawlessness and purify a special people for Himself," zealous of good works.

Through the pages of this book, I have shown how Jesus fulfilled his promise, the promise that his glory would be presented in the clouds as he utilized the Roman armies to fulfill his greatest prophecy, the destruction of Jerusalem, the temple and the entire Jewish political and religious system.

We have seen how he became the mediator of the new covenant by the presentation of his blood in the Most Holy in heaven.

Heb 9:15 For this reason He is the mediator of a new covenant, so that, since a death has taken place for the redemption of the transgressions that were *committed* under the first covenant, those who have been called may receive the promise of the eternal inheritance.

Yes, we have a _**new covenant!**_ When our Lord died, and became that "Lamb of God that takes away the sin of the world," **HE** became that mediator of the new covenant. _**HE fulfilled the promise of redemption**_ from the transgressions which have separated us from God and have rendered us spiritually dead. This redemption was effective retroactively for those faithful ones under the first covenant. Therefore, the _**new covenant**_ was actually **the fulfillment** of the _**old covenant.**_

Yes, the blood of bulls and goats, which was only a stop gap measure anyway, was _no longer necessary._ This does not mean that those who made the sacrifices did not receive forgiveness. But as the Scriptures tell us:

Heb 10:4 For it is impossible for the blood of bulls and goats to take away sins.

But if this was a stop gap measure, then on what basis did they receive forgiveness? Yes! These sacrifices merely pointed the way to Jesus, who became "the Lamb of God." His blood **actually did** take away the sin of the people.

So once again, as I always say, it comes down to a personal level for us. What does this mean for us today living in the twenty-first century?

Jesus said in <u>John 14:6</u> "I am the way, and the truth, and the life;" Throughout this volume, we have seen the expectation of the apostles, and the proof of its happening. The full account of what happened in the fulfillment of this prophecy can also be found in the annals of history, most specifically, with regard to Jesus' greatest prophecy, in the writings of Flavius Josephus. In fact, he documented this in very fine detail in his works, "The Wars of the Jews." You can read about the destruction of Jerusalem and the temple in its entirety in Books 3 through Book 6 of his work.

There is much written on this subject at present, and more volumes are being added all the time. The prophecy pundits have continued to pour out new theories of how the Last Days are still in our future for over a hundred years now, and **every one of them have proven false.** Why? Because our Lord Jesus did exactly what he said he would do. He did return in that first century generation and bring an end to the sacrificial, Levitical system of government. Thus, we are now living in the new covenant, a covenant of grace in which we are promised eternal life for those who believe. Jesus himself made this promise when he said:

John 5:24: Truly, truly, I say to you, he who hears My word, and **believes** Him who sent Me, **has** eternal life, and **does not come into judgment**, but **has passed** out of death into life.

But this is not easy believeism, as some would promote. As James pointed out in his epistle, our faith is made evident by our works. We cannot under any circumstances con the God of the universe. He reads our hearts. But this actually points us to something greater as the Apostle Paul pointed out:

> Php 3:20 For **our citizenship is in heaven**, from which also we eagerly wait for a Savior, the Lord Jesus Christ;
> Php 3:21 who will transform the body of our humble state **into conformity with the body of His glory**, by the exertion of the power that He has even to subject all things to Himself.

Yes! We have a new body awaiting us. It is a spiritual body which will conform to the body of our Lord in his glory. Just exactly what that means is not stated, but we know it will be wonderful! Therefore it is important for us to live our lives in obedience to the commands of our savior, for in this we will be rewarded....not for our works but for our faith. However, it is also true that our works are a mirror of our faith!

So now with all of this in mind, I would just like to ask you a question: Isn't it wonderful to know that our Lord Jesus **did what he said he would do?** And it is not something which can be mocked by some college professor since it is recorded in history for our proof of the facts. But even after all of the data that I have presented in proof of these facts, I would still like to encourage you to look into this matter for yourself.

We are admonished in God's Word to seek truth and pursue it. 1 Thess 5:21 says: "But examine everything *carefully;* hold fast to that which is good;"

Praise God for his awesome grace to us! Thank you Lord, for giving us your promise of redemption. Thank you Lord for keeping that promise.

Bibliography

Aland, Kurt; Black Matthew, Novum Testamentum Graece. The copy from which this material was taken is the 1995 version ISBN 3-438-05100-1 Kunststoff, 3-438-0501-7 Leder

Alford, Henry, The Greek Testament, taken from e-Sword, Version 10.2.1, 2013, Rick Meyers (Free download at www.e-sword.net)

Barnes, Albert, Notes on the Bible, taken from e-Sword, Version 10.2.1, 2013, Rick Meyers (Free download at www.e-sword.net)

Broshi, Magen, The Israel Museum, http://www.centuryone.com/josephus.html

Clarke, Adam, Commentary on the Bible, taken from e-Sword, Version 10.2.1, 2013, Rick Meyers (Free download at www.e-sword.net)

Denton, T. Everett (2011-12-15). Hebrews: From Flawed to Flawless Fulfilled! ASiteForTheLord Publishing. Kindle Edition.

DeMar, Gary, Last Days Madness, 1999 American Vision

Eusebius, Church History
From http://www.newadvent.org

Fox, John, Foxes Book of Martyrs, Chapter 2, taken from e-Sword, Version 10.2.1, 2013, Rick Meyers (Free download at www.e-sword.net)

Gentry, Kenneth, Before Jerusalem Fell, Dating the Book of Revelation, Third Edition, copyright by Gentry Family Trust, April 2, 1999, Victorious Hope publishing, Fountain Inn, SC

Gill, John, Exposition of the Entire Bible, taken from e-Sword, Version 10.2.1, 2013, Rick Meyers (Free download at www.e-sword.net)

Henry, Matthew, Commentary on the Whole Bible, taken from e-Sword, Version 10.2.1, 2013, Rick Meyers (Free download at www.e-sword.net)

Irenaeus of Lyons, *Against Heresies*,
http://www.newadvent.org/fathers/0103530.htm

Meek, Charles, Christian Hope through Fulfilled Prophecy, 2013, Faith Facts Publishing, Spicewood, TX

Meek, Charles, http://prophecyquestions.com/

Mickelsen, A.B., Interpreting the Bible, 1981, Eerdmans Publishing Co., Grand Rapids MI.

Noe, John, Unraveling the End, 2014, East2West Press, Indianapolis, IN

Newton, Sir Isaac, "Observations upon the Prophecies of Daniel and the Apocalypse of St. John"
http://www.gutenberg.org/files/16878/16878-h/16878-h.htm#DanX

Pate, Marvin, General Editor, "Four Views on the Book of Revelation" – 1998, Zondervan Publishing,
Authors:
      Preterist – Kennth L. Gentry Jr.
      Idealist – Sam Hamstra Jr.
      Progressive Dispensationalist – C. Marvin Pate
      Classical Dispensationalist – Robert L. Thomas

Preston, Don K. (2012-06-17). Who Is This Babylon? JaDon Management Inc.. Kindle Edition.

Riddlebarger, Kim (2013-08-15). A Case for Amillennialism: Understanding the End Times, Baker Publishing Group. Kindle Edition.

Riddlebarger, Kim, "What's 1000 years between friends?" http://kimriddlebarger.squarespace.com/theological-essays/amilllecture%20revised.pdf

Russell, James Stuart (2013-12-13). Parousia: The New Testament Doctrine of Our Lord's Second Coming. Kindle Edition. http://www.cogwriter.com/news/church-history/martin-luther-changed-andor-discounted-18-books-of-the-bible/

Sproul, R. C. (2013-07-01). The Promises of God: Discovering the One Who Keeps His Word, David C. Cook. Kindle Edition.

Strong, James (2011-05-07). Strong's Greek Dictionary of the Bible (with beautiful Greek, transliteration, and superior navigation) (Strong's Dictionary) Miklal Software Solutions, Inc.. Kindle Edition.

The Worlds Last Night and other Essays - Harvest Book 2002

Welton, Jonathan (2013-11-01). Raptureless: An Optimistic Guide to the End of the World - Revised Edition Including The Art of Revelation, BookBaby. Kindle Edition

Whiston, William, Translator, The Works of Josephus, Hendrickson Publishers, Peabody, Mass. 1987

Scripture Index

Scripture Index

Scripture Index

Scripture Index

Scripture Index

Scripture Index

Scripture Index

Scripture Index

Scripture Index

Scripture Index

Scripture Index

Scripture Index

About the Author

D. Robert Pike (Rob) is a retired Engineer and husband of his beloved wife Ida. He holds a Bachelor of Science degree from Indiana Wesleyan University, and a Master of Arts Degree from Webster University. In 1998 a powerful spiritual awakening led him to seek the Lord in a deeper more meaningful way.

Through God's help and the encouragement of his wife and his special guys, Bart and Bary Trester, he got his Ph.D in Theology at Trinity College and Seminary. But concerning this degree, Rob states: "I now know that this degree only helped me to understand **HOW LITTLE** I know. Every day, the time I spend reading God's precious Word teaches me something new. This is the beauty of **directly reading** the Bible for one's self. My studies since I earned my Doctorate degree have led me to some important discoveries that need to be known by others. We all need to take the admonition of 1 Thessalonians 5:21 seriously when it says: 'But examine everything *carefully*; hold fast to that which is good.' I certainly **do not** have all of the answers. But it is my hope that this book will purvey truth to all who read it, and it will do so only by God's amazing grace and the power of the Holy Spirit. May these pages bring honor to the great and holy name of Jesus. As Philippians 2:11-12 states: 'so that at the name of Jesus EVERY KNEE WILL BOW, of those who are in heaven and on earth and under the earth, and that every tongue will confess that Jesus Christ is Lord, to the glory of God the Father.' The Lord Jesus **kept his promises**, and that is the story of this book."

Please visit us on the web at www.truthinliving.net.

Made in the USA
Charleston, SC
09 July 2015